Urban Economics

Macmillan books of related interest

Published

Paul N. Balchin and Jeffrey L. Kieve: URBAN LAND ECONOMICS
Brian J. L. Berry: THE HUMAN CONSEQUENCES OF URBANISATION
Gordon C. Cameron: LOCATION, EMPLOYMENT AND THE METROPOLIS
D. J. Dwyer (ed.): THE CITY IN THE THIRD WORLD
Barry J. Garner: LINKAGES WITHIN CITIES
Alan Hay: TRANSPORT FOR THE SPACE ECONOMY
Richard Lecomber: ECONOMIC GROWTH VERSUS THE ENVIRONMENT
Douglas Pocock and Ray Hudson: IMAGES OF THE URBAN ENVIRON-
MENT
C. H. Sharp: TRANSPORT ECONOMICS
Frank J. B. Stilwell: REGIONAL ECONOMIC POLICY
Peter Toyne: ORGANISATION, LOCATION AND BEHAVIOUR

Urban Economics

Theory and Policy

K. J. Button

Lecturer in Economics at the University of Loughborough

First edition 1976
Reprinted 1978

Published by
THE MACMILLAN PRESS LTD
London and Basingstoke
Associated companies in Delhi Dublin
Hong Kong Johannesburg Lagos Melbourne
New York Singapore and Tokyo

ISBN 0 333 18595 1

Printed in Hong Kong

TO ELIZABETH

CONTENTS

PREFACE AND ACKNOWLEDGEMENTS

This book grew out of a course I taught at Loughborough University in 1974–5. It became apparent to me at that time that there was no adequate introductory textbook covering urban economic problems in this country despite the wealth of research material which was beginning to-appear. This slim volume attempts to fill this void, to provide easy access for students to the basic economic concepts in urban studies and to review current policy debates.

Among the many who have encouraged me in this enterprise, I would particularly like to thank Peter Boyes, Jim Hough and Eric Owen Smith for their valuable comments and suggestions. I would especially like to thank Eamonn Judge who undertook the onerous task of reading through the entire manuscript. Without the assistance of this gallant band, the factual mistakes and misrepresentations of ideas would have been even more numerous. Appreciation must also be expressed for the way the department's typists dealt with my flood of hieroglyphics, and in particular I would like to thank Mrs Madge Lowe and Mrs Gloria Brentnall for the care taken over the typing of the final drafts. I would also like to acknowledge the calm and steady hand of David Gillingwater who kindly drew the diagrams.

K.J.B.

Department of Economics
Loughborough University

INTRODUCTION

1.1 The Modern City

The problems of the modern world are numerous and varied but among the most intractable seem to be the economic and social difficulties confronting those who live and work in our major cities. The world's population has expanded rapidly over the past century and this growth has been accompanied by a considerable acceleration in the pace of urbanisation. This process has created severe problems of congestion, crime, housing, education, pollution, overextended public services and unemployment in urban areas. These problems, although differing in their particular characteristics and in degree, are common to all countries, developed and underdeveloped, and seem to be increasing in both number and size rather than diminishing.

In the 1870s somewhere around 1 per cent of the world's population lived in cities of over a million inhabitants; this percentage has since increased at least tenfold. The migration from countryside to city appears even more startling if smaller cities and towns are included. Today the main population pressures are being experienced in the cities of the Third World and it has not been uncommon for the population of some South American cities to have increased by 150 per cent or more over the past decade. The nations of Western Europe have had their industrial revolutions and in many countries, including the United Kingdom, there is now both a fairly stable population and little potential for further rural–urban migration. In this latter group of countries, urban problems revolve around meeting the needs of the existing inhabitants and replacing old and obsolete facilities, especially housing, which were built for workers during the earlier growth phase. On the other hand, underdeveloped countries must generate sufficient investment to meet the basic needs of a rapidly growing inflow of migrants into their cities and construct housing and facilities where none existed before. In the developed world the urban problem can be seen as one of resource allocation; in the underdeveloped world one of resource creation.

As Ursula Hicks [1974] has pointed out, the urban problems of the Western world can no longer be considered as city problems: they are now much too large and more correctly relate to the conurbations and metropolitan areas which now exist. Although the main period of urbanisation has long since passed in the United Kingdom, we have taken a considerable time to recognise its full significance and to realise the complexity of many of the economic problems that it has created. Indeed, it is only in the last few years that the major conurbations outside of Greater London have been incorporated into a framework of comprehensive administration – previously local government and policy in these areas had been in the hands of several smaller authorities.

The traditional methods of planning and governing urban activities have changed radically in the past decades since the inherent urban problems have become more apparent. The city is no longer treated as a piece of land with factories, shops, theatres, houses, parks and roads scattered randomly over it. The city has been recognised as a living organism with people living and moving within it. The realisation of this human and social element has resulted in the growth of a whole new range of studies, including urban sociology, urban psychology and, of course, urban economics.

1.2   Urban Economics

Urban economics is one of the newest and fastest growing specialisms in economics. Although one can trace the foundations of the subject back to the study of urban land economy in the 1920s and extensive work on urban problems was undertaken in German-speaking countries in the inter-war period, modern urban economics is more closely related to regional economics from which it branched at the end of the Second World War. Early work in the field was predominantly American, with pioneering studies of the internal structure of the developing American city being produced by Burgess [1925], Haig [1926] and Hoyt [1933]. Similarly, the majority of studies in the immediate post-war period came from the United States, notably the application of economic analysis to location decisions in urban areas by Walter Isard [1956] and others and work on the theory of land use by William Alonso [1964] and Lowdon Wingo [1961a].

However, urban economics has only been considered a subject worthy of serious study at the highest level in the last decade, the first postgraduate university degree courses concentrating on the new sub-discipline appearing in the United States only in the 1960s (Perloff [1973]). Again, it was not until the mid-1960s that the first textbook, as opposed to research monograph, appeared; this was Wilbur Thompson's volume, *A Preface to Urban Economics* [1965]. Even today, the flow of urban economic texts is painfully slow, partly because of the relatively small number of experts in the field compared to those in other branches of economics and partly because of the present state of the subject. Indeed, at least one author questions the possibility of writing a comprehensive textbook given the current 'state of knowledge' (Rasmussen [1973]). In contrast to this comparative dearth of teaching material, the amount of research into urban phenomena has expanded considerably in the last decade. Combined with a growing interest in the workings of cities and conurbations has been the establishment of specialist research centres (for example at the London School of Economics and at Bristol University) and the founding of a number of academic journals to report the latest findings (for example *Urban Studies, Regional Science and Urban Economics* and the *Journal of Urban Economics*). In addition to the increased interest professional economists have shown in urban problems, urban economics now forms a component part of many academic courses in such fields as sociology and geography and is included in numerous sub-degree and professional syllabi for qualifications in subjects such as town planning.

Despite this rapid expansion of interest in urban economics, no distinct and irrefutable boundary to the subject has yet been agreed upon. There are three distinct problems encountered when one attempts to place a single, comprehensive and workable definition on urban economics.

First, and probably of greatest importance, it is impossible to study the urban economy in purely economic terms; full cognisance must be taken of the historical, political, sociological, planning and geographical perspectives of urban activities. The study of cities must, by virtue of the nature of urban agglomerations, be multi-disciplinary. This is not to say that one cannot concentrate on the economic aspects, but rather that one must always remember the wider dimensions involved. Second, cities form part of a much larger economic system; most cities play important roles in regional activities, while the largest can influence the course of the national economy. Consequently, many urban problems cannot be treated in isolation but must be placed in their much broader context.

Finally, although in many ways it is the least intractable problem, is the difficulty of defining the physical boundaries of urban economies. It is generally agreed that an urban economy is characterised by proximity, production specialisation, affluence and technology (Hirsch [1973]), but this provides little insight into the problems of defining the geographical confines of the urban concentration and this tends to place the urban economist at some disadvantage relative to his colleagues who are concerned with national or industrial economic problems.

Given these difficulties, there have still been many attempts to define the subject-matter of the sub-discipline. McKean, for example, offers a general definition of urban economics as 'the application of economic analysis to the development of information that seems relevant to the urban problems' (McKean [1973] p. 19), but is prevented from narrowing this down by insurmountable difficulties of vagueness and imprecision.

A rather more practical approach, developed to facilitate the delineation of various university economic courses, is offered by Hugh Nourse [1970-1] who differentiates between regional economics, urban economics and the urban public economy. Adopting his definitions, urban economics would concentrate on the spatial analysis of economic, political and social activities within cities; the study of the city as a point within the national economic framework would be left within the realms of regional economics and the spatial aspects of public-sector involvement would be discussed in a course on the urban public economy. Such a framework may be useful for teaching purposes, but it has its limitations. The approach, although emphasising the interdisciplinary nature of the subject, distracts from the interdependence between many of the intra- and inter-urban phenomena involved. It may be legitimate to consider transportation, housing or pollution in a purely urban context (although generally active and pervasive local government makes it seem unlikely that they can be divorced entirely from the urban public sector) but for a full understanding of how cities function one must also examine labour and capital movements and these can only be considered in a wider setting.

The artificial distinctions drawn by Nourse are unacceptable simply because they attempt to constrain a subject which is by its nature diffuse. A far more realistic approach at this stage in the development of the subject is to consider any attempt to systematically apply economic principles to the solving of urban problems as urban economics. By 'economic principles' we mean nothing more than the application of a set of logical deductions which, under certain assumptions and conditions, explain people's behaviour. At present it is impossible to develop a general theory of the urban economy for a multiplicity of reasons, some of which are mentioned below, and consequently this rather intellectually unsatisfying definition seems the best available.

Given this rather simple definition of the subject-matter of urban economics, it is worth pondering for a few moments the question of why it has taken economists so long to become immersed in the problems of our cities.

The first reason is peculiar to the United Kingdom: there has been a strong feeling of 'anti-urbanism' in this country for many centuries and this has been reflected in a general avoidance of any discussion of urban issues except in a most negative fashion. Historically, the tendency has been to accept towns as unpleasant economic necessities and to concentrate upon the supposedly more important problems of agriculture and rural living. This is a theme running through not just the economic literature but is to be found in pre-twentieth-century sociology and town planning. The general problem is summed up by Glass [1972]: 'The absence of any general British texts on urbanism is undoubtedly in keeping with the native dislike of towns.'

A second reason for the slow growth of interest amongst economists in urban matters is the early reluctance of town planners to recognise the importance of social science in the planning process. Urban planning until the 1960s was a physical exercise: town plans involving the preparation of a cartographical picture of how the land-use pattern of a city should develop. This attitude prevented economists and other social scientists actively participating in the creation of urban policy and did little to encourage academic research into urban economic problems. There is a high correlation between the changing attitude of planners and the growth of urban economics.

Third, modern urban economics is not simply concerned with 'efficiency' but also with 'equity' (Chinitz [1974]). In the traditional fields of economics, concentration has focused upon devising rules for achieving the optimum allocation of resources; in other words, to maximise production efficiency. Urban economics is more akin to political economy and deals with housing, pollution, crime, race and poverty, all of which cannot be treated in a purely objective way. Before urban economics could become a viable field of study, it was necessary for economists to realise the wider political and social framework within which they must develop their theories.

The final reason is more straightforward: the basic techniques of 'Marshallian microeconomic analysis', with their emphases on perfect markets and minimal government involvement, were founded on a number of implicit and explicit assumptions which are not tenable in an urban setting. The study of cities implies a study of geographical space but the traditional Marshallian neoclassical economic theory which was developed at the turn of the century makes no allowance for this additional 'dimension'; it was primarily designed to consider the determinants of prices and outputs at some predetermined location. This emphasis was not altogether surprising; in Marshall's day much of the United Kingdom's industry was tied to immobile sources of power and raw materials, and consequently location was almost always predetermined by geographical factors. Although it is possible to circumvent this limitation by modifying the basic theory and treating distance as a cost of either production or consumption, other difficulties have proved more formidable.

A considerable amount of neoclassical economic analysis is couched in terms of perfect markets, with all producers and consumers having perfect knowledge of all prices and of each other's activities. Firms are assumed to be incapable of exercising any individual power over the prevailing price; they are much too small. All factors of importance are traded in open markets so that producers must pay the full costs of their activities and consumers are not forced to suffer from pollution and noise without being duly compensated. It is further assumed that everyone is rational, firms attempting to maximise profit and individuals their welfare. Finally, everything is treated as perfectly divisible and can be produced or consumed in infinitely small quantities if desired.

Compared to this ideal, the urban economy is a very 'imperfect' world and is characterised by widespread externalities (that is costs and benefits which are not reflected in the prices at which goods are bought and sold). The existence of these external effects makes it difficult, if not impossible, to allocate economic resources optimally. In addition, investments tend to be 'lumpy' and often exhibit considerable economies of scale, which makes traditional marginal analysis inappropriate. The assumptions generally associated with the conventional microeconomic approach to problems, namely identical incomes and tastes for all households, uniform utility functions and constant returns to scale are untenable in the urban situation. Indeed, one of the unique features of an urban economy, the 'agglomeration' of economic activity, is only possible when these assumptions are violated. The principal presuppositions of neoclassical analysis, a mythical world of perfect mobility and knowledge, just do not correspond to the realities of the large modern city economy.

With these problems confronting them, it is hardly surprising that economists have been slow to apply their analytical tools to solving the numerous urban problems. It required the development of spatial economic theory in the related field of regional economics to provide the basis for work on modern urban economics. Parallel with the advent of spatial economic analysis came the introduction of new investment-appraisal techniques based upon consumer-surplus theory, such as cost–benefit analysis, which enabled the analyst to take explicit account of the existence of externalities. (Consumer surplus being a welfare concept indicating the benefit a consumer derives from consumption above the actual price he pays for goods.) These new and more powerful tools have enabled advances to be made in the study of the urban economy, but the complexity of urban life is a serious obstacle to rapid progress. It is this complexity which has prevented the widespread use of sophisticated and penetrating mathematical techniques for the creation of a 'general theory' of the urban economy (Richardson [1973a]. To date, mathematical models have proved incapable of incorporating the additional space dimension and of allowing for the non-linear nature of many economic relationships. In addition, as Lowdon Wingo [1961b] intimated over a decade ago, many of the factors influencing urban economic activities are unquantifiable or intangible and, consequently, any attempt to build a comprehensive mathematical model would necessarily result in a myriad of variables that may be significant being omitted. Finally, the models themselves are usually considered in terms of 'goodness of fit', not their power of prediction, and are in consequence of little assistance to the decision-makers who are responsible for the future of the urban economy.

Given these limitations and constraints, how can the economist contribute to the urban debate? Rather than attempt to develop a comprehensive, all-embracing, general theory of the workings of the city economy, the economist should adopt what Needham [1974] has called a 'partial' approach. By this is meant that the analyst assumes that certain relationships within the economic system remain constant whilst considering changes in other relationships. For example, one would use traditional Keynesian multiplier techniques (see Chapter 5) to consider the implications of a large investment in the local economy and implicitly in doing so assume that relationships with the remainder of the national economy (expressed in terms of the propensities to import, consume, and so on) remain invariate. At a micro level, one would use neoclassical supply and demand techniques to look at the effects of a road-pricing policy to alleviate traffic congestion assuming the general location of economic activity was left unaltered (see Chapter 8). This is admittedly a piecemeal approach, revolving explicitly around problem-solving rather than the creation of a comprehensive framework of analysis, but, nevertheless, it appears, at present, as the only practical method of considering the urban economy available.

Accepting the necessity of employing this rather *ad hoc* approach still enables us to form a clear working distinction between urban macroeconomics and microeconomics. The former is concerned with problems involving the city as a whole and its relationships with the rest of both the regional and national economies. It is based essentially upon Keynesian aggregate economic techniques and is the appropriate approach to adopt when considering problems involving urban growth and economic stability. In contrast, urban microeconomics is primarily concerned with problems internal to the city, resting as it does on the firm foundations of price theory. Initially developed to deal with the activities of individuals, households and firms, microeconomics can shed light on location decisions and the workings of the various urban markets for land, transport and housing. Urban microeconomics differs from traditional neoclassical microeconomics in a number of ways. It has been specifically adapted to allow for the distance factor which influences many decisions and has been extended to consider the impact of the excessive monopoly forces which are at work within even the smallest cities. Finally, urban microeconomics incorporates an explicit recognition of the substantial role played by the public sector in metropolitan areas, especially the importance of local government, in the sphere of industrial and residential location and in the provision of social services.

1.3 This Book

Existing textbooks on urban economics are generally designed to meet the needs of the final-year or postgraduate economics students who have a good foundation of economic theory. In addition, many of them, although extremely good in their analytical content, draw upon American experience for illustration and comment. This book, on the other hand, tries to present the main strands of modern urban economics in a non-mathematical way and to set this theory in the context of the current urban situation in the United Kingdom wherever possible. A limited knowledge of basic economic theory is necessary for the reader to understand some of the specialised terminology but the interested layman and non-specialist economist who is not to be deterred by a few diagrams should find no difficulty in following the threads of the arguments presented.

The approach used is essentially a problem-solving one, and attempts are made to suggest possible solutions to the seemingly endless series of crises which seem to beset our largest cities. To really understand the underlying causes of these problems some knowledge of basic urban economic theory is essential and included for that reason. As has been pointed out by Harry Richardson [1973b], however, 'urban economic theory is still in an embryonic and turbulent state'; and consequently the theory we outline is fragmented rather than comprehensive in nature. It is probably true to say, though, that the main ideas we set out are now accepted as conventional wisdom even if the details are not yet agreed upon. Where the theory is particularly weak, though, this is clearly indicated.

Some attempt is made to strike a balance between the amount of urban micro- and macroeconomic theory presented, but since most of the major urban problems in the United Kingdom are of a micro kind, there is something of a bias towards this type of theory.

Macroeconomics is far from ignored, however, primarily because it plays an important role in urban planning. Changes in the administrative system in recent years also suggests that knowledge of urban growth may help the reader to a better understanding of the difficulties confronting the public authorities in large cities whose local economy is closely tied to the economies of adjacent urban areas.

In summary, the remainder of the book can effectively be divided into three distinctive sections.

In Chapters 2–6, we look at the development of urban economic theory. Initially (Chapters 2–4) we consider the contribution of the economist to our understanding of why people and firms decide to concentrate and form cities, and we look at the forces working to create current urban land-use patterns. This is urban microeconomics: we consider firms and individuals rather than the whole city as the units of analysis. The other two chapters in this section are macroeconomic-orientated and attempt to find out why cities grow and to what extent this growth is beneficial to society.

The second part of the book examines various urban economic problems. These are principally micro problems involving transport, the urban environment and housing. In the 1970s these seem to be the subjects under greatest discussion in both academic and more popular literature and certainly are the causes of greatest concern to those living in our conurbations. Whilst much of the theory of the earlier chapters is of general applicability to cities in most Western countries, the problems considered in this second part of the book are more specifically related to U.K. experience.

The final part of the book (Chapters 10 and 11) concentrates on the involvement of government in urban affairs. It specifically looks at the part played by local authorities in organising and controlling certain urban activities and considers the role of economics in urban planning. The urban public sector is a particularly topical subject at the time of writing, with major changes in planning, finance and administration having taken place in the late 1960s and early 1970s – changes which are by no means yet completed.

Since the book is primarily concerned with urban economics, the emphasis is directed towards the main economic issues but, without wishing to be too repetitive, it is important to re-emphasise that, because of their natures, no urban problem can be adequately discussed within the strict confines of any one of the traditional academic disciplines. For a full understanding of city life and urban development, it is necessary also to consider both the sociological and geographical aspects. Where appropriate, some brief mention of the wider implications of particular issues is included but the treatment of non-economic considerations is far from exhaustive.

In an attempt to direct the reader to the wider aspects of urban activity, the book provides extensive references. The referencing also serves to indicate source material which, besides ensuring due credit is awarded to originators of the ideas and theories presented, should enable the interested reader to follow up arguments in more detail. A book of this size and with fairly limited objectives cannot pretend to be comprehensive in its coverage and it is hoped that the lists of references for each chapter will compensate, to some extent, for those topics which have, by necessity, been given only limited space. The decision of what to include and the depth of coverage is obviously subjective.

References

W. ALONSO [1964], *Location and Land Use: Towards a General Theory of Land Rent* (Harvard University Press).

E. W. BURGESS [1925], 'The Growth of the City', in *The City*, ed. R. E. Park and E. W. Burgess (Chicago University Press).

B. CHINITZ [1974], 'Urban Economics: New Approaches', in *Regional Economic Development*, ed. D. J. Firestone (University of Ottawa Press).

R. GLASS [1972], 'Anti-Urbanism', in *The City*, ed. M. Stewart (Harmondsworth: Penguin).

R. M. HAIG [1926], 'Towards an Understanding of the Metropolis', *Quarterly Journal of Economics*, pp. 421–3.

U. K. HICKS [1974], *The Large City: A World Problem* (London: Macmillan).

W. Z. HIRSCH [1973], *Urban Economic Analysis* (New York: McGraw-Hill).

H. HOYT [1933], *One Hundred Years of Land Values in Chicago* (Chicago University Press).

W. ISARD [1956], *Location and Space Economy: A General Theory Relating to Industrial Location, Market Areas, Land Use, Trade and Urban Structure* (New York: Wiley).

R. N. MCKEAN [1973], 'An Outsider looks at Urban Economics', *Urban Studies* (February) pp. 19–37.

O. B. NEEDHAM [1974], 'Three Ways of Studying the Urban Economy', *Urban Studies* (June) pp. 211–15.

H. O. NOURSE [1970–1], 'Are Regional and Urban Economics really different?' *Review of Regional Studies* (Winter) pp. 25–33.

H. S. PERLOFF [1973], 'Development of Urban Economics in the United States', *Urban Studies* (October) pp. 289–301.

D. W. RASMUSSEN [1973], *Urban Economics* (New York: Harper & Row).

H. W. RICHARDSON [1973a], 'A Comment on some uses of Mathematical Models in Urban Economics', *Urban Studies* (June) pp. 259–66.

H. W. RICHARDSON [1973b], 'A Guide to Urban Economics Texts; a Review Article', *Urban Studies* (October) pp. 399–405.

W. R. THOMPSON [1965], *A Preface to Urban Economics* (Baltimore: Johns Hopkins Press).

L. WINGO [1961a], 'An Economic Model of the Utilization of Urban Land for Residential Purposes', *Papers and Proceedings of the Regional Science Association*, pp. 191–205.

L. WINGO [1961b], *Transportation and Urban Land* (New York: Resources for the Future Incorporated).

2 THE ECONOMICS OF GEOGRAPHICAL CONCENTRATION

2.1 Urbanisation

The process of urbanisation in both the developed Western world and the less developed areas of Africa, Asia and South America is creating immense difficulties for urban authorities. Before looking at these problems, it is first important to understand the economic forces at work causing this expansion in the urban population. The explanation is not simple and is not entirely economic in nature. The reasons why urbanisation occurs are complex and it would be incorrect to pretend that they are yet fully understood; nevertheless, some general principles are beginning to emerge.

What we can say is that there is an increasing tendency for both public and private sections to favour urban concentration. When people and industry are geographically concentrated in urban areas, public services may be provided more cheaply than if the population was spread evenly over the whole country. To individuals, cities offer a range of services and amenities which would be unobtainable in rural areas or only provided at much higher prices. Firms find they can produce more cheaply in cities than elsewhere and this proves a considerable attraction when they are taking location decisions. In this chapter we explain some of the attractions of urban areas to firms and industries and attempt to isolate some of the influences on the location decisions of individuals.

Before going into the economic advantages associated with urbanisation, it is useful to give a brief economic history of urban areas. This serves two main purposes besides being of interest in itself. First, it provides the reader with some understanding of why cities exist and also how modern cities fit into the long-term urbanisation process. Second, the durability of buildings and property, not to mention the relative immobility of people, means that many modern cities are a legacy of the past, and consequently some of their current economic characteristics and problems can be traced back to their origins and to changes that have occurred subsequently. The durability of buildings is a problem in itself since it means that many industrial and residential decisions taken today are constrained by the locational and building decisions of previous generations. The traditional economic forces of supply and demand respond slowly in this type of environment.

2.2 A Brief History of Urbanisation

A city may be defined in a number of ways – legal, demographic, geographic or economic – but all cities have the basic characteristic of being spatial concentrations of people and economic activities. In economic terms, a city is seen as an interrelated network of economic markets – housing, labour, land, transport, and so on – situated in a limited spatial area. For administrative reasons, central government often finds it convenient to use minimum population levels or other institutional definitions to describe cities, but this is not the economic approach. Consequently, urban economics treats any large geographical concentration of economic agents as a city and this is the definition we apply here.

There is considerable debate as to when the first cities appeared, but there is strong evidence to support the school claiming the sixth millennium B.C. as the period when urbanisation began. Again, there is no consensus as to where the city was born, although the discovery of Catal Huyuk on the Anatolian plateau of Turkey suggests early urban development in this region. Despite this fairly long history, it has only been in the last 100–150 years that urbanisation has really gained momentum. Today somewhere around 80 per cent of the United Kingdom's population and over 70 per cent of the United States' live in urban communities and the process is a continuing one (Best [1968]). This expansion of urban living raises two questions. First, what were the origins of the city and what factors were instrumental in initiating the trend towards urban living? Second, why has the process of urbanisation accelerated so rapidly during the past century? These are questions which stand by themselves: there has not been a gradual and progressive movement towards urbanisation but rather a number of discrete steps or stages of which the present rapid increase in city sizes and numbers represents a quite distinct and dramatic departure from any previous development.

There is a major dichotomy of opinion over why the urbanisation process began. Traditional theory holds that urbanisation was initially a slow process which progressed from village life. The introduction of agriculture and the replacement of the nomadic existence of neolithic hunters and herdsmen necessitated the establishment of more permanent and stable settlements. Following on from this came an increased division of labour and an expansion in communal economic undertakings – a trend which accelerated as the size of villages grew and greater economies of specialisation became possible. Once the urbanisation process had begun, market forces tended to attract more people and industry to the city. Industry was attracted because the city offered 'agglomeration economies' in the form of a large captive home market, supplies of both skilled and unskilled labour and the availability of supplementary industries. To the individual, the city offered a wide range of services and, generally, security and well-paid employment. In many ways, once the urbanisation process had begun, it became self-reinforcing, market forces favouring a continued flow of factors and population into the city. It has frequently been argued that urban life could never have evolved without the initial existence of agricultural surpluses to support the inhabitants and that cities are characterised by their sheltering of non-agricultural specialists (Sjoberg [1967]).

This, the traditional approach, has been criticised by Jane Jacobs [1972], who argues that cities and urban life preceded rural developments. Miss Jacob's thesis is that cities grew out of trading centres where nomadic hunters met with local inhabitants who were willing to trade minerals and other raw materials found in the area for food and hides. This trading took place in the locality of ore deposits or some other source of natural wealth which the hunters valued. After a time, traders were attracted to the trading centre and some local producers turned to buying and selling. These groups eventually combined to create a merchant class. The next phase involved the establishment of industry in the area. Initially, local inhabitants processed their raw materials, manufacturing goods from the resources obtained in trade (for example the production of hide garments and bags from leather traded by the nomads and the manufacture of weapons and other utensils from the local supplies of minerals). To begin with, the merchants and craftsmen would also acquire their seeds, meat and other foodstuffs as part of their trade with the nomads, but eventually the expanding city encouraged the establishment and development of adjacent agricultural communities and the familiar rural periphery to the urban core was born. The city itself continued to grow, primarily because interactions between its inhabitants generated fresh ideas and products, which introduced a new dynamic and inventive element into the local economy. Clearly this approach advances the view that urban life must have preceded agriculture and was a necessary prerequisite for it.

These two explanations of the underlying causes of urban development may initially appear mutually exclusive, the validity of one theory precluding the acceptance of the other. Obviously, if agriculture did precede urbanisation at Catal Huyuk, then it cannot also be a product of it. In fact, it is quite conceivable that both lines of thought are correct (and equally other explanations for the emergence of cities may be just as valid). Sjoberg and others have pointed to the independent and unrelated nature of urban development in separate and geographically distinct regions: the classic example being the existence of cities in the New World prior to the sixteenth century which were completely free of any interference from European or Asiatic sources. It is therefore quite possible, if Sjoberg is correct, that cities grew up in different regions for entirely different reasons. The validity of this or any other approach is unlikely to be satisfactorily tested by economic debate alone and can only be probed by archaeologists and, possibly, social anthropologists. Even so, it seems unlikely that a firm and unquestionable conclusion will ever be reached.

The answer to the second question, concerning the rapid extension of urban living since the mid-nineteenth century, is of more importance to the economist if he is to fully understand contemporary urban problems. Earlier periods of urbanisation have generally resulted either from an expansion of imperialism (for example associated with the Persian and Roman Empires) or a growth in trade (for example the creation of important oasis cities along the 'Great Silk Road' in Turkestan). In these circumstances, cities were established as either military centres, for the mutual protection of the inhabitants and as a means of controlling the local population, or as staging posts where traders could rest and replenish their supplies. The recent upsurge in urbanisation is an entirely different phenomena. The region where this expansion was initiated – north-western Europe – has no long tradition of urbanisation and has, in fact, been remarkable for its rural nature in the past. In a wide-ranging essay, Kingsley Davis [1967] has gone so far as to comment that the absence of any existing parasitic cities was partially responsible for the growth of a 'revolutionary degree of urbanisation' in the region. The lack of older cities may have been a necessary condition for the new wave of urbanisation, but it was not a sufficient one: a positive stimulus to city growth was required to transform the predominantly agricultural nature of the area's economy. The advent of industrialism provided the necessary impetus.

The late eighteenth century was dominated by the upsurge in industrialisation that occurred. Cities grew in the north of Britain where, previously, urbanisation had been minimal, the important cities of the previous era being in the south, notably Norwich and London. After 1750 the balance changed and urbanisation took root in the northern provinces, especially West Lancashire and Yorkshire. Although exact data relating to this period are sparse, the introduction of the Census in 1801 does provide some idea of the rapid growth in urbanisation that took place in the later years of the Industrial Revolution (see Table 2.1). These statistics, relating

TABLE 2.1   *Growth in population of the main U.K. cities*

City	Population (thousands)					
	1801	1811	1821	1831	1841	1851
Greater London	1117	1327	1600	1907	2239	2635
Birmingham	71	83	102	144	183	233
Manchester	75	89	126	132	235	303
Liverpool	82	104	138	202	285	376
Glasgow	77	101	147	202	275	343
Bradford	13	16	26	44	67	104
Leeds	53	63	84	123	152	172
Sheffield	46	53	65	92	111	135

to the main cities, although showing that the population living in the ten largest cities grew from 16 per cent to 23 per cent of the total between 1801 and 1851, underestimate the extent of urbanisation considerably, neglecting the movement from the countryside into the smaller towns.

The availability of new sources of power in the early eighteenth century, coupled with the invention of the steam engine, enabled the rapid introduction of large-scale factory production and with it the extension of, first, trade and, later, skill specialisation. Factories, combined with new machinery, produced economies of scale and this in turn resulted in increased plant size. The uneven spread of raw materials (in particular coal and iron ore), the peculiarities of local climate (especially important in the textile industry) and high transport costs tended to concentrate industry in certain advantaged areas. The expanding industrial labour force required housing and other services which could only be provided in an urban environment. Consequently, industrial towns and cities grew, and with this growth came the reinforcing expansion of commercial and retailing activities to meet the rising demands of the local inhabitants and firms.

This rapid burst of urbanisation, which both drew men away from the land and, at the same time, increased the demand for agricultural produce, could not have been sustained but for equally dramatic parallel changes in other complementary sectors. At the same time as industrial technology was transformed, there were advances made in farming techniques, food preservation and transportation. In addition to the extraordinary improvement in home agricultural productivity, new sources of food became available in both the New World and the emerging Asiatic and African colonies which, with the combination of both faster and more reliable transport, together with refrigerated methods of storage, supplied the necessary foodstuffs to enable the expanding industrial centres to eat. The advent of the age of automation reinforced and accelerated the urbanisation process and from the industrial cities grew the modern American metropolitan regions and the U.K. conurbations.

Since the 1950s there has been a moderate decline in the absolute populations in most of the major U.K. conurbations. People have, partly as a result of enjoying higher incomes and partly due to deliberate planning policies, moved into new housing estates on the outskirts of cities or into the New Towns that have been built. Nevertheless, a third of the population of England and Wales live in the six major conurbations and 15 per cent of the total in the largest, Greater London. Although these traditional urban centres have now stabilised, there are many other cities where growth continues. The difference between the post-war period and the pre-war era is the greater control exercised by local and central government: urbanisation is encouraged but is to be spread over a much larger number of centres.

2.3 Agglomeration Economies

Having briefly considered why urbanisation has occurred in the past, we now turn to examine why industry and population should continue to concentrate in cities today. We also need to find out why particular firms and individuals select one city in preference to another. To fully understand these two related issues, it is necessary to examine the returns or benefits obtained from locating in an urban area.

Urban areas are characterised by their concentration of different economic activities. Some cities are also noted for their specialisation in a particular industry, for example the boot and shoe trade of Northampton and the steel industry in Sheffield. This latter phenomena can be explained in part by the availability of local raw materials, as is the case with the coal-mining towns, but this is far less common than it was a century ago. Many cities continue to specialise in the production of a particular commodity despite the fact that local supplies of raw materials have long since become exhausted and are now imported from outside the area. Similarly, some urban areas have a high concentration of one particular type of 'mobile' industry which has never been tied to a source of raw material – the car-manufacturing centres of the West Midlands provide a clear example of this. In this and the following section, we are interested in the basic economic forces which encourage firms to concentrate and to explain why particular types of mobile industry should elect to locate in a specific city.

Before proceeding, an important point of definition should be brought before the reader concerning the term 'concentration'. To the *urban economist*, industrial concentration refers to the geographical concentration of industry in a given area or city. To the *industrial economist*, the same term refers to the control of an industry by a limited number of people. We use the former definition throughout the book unless otherwise stated.

One of the main reasons industry concentrates geographically is because of so-called 'agglomeration economies' that they can enjoy. These economies are composed primarily, although not exclusively, of what economists call 'externalities' or, more specifically, 'external economies'. In general, external economies might be defined in terms of the response of one firm's output to the activities of others. This definition, although conveying the basic idea of one firm's activity affecting another's, is not altogether satisfactory (Mishan [1971]). A more useful definition of externalities has been provided by Ralph Turvey [1966], who described them as 'the impact of the activities of households, public agencies or enterprises upon the activities of other households, public agencies or enterprises which are exerted otherwise than through the market. They are, in other words, relationships other than those between buyer and seller.' Agglomeration economies may occur when close geographical proximity generates external benefits for the firms and industries involved.

Not all agglomeration economies are external: when there are benefits to be enjoyed by a single firm expanding in a particular area, some of the economies, such as those resulting from increased scale, will be strictly internal. However, where agglomeration economies accrue to a number of separate firms in the same industry congregating in a particular city, these are said to be external to each individual firm but internal to the industry as a whole. In addition, agglomeration economies can take a wide variety of forms and appear on both the demand and supply sides of the production equation. Again, although some types of agglomeration economy are enjoyed by all firms in a city, other categories apply only to firms in particular industries.

There is no hard-and-fast rule for categorising agglomeration economies: their nature and impact will vary with the size and location of the city and with the type of firm involved. However, we can usefully distinguish ten broad types of agglomeration benefit which may, to varying degrees, influence the decisions of businessmen when deciding whether or not to locate near other producers.

(1) *The potential size of the local market.* Large concentrations of people and industry create marketing economies. In America, Ullman [1962] has demonstrated that as the population size of a city grows, it leads to a greater degree of self-sufficiency and this, in turn, increases the potential market for locally based firms and businesses. Expansion in the local market is preferable to expansions in external markets because it involves lower transport costs which are in turn reflected in lower total production and distribution costs. It also tends to reduce actual marketing costs since information about various products tends to spread more easily within an area than it does between areas.

(2) *A large local market* can also reduce actual production costs as it enables a higher degree of specialisation and introduces the possibility of economies from large-scale production. Adam Smith first pointed to the advantages of specialisation some 200 years ago with his example of a pin factory, but his basic arguments are still valid today. By situating in a large urban area, a producer is assured of a sufficient market for his goods to enable him to employ bigger and more efficient pieces of machinery and to introduce more productive and automated techniques into his factories. When the local market is small, such economies can only be reaped if there is a large 'export' market to other urban areas and this can usually only be reached by incurring high transport costs.

(3) Related to scale economies is the requirement of a *threshold level of population* before certain public services are provided. This is true of a large number of different public services but is particularly the case with transport. Only the largest urban areas are served by airport facilities and there is a minimum size needed before mainline railway services are provided. There is a similar situation with regard to inter-urban road provision: this is reflected in a Ministerial statement in 1971 setting out the objectives of the U.K. motorway-building programme: 'Every large city and town with a population of more than 250,000 will be directly connected to the strategic network and all with a population of more than 80,000 will be within ten miles of it.' Although this objective has yet to be fully realised, larger cities generally offer superior access to national markets. Good inter-urban transport increases the potential market area a firm may serve economically and at the same time reduces the costs of 'importing' raw materials and components into an area.

(4) *Geographical concentration* of a specific industry in a particular location tends to encourage the establishment of complementary industries to meet its demands for imports and to provide facilities to market and transport the final product. In the case of Coventry and Oxford, the establishment of a substantial car-manufacturing industry was quickly followed by firms moving into the cities producing components and by the appearance of specialist transporter concerns. In commercial centres, such as London, the main financial institutions have been supplemented by the growth of complementary legal and insurance facilities. In many cases, these complementary firms have been accompanied by government-

assisted agencies to retrain labour and provide information services for the primary industry in the area.

(5) A further agglomeration economy associated specifically with the geographical concentration of like firms is that *a pool of skilled labour tends to accumulate and a system of job placement geared to the needs of the local industry develops*. This has clearly happened in the motor towns of the West Midlands and in the textile centres of Yorkshire and Lancashire.

(6) Just as skilled labour pools develop, so do *pools of managerial and entrepreneurial talent*. This applies not simply to those directly involved in the industries but also to those who are taken on in contractual roles, for example accountants, work-study experts, and so forth.

(7) *Financial and commercial facilities* tend to be superior in large cities. They are more attuned to the local specialist needs of the industry in the area and consequently able to offer greater assistance in the financing and control of investments.

(8) Urban concentrations can usually offer a much wider range of facilities – recreational, social, educational, and so on – than smaller centres and this is an attraction to good management. It is frequently the general level of amenity in an area which attracts top management as much as high salaries.

(9) Businessmen prefer to concentrate because it enables *face-to-face contact*. This, they claim, enables a far more efficient operation of the management process, enhances confidence and enables ideas to flow more freely. Despite the improvements in communications, there seems to be a considerable degree of truth in this argument – businessmen do like to know personally the men they are dealing with.

(10) A rather more dynamic type of agglomeration economy is *the greater incentive for firms to innovate* when there is geographical concentration. This is a point emphasised in Jane Jacobs's thesis but has been studied more rigorously by Ogburn and Duncan [1964]. They found that in the period 1900 to 1935, of 600 major innovations recorded in the United States over half occurred in cities with populations in excess of 300,000. There are a number of reasons why the incidents of innovation might be correlated with concentration. A large number of firms producing similar goods in a city motivates competition, which, in turn, encourages innovation. The geographical concentration itself tends to produce a freer flow of

information between the manufacturers of a commodity and their suppliers and customers. A considerable amount of innovation is the result of learning exactly what customers require and discovering the particular problems of suppliers. Finally, communications in general are superior in large concentrations and this means news of an innovation spreads relatively quickly, leading to its rapid adoption by all firms in the area.

2.4 The Simple Theory of Inter-Urban Location

Having considered the advantages to industry of spatial concentration, both for firms in the same line of business and for those providing different but complementary goods and services, we now turn to look at the inter-urban location decision. Why do firms and people prefer to locate in one city rather than another? Obviously many firms are inert and once they are established at a certain place, a decision frequently taken in the distant past when the location provided necessary raw materials or was an important link in the communications system of the day, they expand (or stagnate) there rather than move to another city which may offer a higher financial return. In some instances there is a simple rationale behind this, especially if the costs of search for a better location and removal are large and the probable gain from the new situation small. Similarly, individuals, because of family and social ties, are frequently reluctant to move from the towns in which they were born despite the prospects of higher earnings elsewhere. In this section we are less concerned with these categories of firm and individual and concentrate on the more mobile elements in society.

In general, people attempt to locate so that they maximise their welfare over time. Firms are usually considered to prefer locations offering the highest profits or which meet some other commercial objective. Although urban areas contain both people, who, in turn, form the workers, and employers, Hoover [1948] has argued that the latter are more important in the determination of the location of economic activity. Two reasons are given for this:

(*a*) businessmen, because they have more to lose, are generally better informed about the potential profits associated with different urban areas than the worker is about living costs and wages; and

(*b*) there seem to be more changes in the patterns that determine firms' preferences than in the patterns that determine consumers' preferences. An example of this is technical change, which alters the firm's, but not the worker's, preferences.

It is for these reasons that we consider the location decisions of firms first. Any producer has three types of cost to consider when deciding the optimal location for his factory. First, there is the cost of obtaining the raw materials used in the production process and of transporting them to the chosen city. Second, there are the actual costs of production, the processing costs, which will include the costs of labour and local services. Finally, there are marketing and distributional costs entailed in getting the finished product to the consumer. When seeking the optimal location, a businessman should know all of these costs and also the spatial pattern of demand for his output. In general, the costs associated with each city depend upon transport into the area (important in the procurement of raw materials and in distributing the final product) and the local production conditions (including agglomeration economies).

Initially, let us consider the simplest location decision when the firm in question produces a product which sells for exactly the same price irrespective of where it is manufactured. Further, assume that the costs of producing this commodity vary from city to city but that there is one particular location where total production costs are minimised. This is not an unrealistic situation; many goods do have a uniform national selling price and, because each city will have associated with it a production cost combining raw material, processing and transport costs of varying magnitude, it is not difficult to envisage a case where one city offers the lowest over-all cost of production. If these conditions hold, clearly any entrepreneur intent on profit maximisation will elect to locate in the cost-minimising city.

Suppose the intention is not profit maximisation however. What if the entrepreneur wishes to maximise his revenue? To enable us to consider this possibility we need to introduce the concept of a *space cost curve*. In traditional economic theory it is assumed that the costs of production vary with output, increasing costs occurring when the cost of each incremental unit of output rises as output rises and decreasing costs when incremental costs fall with expanding output. A space cost curve differs from this traditional concept in so far as output is assumed given (or fixed) but the costs of producing it vary with location. Two types of production cost are generally considered important: *basic costs*, which are independent of location (for example labour paid at a nationally negotiated wage rate) and *location costs*, which depend upon the particular city chosen (for example transport costs to the national market). It is the latter category we are primarily interested in since it determines the least-cost site. Assume once more that the space cost curve takes a V-shape with respect to distance from the national frontiers. This simply means that there is one city where location costs are minimised and, moving away from this city, location costs will begin to rise. The constant price means that the fixed output will sell for the same amount wherever it is produced but costs of production will vary, as in Figure 2.1(*a*). The profit-maximising firm will again select the least-cost city, city *H* in the diagram, because this offers the maximum net revenue. It is also clear that a firm intent on cost minimisation will also prefer city *H*. Revenue maximisers will have no strong reason for preferring *H* to any other city between *E* and *K*; they all offer the maximum possible revenue without forcing the firm into a loss-making situation.

Of course, one might argue that revenue is not the same wherever the output is sold: it will be higher in some cities than in others depending upon the local conditions of supply and demand. It is possible that the highest price will be obtained in the city offering the lowest production costs, but this is not necessarily the case and in many industries most certainly does not hold. Let us therefore assume that city *F* is the one where prices are highest and the fixed output of the good will be sold for the maximum revenue, moving away from *F* prices fall as the national frontier is approached (Figure 2.1(*b*)). In these conditions, the profit-maximising firm will locate at *G*, where the divergence between the revenue curve and the space cost curve is greatest. The cost-minimising firm will still prefer to produce in city *H* but the revenue maximiser will have a decided preference for city *F*, where the revenue curve is at its zenith.

The above analysis is obviously a simplification and it is important to pinpoint the vital assumptions made. First, we have used a two-dimensional analysis and depicted the spatial economy as a series of cities located along a straight line. This is hardly realistic. In fact, the spatial economy has depth as well as length and should more correctly be represented as a surface or plane rather than a line. This is not a major problem to overcome however, and mathematical models have been developed to incorporate the

additional dimension. Second, we have assumed that the output
under consideration is fixed but, in the majority of industries, this is
not the case. If we make the more realistic assumption that output is
variable, an additional set of possibilities must be incorporated into
the analysis – it then becomes possible for one city to be the
minimum-cost location at one level of output but another city may
have lower costs at a higher (or lower) level of production. Again,

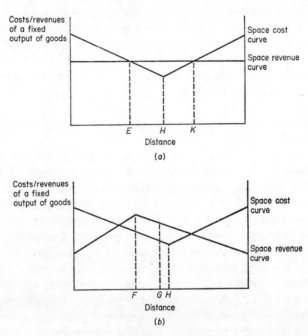

FIG. 2.1   *The space cost curve and inter-urban location*

one would have to resort to mathematics in order to incorporate
this possibility. Third, there may not be a unique cost-minimisation
location (or revenue-maximising one for that matter) but rather a
number of cities where the space cost curve is at its lowest. This
may be because different cities within the country offer identical
facilities, which is the obvious example, or, perhaps less apparent,
because they can offer alternative methods of production at identi-
cally low costs. An example of the latter may be when one city has
an abundant supply of skilled labour which can be combined with

expensive raw materials, while another city has less skilful workers but readily available and cheap transport to keep raw-materials and distribution costs down. In these circumstances it is quite conceivable that the space cost curve could register a minimum for both cities. Finally, we have considered a single firm in isolation assuming its locational decision to be completely independent of other competing firms: in fact, there are considerable interdependencies. In the real world, competing firms often attempt to locate away from rivals, while other firms try to guess the probable future location of supplementary industry so that they may establish themselves near them. In other words, there is imperfect knowledge about the likely response of other firms to one firm's location decision. We say a little more on this subject in the next chapter in the context of intra-urban location.

2.5 The Location Decisions of Households

Firms locate to maximise profits or revenue, or to minimise their production costs; people take a much wider range of factors into account. Obviously, pecuniary benefits and job opportunities come high on the list of priorities for most households, but they are not the sole determinant of families' choices of location. If an area or city offers a considerably higher level of income, this may attract households, causing them to uproot from other urban centres or rural districts, but small income differentials are unlikely to have a significant impact. As far as large income differentials do occur across space, and people have full knowledge of them, they are likely to encourage households to locate in prosperous areas and cities where the most dynamic and productive industry is.

Since income is not the unique determinant of household location, what other factors are important? Local and cultural ties clearly play a role; people are often willing to move between urban centres within the same geographical region but are reluctant to move to any other part of the country. Such people attach a high positive value to a familiar cultural environment and to the social values and characteristics of their native region. A similar effect is experienced in rural areas where households do not identify with urban life-styles and prefer to remain outside of the cities, even in their native region, despite having lower incomes.

People also place considerable value on the range and quality of the amenities and social facilities in different urban areas. Individuals are often willing to live in large cities, such as London, and be paid relatively low incomes to enable them to make use of recreational, cultural and social facilities. Only large urban concentrations can offer such a range of facilities because of the high turnover needed to make them viable economic propositions. Also, many of these facilities are supplementary to each other and a minimum threshold level of custom is needed before they will be provided. As units, households are often willing to sacrifice money income for the sake of individual members; in particular, location decisions may be influenced by the quality of education for the children or of health services for the sick and aged. In these cases, households are taking a much wider view of income than the conventional wage rate. They are considering the free, or cheap, public services available and the range of opportunities upon which they can spend their monetary incomes. The difficulty for the economist is that these considerations are usually of a qualitative or subjective nature and this makes it very difficult to develop theories which are easily tested. Some of the models which have been developed are considered in Chapter 4 which deals with urban labour markets.

2.6 Summary

Cities are becoming both larger and more numerous. For firms there are positive advantages to be enjoyed by locating together, either with firms of a similar type or with those of a supplementary nature. Geographical concentration permits the benefits of agglomeration and scale economies to be reaped and transport costs to be minimised. To the individual, cities offer a wide range of social and recreational facilities and permit a higher standard of living to be enjoyed. There is clearly a link between the attraction of cities to firms and to individuals. The market and labour supply of a large urban area benefits firms locating there but the individuals also gain from having a wider range of jobs to choose from and the prospect of higher incomes. Whether it is the availability of labour which attracts industry initially, or the opportunity of employment which attracts workers, is something of a 'chicken-and-egg' problem (see Burns [1964]), but in all probability it is a simultaneous process with almost instantaneous adjustment between job opportunities and population increase.

References

R. H. BEST [1968], 'The Extent of Urban Growth and Agricultural Displacement in Post-war Britain', *Urban Studies* (February) pp. 1–23.

L. S. BURNS [1964], 'People or Jobs ... or Chickens and Eggs', *Land Economics* (May) pp. 231–4.

K. DAVIS [1967], 'The Urbanisation of the Human Population', in *Cities: A Scientific American Book* (Harmondsworth: Penguin).

E. M. HOOVER [1948], *The Location of Economic Activity* (New York: McGraw-Hill).

J. JACOBS [1972], *The Economy of Cities* (Harmondsworth: Penguin).

E. J. MISHAN [1971], 'The Post-war Literature of Externalities: an Interpretative Essay', *Journal of Economic Literature* (March) pp. 1–28.

W. F. OGBURN and O. D. DUNCAN [1964], 'City Size as a Sociological Variable', in *Contributions to Urban Sociology*, ed. E. W. Burgess and D. J. Bogue (Chicago University Press).

G. SJOBERG [1967], 'The Origin and Evolution of Cities', in *Cities: A Scientific American Book* (Harmondsworth: Penguin).

R. TURVEY [1966], 'Side Effects of Resource Use', in *Environmental Quality in a Growing Economy*, ed. H. Jarrett (Baltimore: Johns Hopkins Press).

E. L. ULLMAN [1962], 'The Nature of Cities Reconsidered', *Papers and Proceedings of the Regional Science Association*, pp. 7–23.

3 INTRA-URBAN LOCATION AND LAND USE

3.1 Introduction

Chapter 2 has been concerned with outlining the main reasons why firms and individuals congregate to form cities. We now turn to look at why, once the decision to locate in a city has been made, particular urban sites are chosen. This chapter is therefore concerned with intra-urban location theory and practice. Some firms are obviously restricted in their location choices by the availability of local resources; many local utilities fall into this category, as do extractive industries. We are less concerned with these firms and concentrate on those which have a fairly high degree of mobility and can choose between alternative sites.

There is no single and comprehensive theory which can explain all location decisions, but this is not surprising. Intra-urban location decisions are made by large numbers of separate individuals and firms with different sets of priorities and objectives. We attempt to explain some of the reasons why particular sites are preferred, initially looking at firms and then households, but the explanations given are, by necessity, limited by their underlying assumptions. The weaknesses of these models are examined in Section 3.6, when we consider some of the empirical work that has been carried out to test various location theories. Nevertheless, location theory does provide some useful general guidelines and insights into the pattern of urban activities.

3.2 Patterns of Urban Land Use

Geographically, location patterns within cities are far from uniform and one of the apparent delights of geographers is to categorise different types of cities by their land-use characteristics. Cities can broadly be divided into three distinct groups, which are generally referred to as concentric, radial and multi-nuclei. These various city types are usually the result of different growth patterns that have occurred in the past.

The theory of concentric cities was initially developed by E. W. Burgess [1925]. These cities are typified by regular outward circles of different land usage centred around a single core or, in American terminology, central business district (C.B.D.) – see Figure 3.1(*a*). The C.B.D. is a concentration of all the main businesses, offices and retail outlets in the city and is frequently the oldest part of it. Surrounding the C.B.D. is usually a ring of residential property which in the past provided accommodation for those working in the C.B.D. but, with the growth of suburbia, has become run-down and now houses the poorest sections of the community. Surrounding this first ring is another, comprising better-quality and newer houses which provide homes for middle-income workers. Further out are more expensive houses which form the commuter belt and are where the highest-income earners live. The pattern is not static but changes in the sense that as the C.B.D. expands and the city grows, the core engulfs areas of poor housing for redevelopment and the lower-income groups living there are forced to move further out. Hence, there is continual pressure for each successive circle to move outwards over time and for land and houses to pass from higher- to lower-income groups as the city grows (this is known as filtering').

The central business district itself is a relic of previous stages of urbanisation when inadequate transport and communications necessitated close physical proximity for maximum economic efficiency. The continued existence of the C.B.D. is more difficult to explain with the improvements in transport which have taken place in the twentieth century. One explanation is that of William Alonso [1966] who feels that 'A strong centre is needed socially, economically and psychologically, for it is here that urban life is lived in full, and virtually all activities in the metropolitan area focus towards it. . . . The down-town area is the brain tissue of the metropolis, a complex evolving and little understood organ.' This emphasises the multifarious roles an urban core area fulfils – it is a community, as well as an economic centre. Indeed there is evidence of a limited number of very high-income households actually moving back from the perimeter to the C.B.D. because of the value placed upon easy access to the core for business and social reasons.

A particular type, or special case, of the concentric city, is the axial structure – see Figure 3.1(*b*). This model, initially isolated by Babcock [1932], allows for the influence of transport axes on the simple concentric pattern. Movement in this type of city concentrates along a number of main radial routes and, consequently, sites along these arteries offer a high degree of accessibility to the city centre. The C.B.D. tends to extend along these routes forming a star-shaped pattern which is reflected in each of the successive residential rings.

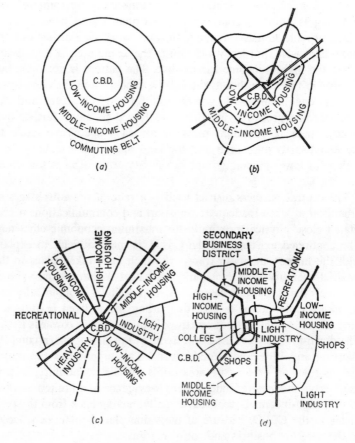

FIG· 3.1   *Urban land-use models*

Radial-sector cities are composed of a number of segments, rather like an orange, radiating out from the C.B.D. – Figure 3.1(c). Each segment is devoted to a particular land use. The model was initially developed by Homer Hoyt [1939] to explain residential land-use patterns, but has since been extended to cover all urban activities. The segments have resulted from decisions taken by firms and individuals. The firms have concentrated together to reap agglomeration economies, high-income groups have located on the best radial transport routes, while physical constraints have encouraged the siting of recreational facilities in other segments.

Multi-nuclei cities do not have a single core but rather a number of separate centres, although one may be dominant in size and importance – Figure 3.1(d). Many larger cities are of this particular type, especially those that have grown as the result of several smaller towns expanding and merging together. The major U.K. conurbations, for example West Yorkshire, are extreme cases created by the continued outward growth of urban concentrations which are cities in their own right. The multi concept does not contradict the existence of radial or concentric patterns of land use; indeed, each sub-centre within the city may be of either a radial or concentric nature.

These models do not describe all urban forms. The intervention of the public sector, especially in the provision of housing, increased affluence and improved transport, have tended to distort the stereotypes so loved by geographers. Moreover, topographical and environmental influences have affected the development of various cities over time. Checkland [1964] offers an example of this when he points to the extension of higher socio-economic housing westward over the years in the United Kingdom affecting urban land-use patterns.

3.3 Rent as an Influence on Intra-Urban Location

The most frequently encountered pattern of urban land use is the concentric city with business and retailing located at the city centre and rings of residential housing surrounding it. A useful model explaining this particular pattern of urban activity can be developed from ceiling-rent curves. In the case of a firm, these curves indicate the maximum commercial rent which can be paid at different locations and still enable the firm to earn normal profits (that is profits

sufficient to keep it in its current line of business). To households
these curves show the maximum commercial rent that will be paid
to live in a particular type of house at different sites.

The concept of commercial (or market) rent used in this type of
analysis calls for some explanation. Commercial rent is composed
of two elements: transfer earnings and economic (or scarcity) rent.
Transfer earnings are a sort of opportunity cost showing the maximum amount the landowner could earn by putting his land to some
other use. Economic rent represents a premium above transfer earnings obtainable because there is usually competition to secure scarce
land. In general, urban commercial rents contain high transfer
earnings because of the over-all usefulness of the land and the
possible returns from transferring it between uses. However, because
urban land is fairly fixed (inelastic) in supply, and becomes increasingly so near the city's centre, economic rent is also high for particular sites and forms an increasing proportion of total rent as the
C.B.D. is approached. Any increase in demand for C.B.D. sites is
therefore reflected in substantial rises in commercial rent. On the
city's outskirts, however, any increase in the demand to use land for
a specific purpose only produces a small change in economic rent
(land being that much less scarce), and *ipso facto* in commercial
rent.

If we take a simple case where there are two firms, one a retailer
and the other an accountant, seeking sites to establish their business,
and one household seeking a home in which to live, then three
ceiling-rent curves can be defined. (We indicate the maximum rents
each party is willing to pay on the vertical axis of Figure 3.2 and
the distance of various possible locations from the C.B.D. on the
horizontal.) The retailer will be primarily interested in locating at
the market centre where he is accessible to the maximum possible
number of shoppers and is likely to do the greatest amount of business. He will be very reluctant to move further out. The ceiling-rent
curve for the retailer is likely, therefore, to taper off very steeply
with distance from the C.B.D. and this is shown by *RR* in the
diagram. The accountant will prefer to rent a site at the city centre
but, because his business is less dependent upon passing browsers'
impulse buying than the retailer, he will not be adverse to locating
a little way out. The accountant's ceiling-rent curve, therefore, will
be less steeply inclined than the retailer's and may be shown as *AA*
in the figure. The household would again like to locate near the city

centre, where the majority of employment opportunities and recreational facilities are situated, but is less dependent upon general accessibility to the C.B.D. than either the retailer or accountant and consequently its offer curve, *HH*, is less steep.

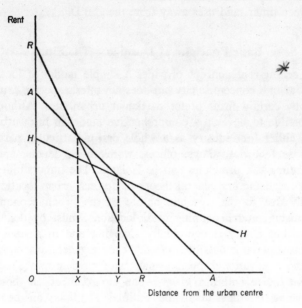

FIG. 3.2   *The effects of rent on location*

Since the retailer is prepared to pay a higher rent than the others for a site near the C.B.D., he will locate between *O* and *X* by outbidding the other parties -- in this range the *RR* curve is above both the *AA* and *HH* curves. The accountant will outbid the household for sites between *X* and *Y*, leaving the area beyond *Y* for residential occupation. This is a useful method of explaining not only land-use patterns but also shows why rents are higher in the C.B.D. than over the rest of the city: they represent payments for prime sites with high earning potential or offering great utility to households.

The high rents for land at the centre of urban areas also have *answer to Xmas tutorial* further important effects. Land is an input into the production process and consequently firms which are land-intensive (that is require a lot of land in their activities) will tend to locate further from the city centre than those which use relatively little land. Effectively, those firms using land-intensive techniques trade off the high rents in the core area against the disadvantage of not having a central location and frequently find a suburban site the best proposition. This is why many firms now have their factories on the outskirts of cities or, as in the radial model of location patterns, sandwiched between other land uses away from the C.B.D.

3.4 Some Basic Principles of Location – The Firm

The ceiling-rent concept provides a simple model of location behaviour in a concentric city but does not offer a specific explanation of why certain firms prefer particular urban sites. Although it is impossible to develop a comprehensive model of intra-urban location, either for industry as a whole or for particular parts of it – such as factories, shops, offices, warehouses, depots, and so on – certain basic principles can be isolated. The impossibility of creating a satisfactory general theory of optimal urban location is primarily due to the dynamic nature of the urban economy. Any optimising model, defining ideal locations, must by definition be static, but a city is continually changing and in a state of flux. Nevertheless, it is possible to isolate certain general principles showing how a rational businessman with predetermined objectives *should* locate within a given urban environment. In these rather restrictive circumstances, the optimal location can be defined, although as Brian Goodall [1972] has observed, 'Actual and optimal do not coincide.' In many cases firms cannot locate at the optimal site because they have insufficient knowledge to determine the best location or, alternatively, the site may already be occupied.

In the previous chapter we saw that firms' inter-urban location decisions were influenced by the possibilities of agglomeration economies and the availability of resources. In selecting a site, additional factors also assume an importance. These specific intra-urban influences can be divided into three main categories.

(i) *Transport Provision.* Industrial location decisions are extremely sensitive to the quality of urban transport. Ideal urban sites must provide adequate transport – both public and private – to ensure uninterrupted supplies of inputs and free movement of finished products to their markets. Included within this is a transport system capable of getting all employees to their work with the minimum of friction. In the case of retailers, the transport system should be adequate to provide a satisfactory degree of accessibility to their shops for potential customers.

(ii) *Interdependence of Decisions.* Firms are initially attracted to cities by the possibility of agglomeration economies and consequently will wish to eventually locate near complementary firms and away from competitors. Their final siting will depend, therefore, to a large extent on the location decisions of other firms in the city.

(iii) *Competition for Factors of Production.* Labour wage costs tend to vary considerably between regions and cities but relatively little within an urban area. This is the result of a relative lack of geographical mobility between areas but much freer movement of workers between similar jobs within the same area. The influence of this mobility is that wages for any occupation within urban areas tend to be very much the same both between firms and over the geographical area of the city. As a consequence, labour costs are assumed to have little influence on intra-urban location decisions.

Remembering these peculiarities of the intra-urban location decision, we can now consider some of the basic principles that underlie a firm's decision to set up business at a particular site. Initially we consider a profit-maximising firm which wishes to establish in an urban area where its potential customers are unevenly spread. Further, let the volume of business that will go to the firm be unaffected by its eventual location and also let its production costs be invariate with respect to siting. In these circumstances the only factor affecting location is the cost of delivery and distribution. William Alonso [1964] has demonstrated, using the example of a baker, that in this situation the firm should locate at the median (or middle) distance from his customers – this will minimise the sum of distances over which he has to deliver.

A simple example clearly illustrates the point. If we assume that the firm has customers located along a straight line, as illustrated in Figure 3.3, and that a single trip is made to each customer every day, then the ideal location for the firm is at site *D*. This is effectively the centre of gravity. If the mean distance is chosen, namely to locate adjacent to customer *E*, the distribution of goods will involve travelling 28 miles (that is $5+4+3+2+6+8$ miles) but at the median site adjacent to customer D, distribution is reduced to 26 miles (that is $3 + 2 + 1 + 2 + 8 + 10$ miles).

However, few firms have this opportunity of locating in a vacuum, but must take account of the sites selected by their competitors and suppliers. In the pioneering work of Harold Hotelling

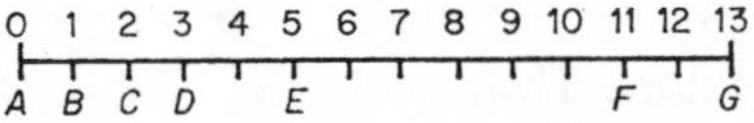

FIG. 3.3

[1929], the activities of two competing firms in the same industry were examined. The urban environment in which they are locating is somewhat different to that in Alonso's model because it is assumed that customers are spread evenly over the city. These customers are considered insensitive to price (the price elasticity of demand is zero), which is the same for both selling units, but are interested in minimising the distance they must travel to purchase the goods. Hotelling's model therefore applies primarily to retail concerns which do not operate delivery services but rely on customers coming to them. As with Alonso's example, the total volume of sales remains constant but now it is divided between two suppliers competing with each other for the largest share.

Under these conditions the firms will tend to locate adjacent to each other at the city centre. The reason for this is fairly straightforward and can easily be illustrated with an example (Figure 3.4). The city boundaries extend from A to B in the diagram and we initially assume the two firms, X and Y, are situated on the quartiles so that X has AM customers and Y has MB. This location pattern will minimise the distance customers have to travel to collect their goods, and is thus a social optimum, but competitive forces will encourage the firms to move to other sites. X, for example, can increase its profits by moving to a site just to the left of Y – this will increase X's share of the market from one-half to three-quarters but in the process reduces Y's share to one-quarter. The move would provoke retaliation from Y which would benefit from relocating just to the left of X's new site – Y would then have just under three-quarters of total sales and X slightly over one-quarter. X would then presumably relocate, and so on and so forth. Eventually a stable situation would be reached when both firms locate at M. (It is worth noting that no stable pattern emerges if three firms are involved – the reader may like to trace through the effect of an additional firm, Z, entering the market.) This type of analysis helps to explain why certain categories of business concentrate in particular parts of a city, although it is by no means a complete explanation as we shall see below.

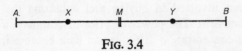

Fig. 3.4

The assumptions we have made to date have been very restrictive, but the basic competitive forces that encourage firms to concentrate in particular urban areas have been introduced. We now proceed to relax some of the assumptions and to see how the introduction of additional considerations can influence location patterns and the degree of spatial concentration.

So far we have assumed that although transport costs may vary between sites, they are the same for all firms. In reality some firms are more efficient than others and consequently have lower delivery costs. Assuming other things are equal, firms with low transport costs should capture a larger share of the market than their less efficient rivals. In Figure 3.5(*a*) we assume firms X and Y have identical production costs but that X's transport costs – as indicated by the gradients of the cost curve – are lower than its competitors. With customers spread evenly over the city, the firms will locate apart with a geographical market of AN going to firm X and NB to Y. The more important transport costs are in relation to the total selling price, the greater will be the tendency for spatial dispersion of competitive firms in the city.

Of course, transport costs can be identical for the two firms, but their production costs may differ. If we assume Y is the more efficient producing unit, then we can see by comparing the vertical cost lines in Figure 3.5(*b*) that it will enjoy a larger share of the market than X. If one firm can produce the goods more cheaply but its competitor is a more efficient distributor, then there is no *a priori* way of determining which will have the largest volume of sales without actual knowledge of the relative cost differences.

The assumption has been that the price at which the good is sold is the same for all customers; in fact, there may be price discrimination. In Figure 3.5(*a*), for example, it may be possible to charge customers located around the sites of X and Y higher prices than those situated at positions near N. Buyers near N have the choice of either purchasing from X or Y, and any attempt by one firm to raise prices will result in customers switching to its competitor. On the other hand, customers located near either of the firms will have less incentive to change supplier if prices rise because of the higher transport costs involved in buying and collecting the commodity from the other firm. The power of price discrimination encourages geographical concentration at the urban core because it means distance is less important in a firm's calculations – a firm will lose few customers by taking a central position.

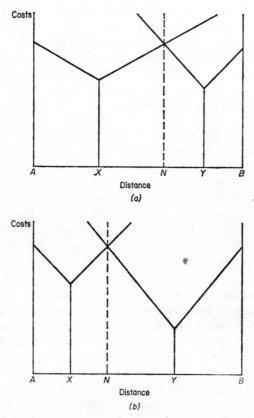

FIG. 3.5   *The effects of differing transport and production costs on industrial location*

A further complication is that a city's population is seldom evenly spread as our multi-firm analysis has assumed, but tends to be bunched (as in Alonso's single-firm model considered earlier). This frequently leads to the existence of several sub-markets. The economic forces in these cases tend to encourage location at the largest sub-market. Hence an uneven spatial distribution of population is an incentive for firms to concentrate at a number of different-sized centres rather than be spread evenly over the city.

A further refinement is necessary when costs of production vary with a firm's output. If costs of production increase with output (marginal cost is rising), then transport costs become relatively less important to the producer who can pass them on to his customers – this tends to encourage the spatial concentration of firms at a central site. If costs are falling with production (marginal cost is decreasing), producers can only pass a decreasing share of transport costs on to buyers without losing customers. In this latter case, firms will be more concerned in selecting sites near customers so that distribution costs are minimised: decentralisation results.

In the last few paragraphs we have been concerned with the economic forces which affect the degree of spatial concentration of an industry within a city. These forces have been summarised by Melvin Greenhut [1956]. The degree to which firms in a single industry or line of business will concentrate at the urban centre depends upon:

(*a*) the sensitivity of consumers to price;
(*b*) the cost of transport relative to the final selling price;
(*c*) a firm's knowledge of the actions and decisions of competitors;
(*d*) the density of the urban population;
(*e*) the degree of price discrimination possible; and
(*f*) the variability of costs in relation to output.

3.5 The Market-Area Theory of Location

In the previous section we looked at some of the basic principles of location theory which influence the urban pattern of industrial activity. This section, although containing some useful insights on how firms arrive at their location decisions, does not offer a general theory of intra-urban location. One attempt to develop such a model makes use of central-place theory. This approach treats each firm as a local monopoly with its own market area; in this respect it differs from the models discussed so far which have been founded on ideas of competition.

Empirically we observe that many firms locate near their customers (for example certain retailers often locate in residential districts), while others prefer a more central site. Central-place theory explains this in terms of the market area they intend to serve. Small retail outlets serve a local market and consequently want to ensure that local customers have easy access to their services. Other businesses, such as insurance companies, are more concerned with acquiring a central position so that they are accessible to the urban population at large.

Market areas are effectively spatial monopolies where a single firm supplies a particular good or service to customers over a given geographical area. Viewed in terms of local monopolies, intra-urban location decisions can be related to central-place theory (Losch [1954]). This type of analysis has been widely used to study urban growth and city hierarchies, but it can also provide useful insight into location patterns. Central-place theory assumes the urban population is spread evenly over the city and describes a situation where the demand for a particular product is just sufficient to support the existence of a single supplier in each geographical market. A 'threshold' level of demand is then said to exist in each market; strictly this is defined as a demand sufficient to support one firm's activity given the local production conditions. (Hence the theory explains why small shopkeepers can survive in a residential estate but an insurance company cannot – the local demand for insurance is insufficient.) The area over which this monopoly power extends depends upon the 'range' of the good sold. This range is determined by the distance over which customers are either willing to come in order to collect the good or are prepared to pay carriage. Transport considerations therefore dominate the area of local monopoly. Boundaries to markets occur at points where customers become indifferent as between producers.

Firms will tend to locate at the centre of their market area, at the central place. The number of central places in any city will depend upon its size and the type of firm under consideration – there will obviously be more central places for grocers than for insurance brokers. An expanding city will attract new firms as the number of potential local monopolies increases. The actual siting of these new firms will depend upon the distribution of the population, the locations of existing central places and the accessibility of the alternative locations. Over time there will also be a movement of firms within the city as demand patterns change and transport costs vary; by altering thresholds and ranges these changes will cause shifts in market areas.

As the city expands in size, the local population may decide against allowing more firms to establish within its boundaries. This action will have two effects:

(i) it will increase the spatial monopoly powers of established firms and extend their range; and

(ii) it will force up transport costs to outlying customers as the market area of each firm is expanded.

These adverse effects may be offset, however, by increased efficiency on the part of the firms. As market areas are expanded, each firm will produce more and consequently may be able to reap economies of large-scale production. Increased transport costs could be cancelled out by lower production costs in these circumstances.

When considered in terms of local monopoly power, intra-urban decisions are therefore influenced by the potential market area for the commodity sold, prevailing transport costs and the attitude of the local authority to the entry of new firms into the city. Empirically this approach offers a useful explanation of the sitings of different types of retailing outlet and of office locations within an urban area, but is less satisfactory in accounting for the location of manufacturing firms which serve a regional, national or even international market.

3.6 Empirical Studies of Intra-Urban Location

So far we have looked at a number of theories which have been developed to explain location within cities; there is a second approach which is to examine the actual location decisions of firms. Studies of this type fall into two categories. First, there are those that consider census and other official data in order to compare this with the theoretical models of location. Second, there have been a number of attempts to directly question businessmen in order to elicit information on their motivations and objectives in selecting a particular site to carry on their activities. Little comparable work has been undertaken on residential location to date.

The majority of work in both these fields has been carried out in the United States, although there is a growing literature on the U.K. experience and the location of firms within London in particular.

In one of these latter studies, Goddard [1967] considered the sitings of thirty-five different office activities within Greater London and looked at three – advertising agencies, publishing and construction-engineering offices – in some detail. He found that many of the underlying assumptions of intra-urban theory are no longer valid – in particular, the forces which have previously encouraged firms to locate within the C.B.D. (principally linkages with other firms and with customers) are much weaker today than in the past. This change has come about as the result of improved communications – telephones, telexes and greater consumer mobility – which have significantly reduced the advantages of a central location.

Goddard's findings support a number of earlier studies made in the United States – these found a long-term trend for firms to drift from the C.B.D. In one piece of work, Vernon [1959] looked at thirteen major metropolitan areas and discovered a continuing decentralisation process throughout the study period (1898–1954). Similarly, Meyer, Kain and Wohl [1965] in looking at thirty-nine cities over the period 1947–58 found that in all cases employment grew much faster in the outer urban areas than at the core, where, in many instances, there was an actual decline.

These studies suggest that the importance attached to transport costs in location models tends to be excessive and that many of the disadvantages of locating away from the core have disappeared as communications have improved. The outward movement of the population may also exert important influences.

An alternative hypothesis is suggested by Cameron and Johnson [1969], who argue that the decentralisation process may be the result of firms not being willing to pay for redeveloping their central-area premises (or being discouraged from doing so by the local authority) when there is cheaper land available on the urban periphery. Whereas the improvement-in-communications thesis concentrates on the fall in demand for C.B.D. sites, this alternative approach is supply-orientated.

In order to isolate the factors influencing location decisions, and consequently in an attempt to determine the appropriate assumptions for model building, several attempts have been made to directly question businessmen on their location choices. A number of questionnaire studies in London indicate that access to customers tends to dominate location decisions. The South East Joint Planning Study [1971] found that 64 per cent of manufacturing firms in Inner London thought access to customers was an important factor in holding them in London. Similarly, Hoare [1973] found that 80·1 per cent of the businessmen he questioned considered this an 'important' influence on their location in London. Access to markets seems to be of significantly greater importance in both instances than access to supplies. In addition, these studies emphasise that firms consider locating in London to be far more important than being at some particular site within the city: the inter-urban decision dominates the intra-urban. (Indeed, 46·1 per cent of those questioned by Hoare felt that simply having a prestige London address was important.)

A further study of office moves by Wabe [1966] suggests that the size of the individual firm can be important in the location decision. By examining a sample of firms drawn from the records of the Location of Offices Bureau he was able to determine why particular firms relocated within London in 1965. He found that, in general, smaller firms were less likely to move to periphery sites than large ones, especially if the latter were head offices for companies dealing in a regional or national rather than a purely local market. He concludes: 'Of all the groups of firms that moved [away from Central London], the small firms are probably able to make the highest percentage addition to trading profit. To balance against this is the fact that small firms are usually specialist firms who have strong locational ties with the centre . . . if they do consider it possible to move they usually move only a short distance.' Again, the importance of access to customers is apparent.

From these several studies, there does emerge some general support for the market-area theory, at least in office location. Firms moving away from the central area seem to be those serving a super-urban market and are consequently less concerned about retaining a central site as land values rise. Providing these firms can find offices in suburban areas with good inter-urban communications, they will vacate the C.B.D. although they may have small prestige offices in the capital. Smaller firms serving only a local market appear to prefer a central site in order to maximise their catchment area and, once located, significant rises in land values are necessary to force relocation and then it is usually not far from the C.B.D.

One final point to emerge from empirical work in this field is the general locational inertia of industry and the poor information upon which decisions are made. Firms appear inadequately informed about the potential of alternative locations and have little idea of the relative costs and benefits associated with different sites. Where moves do occur they are often for reasons other than simple profit maximisation and fall into that category of objectives known as 'satisficing', which includes environmental, social, recreational, political and other considerations besides the purely pecuniary (Townroe [1971]).

3.7 Residential Location

Early work on location theory concentrated almost exclusively on the siting of industrial and retailing premises. In the urban context this seems rather strange since the largest part of the land area in most modern cities is devoted to housing. The early work on industrial location simply assumed that people respond to the establishment of different firms and, in order to take advantage of employment and consumption opportunities, locate around them. John F. Kain [1968], for example, said, 'Manufacturing determines the location decisions of households, not vice versa.'

In terms of microeconomics, this lack of any satisfactory theory of residential location left a serious gap in the economic theory of consumption, housing representing the largest single expenditure in most households' budgets. To the urban economist, an adequate theory of residential location is necessary to understand how the urban land economy functions.

The difficulty with studying residential location is that in deciding to live in a particular house, a family is making more than a simple location decision. A house provides a whole range of facilities (for example living space, prestige, amenity, and so on) which must be considered in conjunction with its geographical position. It is unlikely that a house will fulfil all the requirements of a family, and consequently trade-offs are necessary between the attributes and shortcomings of each property. A less preferred site may be chosen, for example, because the building meets all the other requirements of the family. The exact values people attach to different sites and buildings is by no means clear, although at least one economist (Kaiser [1968]) feels that location comes low on the list of priorities. Brian Goodall [1972] argues, however, that there comes a point when the physical characteristics of a house are offset by locational factors if only because of transport-cost considerations.

Three main factors appear important in determining residential location. A family's income is certainly a significant consideration; high income both increases the selection of sites available and the potential size of plot. Empirical evidence also suggests the age of the property bought varies inversely with income (as the concentric theory of cities would suggest). High-income groups appear to have a preference for sites offering good accessibility to the city centre and to transport facilities. These factors attract the higher-income earners to the outskirts of the urban area, where there is space to build, and to sites adjacent to the main transport routes.

Income is not the only determinant of location – at least as important is the access the property offers to local amenities and employment opportunities. Certain urban sites have the advantage of close proximity to either major recreational facilities or work places and are therefore much sought after.

A final, but still important, consideration is the quality of neighbourhood. People in the same social class tend to concentrate together and, although this can partly be explained in terms of income, this seems to suggest similarities in taste. There are 'snob' effects associated with particular neighbourhoods and also a feeling of security is often experienced when living near people in a similar social class; there is less risk of adverse environmental change. Inasmuch as relatives/family tend to be of the same social class, this also influences locational behaviour. Concentration is particularly pronounced amongst immigrant groups, which tend to group together partly because of their individual cultures and partly because they have difficulty mixing with other sections of the community.

Early theories of residential location were little more than extensions of the existing models of either agricultural or industrial location. The first specific model of housing location was that of Park, Burgess and McKenzie [1925] who, in their study of concentric cities, decided that the wealthier sections of the urban community elected to live on the periphery of the urban area because they place great weight on large and new buildings. Periphery areas offer plenty of cheap, undeveloped land for this purpose.

More recent work has concentrated on the importance of income and accessibility. These models have attempted to show that families try to select a site which will maximise their utility (or welfare) subject to their income. One such model has been developed by William Alonso [1965]. In this it is assumed that a family spends its income on (*a*) a piece of land upon which to live, (*b*) commuting, and (*c*) 'other goods'. It is also assumed that land becomes cheaper with distance from the C.B.D. and that transport costs are directly determined by the distance covered. If income rises the family can either spend more on commuting and live further from the C.B.D. on a larger plot of land or else it can buy more of the 'other goods'. The final choice will depend upon the particular preferences of the household but, as a general principle, it will select that combination which increases its welfare by the greatest amount. This will be achieved by both increasing the consumption of other goods and moving to a large site; people who wish to buy a relatively large amount of land will move out further than those who give a higher priority to 'other goods'.

Alonso's model assumes that commuting costs only vary with distance and that all workers are employed in the C.B.D. It also takes no account of the actual characteristics of residences other than their location. Jay Siegal [1970] relaxes these assumptions and concludes that residential location decisions are determined by three things: accessibility, environmental quality and the particular characteristics of each site. The household maximises the utility it obtains from these characteristics given its income. If the head of the family also has the choice of where to work, he must make two simultaneous decisions: where to live and where to work. A utility-maximising approach is again employed.

3.8 Intervention in the Urban Land Market

The principles of intra-urban location discussed in previous sections rely upon the operation of market forces with no interference from national or local authorities. In reality, government is far from passive in the workings of the urban land market. Controls extend to all types of urban activity – industrial, commercial and residential – and lead to distortions in the normal market processes.

In practice, it is impossible to isolate the effects of urban location policy from that of regional policy, although one or two general points do emerge. Office and industrial location is clearly an integral part of a successful regional policy, but the operation of this policy also has profound effects on the patterns of urban land usage. To varying degrees, industry has been encouraged to move from the congested South-eastern and West Midlands regions since the depression of the 1930s and to establish in the Development Areas. This policy has included the stick of Industrial Development Certificate controls and the carrot of subsidised trading estates built on the outskirts of the older industrial centres of the North-east and North-west. The over-all effect has been a shift of industry from central sites to periphery ones, although exact quantification of the impact of the policy is difficult to assess.

Official policy has also influenced office location in recent years. The Location of Offices Bureau was established in 1963 to encourage offices to be relocated away from Central London, and via its advertising seems to have had some degree of success (in 1970, for example, 906 firms moved from the centre taking 75,000 jobs with them), and there appears to be considerable relocation at periphery sites. Harry Richardson [1971], however, points to a contradiction in this policy because office development in the remainder of the South-east has also been severely restricted since 1965. This has prevented relocation being fully realised and many firms wishing to move to the outskirts of London have been prevented from doing so by this legislation.

The urban housing market is also subject to quite rigid controls (see Chapter 9). A government circular in 1955 initiated the well-known 'green-belt' policy which prevented the development of agricultural–rural land around the boundaries of our major cities. Based upon the assumption of extremely slow population growth, this policy was intended to prevent exploitation of the countryside and to provide urban dwellers with recreational facilities. In reality, developers have moved beyond the designated green belt and constructed housing estates for high-income commuters further out. Effectively, the concentric pattern of many cities has now been modified and between the rings of high-quality housing around the edge of cities is sandwiched a belt of undeveloped land. London is an example of this trend, with a green belt some forty or so miles from the centre, and surrounded by an outer commuter belt.

Local authorities exercise more direct controls through their powers to grant planning permission and through their own house-building activities. Council housing and road systems cover a large part of the urban area but are difficult to incorporate into traditional economic models. Planning is playing an increasingly important role in determining intra-urban location patterns; to assume perfectly free markets is a little unrealistic. Given the constraints imposed by official policy, and the geographical features of each city, the basic economic principles we have outlined above provide an adequate explanation of most location choices and they also provide useful guidelines to enable planners and politicians to understand the implications of their actions.

3.9 Summary

No general theory of intra-urban location has yet been developed, and it seems unlikely that any such theory will emerge in the foreseeable future because of the diverse objectives of the firms, businesses and individuals which comprise a city. Retailers want a site to maximise access for customers; industry seeks good transport links with suppliers and potential markets; while offices attempt to concentrate together to take advantage of their mutual services. Central-place theory provides a partial explanation of certain types of location decisions but is of only limited use when considering firms serving a super-urban market.

The general principles of location outlined above have a considerable degree of applicability and help to explain certain features of urban land-use patterns but do not represent a theory in themselves. The best that can be said for intra-urban location theory in its current state is that it offers some limited assistance to those trying to understand the workings of the urban economy and also helps politicians and planners in drawing up policy, but it is still, in many ways, one of the least satisfactory parts of urban economics.

References

W. ALONSO [1964], 'Location Theory', in *Regional Development and Planning: A Reader*, ed. J. Friedmann and W. Alonso (Cambridge, Mass.: M.I.T. Press).

W. ALONSO [1965], *Location and Land Use: Towards a General Theory of Land Rent* (Harvard University Press).

W. ALONSO [1966], 'Cities, Planners and Urban Renewal', *Urban*

Renewal: The Record and Controversy, ed. J. Q. Wilson (Cambridge, Mass.: M.I.T. Press).

F. M. BABCOCK [1932], *The Valuation of Real Estate* (New York: McGraw-Hill).

E. W. BURGESS [1925], 'The Growth of the City', in *The City*, ed. R. E. Park, E. W. Burgess and R. D. McKenzie (University of Chicago Press).

G. C. CAMERON and K. M. JOHNSON [1969], 'Comprehensive Urban Renewal and Industrial Relocation – the Glasgow Case', in *Regional and Urban Studies*, ed. S. C. Orr and J. B. Cullingworth (London: Allen & Unwin).

S. G. CHECKLAND [1964], 'The British Industrial City as History: the Glasgow Case', *Urban Studies* (February) pp. 34–54.

J. GODDARD [1967], 'Changing Office Location Patterns within Central London', *Urban Studies* (November) pp. 276–83.

B. GOODALL [1972], *The Economics of Urban Areas* (Oxford: Pergamon).

M. GREENHUT [1956], *Plant Location in Theory and Practice* (University of North Carolina Press).

A. G. HOARE [1973], 'The Sphere of Influence of Industrial Location Factors', *Regional Studies*, pp. 301–14.

H. HOTELLING [1929], 'Stability in Competition', *Economic Journal* (March) pp. 41–57.

H. HOYT [1939], *The Structure and Growth of Residential Neighbourhoods in American Cities* (Washington: Government Printing Office).

J. F. KAIN [1968], 'The Distribution and Movement of Jobs and Industry', in *The Metropolitan Enigma*, ed. J. Q. Wilson (Harvard University Press).

E. J. KAISER [1968], 'Location Decision Factors in a Producer Model of Residential Development', *Land Economics* (August) pp. 351–62.

A. LOSCH [1954], *The Economics of Location* (Yale University Press).

J. R. MEYER, J. F. KAIN and M. WOHL [1965], *The Urban Transport Problem* (Harvard University Press).

R. E. PARK, E. W. BURGESS and R. D. MCKENZIE [1925] (eds), *The City* (University of Chicago Press).

H. W. RICHARDSON [1971], *Urban Economics* (Harmondsworth: Penguin).

J. SIEGAL [1970], *Intrametropolitan Migration of White and Minority Group Households* (Stanford University Press).

The South East Joint Planning Team [1971], *Strategic Plan for the South-East – A Framework* (London: H.M.S.O.).

P. M. TOWNROE [1971], *Industrial Location Decisions: A Study in Management Behaviour* (Centre for Urban and Regional Studies: University of Birmingham).

R. VERNON [1959], *The Changing Economic Function of the Central City* (Committee for Economic Development).

J. S. WABE [1966], 'Office Decentralisation: an Empirical Study', *Urban Studies* (June) pp. 36–55.

4 THE URBAN LABOUR MARKET

4.1 Introduction

Besides containing industry and commerce, cities are concentrations of people, and the urban labour market determines whether these people will have work and, if so, the wage rate they will be paid. In less developed countries the paramount problem is providing sufficient employment for the rapidly expanding urban populations; in the Western world the economist is more interested in labour flows between urban areas and between jobs within urban concentrations and with wage differentials between various forms of employment at different locations. This chapter concentrates on these latter problems.

Comparatively little is known about the working of the urban labour market in a developed economy. This is particularly surprising because of its importance as the major urban factor market (indeed, Wilbur Thompson [1965] has argued that 'the urban economy is above all else a labour market') and the role it plays in linking many of the various parts of the local economic system. Employment considerations, as we saw earlier, affect both the inter- and intra-urban location decisions of households and, in turn, are a determinant of, and a response to, a city's housing, environmental and transport situation. Workers are unique in the sense that they are not only factors of production but also consumers of urban facilities, residents, voters and, frequently, public employees. This multiplicity of roles would suggest that considerable effort would need to be put into gaining a clearer understanding of the workings of the urban labour market.

Although a large number of studies have been made of the sociological and psychological aspects of the market, particularly with respect to race relations and poverty, our understanding of the economic mechanisms at work are much less well-developed. The relatively sparse literature on this aspect of urban economics is partly explained by the emphasis labour economists have put into the study of national and regional labour markets in recent years. There is a natural tendency, because of the way U.K. trade unions and firms are organised, to delineate by type of industry rather than by geographical area. Hence most labour economics has concentrated, until comparatively recently, on particular sectors, regardless of their location (for a survey see King [1972]). This type of work sheds little light on why wage rates differ between cities and between those employed in similar jobs but living in different parts of the same city. Where earlier attempts were made to consider the spatial aspects of labour markets, they tended to be descriptive rather than analytical and frequently bordered on geography rather than economics. In this chapter, we try to draw together the skeleton of what is known, but at present there is very little flesh on the bones. Initially, however, we need to define the boundaries of an urban labour market.

4.2 The Idea of a Local Labour Market

There is no single labour market in a city but rather a multiplicity of sub-markets, demarcated by various criteria but linked by mobility – both geographical and occupational. Many labour markets extend outside of individual cities – in the case of higher management they may be national or even international, while others are much more localised, especially for manual workers (Goodman [1970]). The geographical boundaries of any labour market are determined primarily by the pecuniary and psychological costs of extensive travel to and from work and the alternative costs of migration to different areas. Lower-income earners cannot afford long commuting trips and the benefits of removing to another city are likely to be relatively small. On the other hand, those in higher-income categories may be prepared to travel some distance between home and work every day and, in some circumstances, migrate considerable distances to obtain a 'better' job. This feature of urban labour markets is partly reflected in the various land-use patterns discussed earlier where high-income earners live on the outskirts of large cities while manual and lower-paid workers locate nearer the central area.

A secondary constraint on labour mobility is the system of communication linking employer and worker. White-collar workers, partly by virtue of the nature of their work but also because of the effort employers put into seeking suitable employees, tend to be much better informed about alternative jobs than do manual workers. The latter frequently rely upon informal networks of friends and upon advertisements in local newspapers when seeking new employment. This limits the geographical range of the effective labour-catchment area. The communications factor is of considerable importance in the urban context because it means that in our largest cities there may well be a number of quite separate neighbourhood labour markets created by local informal communications systems. This situation is particularly likely to occur when different parts of a city specialise in different types of economic activity and create peculiar local conditions of labour demand, as well as supply.

Attempts have been made to rigidly define local labour markets using these concepts of access to work and boundaries to occupational communications networks, but they have proved to be very imprecise. In the urban context a much more useful approach is the one quoted by Hunter and Reid [1968] which defines a local labour market as 'a geographical area surrounding a central city (or cities a few miles apart) in which there is a concentration of labour demand, and in which workers can change their jobs without changing their residences'. Further, Hunter and Reid consider that 'the essential points about a local labour market are that the bulk of the area's population habitually seeks employment there, and that local employers recruit most of their labour from that area'. This type of definition is vague (for example does 'bulk' mean 51 per cent or 90 per cent?) but it does convey the basic characteristics of a local labour market without being too restrictive. It is also a definition which should be familiar to economic geographers who think in terms of 'employment fields' and 'labour sheds' which are cartographical descriptions of sources of labour supply to certain economic activities (for example a group of factories or a central business district of a large city).

4.3 The Gravity Model of Labour Movements

Neoclassical economic theory assumes that the wage rate for any occupation is determined by the interaction of supply and demand in the labour market. The higher the wage rate, the greater will be the supply of people willing to take employment but the lower will be the demand for their services. Men will continue to offer them-selves for employment until the marginal man's income just com-pensates him for the disutility of the job. Employers will keep taking on more men until the value of the incremental man's work (the marginal revenue product) just equals his wage. When the supply of labour just equals the demand for labour services, an equilibrium is reached and no more workers will be employed at the prevailing wage rate and no more will offer themselves for employment.

Wage rates for any job can, according to this theory, only differ between urban areas for short periods. If one city has a higher wage rate, it will attract workers from other cities and rural areas which will (a) increase the supply of labour in that city, pulling the local wage down, and (b) reduce the supply of labour in other cities, pushing their local wage rates up. In terms of labour movements, prosperous cities offering high wages will act as magnets and 'pull' people towards them, while, at the same time, other cities, where industries are in decline, and rural areas, where economic activity is stagnant, will have a much weaker demand for labour and the lower wages they can offer will 'push' workers away. This mechanism means that, in the long term, an optimal geographical distribution of workers is achieved because no worker will be able to gain by moving to a new location.

In reality, we know from experience that wage rates do not equal out over time. Within any country, the strength of economic forces will depend not only on wage rates but also upon the difficulty of physically relocating, the relative attractiveness of a prosperous city will be greater if removal, resettlement and other relocation costs are minimal. In many cases, these relocation costs are considerable, especially if one also includes the social costs associated with break-ing existing neighbourhood ties and forming new ones.

The gravity model, adapted from Newtonian physics by Reilly [1929] and others, attempts to explain inter-urban movements of labour in terms of the relative attractiveness of different cities and the friction associated with moving between them. In its simplest form, the model assumes income differentials approximate to the relative attractiveness of different urban areas and the geographical distance between cities to the impedance of moving between them. However, this model suffers from several obvious limitations. The attraction factor ignores environmental and amenity considerations, while the friction element, although a reasonable surrogate for removal costs, does not reflect the full social costs of relocating.

The most elementary formulation of the gravity model states that migration from city X to city Y will be positively related to the relative income levels in the two cities and inversely related to the distance between them. In other words, we can explain migration between the city pairs in terms of

$$M_{xy} = \frac{KA_y{}^\alpha}{d_{xy}^\beta},$$

where M_{xy} is the probability of a worker moving from city X to city Y, A_y is the attraction of Y (in this case the higher income which can be earned) and d_{xy} is the geographical distance between the cities (K, α and β are parameters to be estimated mathematically from empirical data).

Extending this simple framework to include a wider range of socio-economic variables, as well as relaxing the implicit assumption that all workers have full knowledge of relative wage rates and removal costs, is theoretically straightforward. Unfortunately, these additions complicate the model and make calibration difficult, even assuming the relevant data are available. One crude attempt to calibrate a gravity model in the United States, by Ida Lowry [1966] for instance, produced poor results unless migrants were sub-divided by a number of socio-economic characteristics (for example age, income, education, and so on).

A variation on the straightforward gravity approach is the intervening-opportunities model. This approach assumes a worker is intent upon migration from city X and considers the probability of his moving to Y not in terms of the distance between the city pairs, but rather in relation to the alternative opportunities of employment between them. At its simplest, the intervening-opportunities model may be expressed as

$$M_{xy} = \frac{KA_y}{A_{xy}},$$

where M_{xy} and A_y are as above and A_{xy} represents income-earning opportunities geographically between cities X and Y (K is a constant to be calculated as before). A model of this kind, based upon Swedish data, produced quite encouraging results (see Isbell [1944]), but the approach suffers from similar defects as the gravity model.

The underlying theory is simple to understand and the model straightforward to calibrate in the form specified above, but increased realism requires a much more complex description of 'opportunities', which is difficult to formulate, and the model becomes more cumbersome to calculate as additional influences are incorporated.

Models of the gravity and opportunities kind are useful guides when attempting to explain why labour moves between cities, but they are too limited to provide a complete explanation. The majority of people remain in the city where they were born and brought up; in reality, mobility is very limited. This is partly due to the psychic gain of living in familiar surroundings, near friends and family, but it also reflects a preference for security. It is much easier to find work in a town with which one is familiar than in an entirely unknown environment. Besides neglecting these factors, both approaches also ignore longer-term considerations: people do not necessarily consider simply the short-run gains from relocating but also take account of the longer-term prospects, looking at net earnings over the whole of the remainder of their working lives. (The importance of expected future earnings has been substantiated to some extent by the empirical work of Samuel Bowles [1970] in the United States.)

4.4 Intra-Urban Wage-Rate Differentials

In order to develop theories of intra-urban location, it is frequently assumed, as we did in Chapter 3, that labour engaged in a particular occupation will receive the same rate of pay irrespective of the location of its employment within the urban area. In other words, it is assumed that wages differ between cities but not within them. In regional studies or in the consideration of smaller urban areas, the assumption of a constant spatial wage level across cities may be justified, but in the case of large metropolitan areas there may in fact be quite pronounced differentials in spatial wage rates which, judging from findings in the United States, do not seem to be narrowing over time (Buckley [1969]).

The frequently made assumption of common wage rates across urban areas is a relic of classical economic theory dating back to Adam Smith [1776]. In *The Wealth of Nations*, for example, we find it stated:

The whole of the advantages and disadvantages of the different employments of labour and stock must, in the same neighbourhood, be either perfectly equal or continually tending to equality. If in the same neighbourhood, thère was any employment evidently either more or less advantageous than the rest, so many people would crowd into it in the one case, and so many would desert it in the other, that its advantages would soon return to the level of other employment.

Despite these natural long-term economic tendencies, within any urban area wage differentials do exist both between occupations and also within them. In this section, explanations for these differences are presented; some of these are of a purely economic nature, but wage differentials may also occur because of discrimination and other social factors. We consider these latter features of the urban labour market in more general terms later in the chapter.

Different groups within an urban area will earn different amounts, irrespective of their location within the city; this is simply the result of differences in skills and education. People with training tend to be more productive than those without and hence can command higher wages. In the longer term, low-paid workers will attempt to undertake more training in order to push their wages up, but initial costs are high, making this a slow process. Inter-job mobility, therefore, tends to be very poor, especially in a highly specialised economy such as we find in most urban areas. But even accepting differences in pay between occupations, we still need to explain why wages differ for the same occupation in different parts of a large city.

The only major U.K. study of inter-plant wage differentials within cities (MacKay [1970]) shows considerable variations in wage rates. In 1959, for example, standard weekly earnings for fitters in Glasgow varied between £9·3 in the lowest wage unit up to £15·6 in the highest. Considering a range of engineering occupations in the city, MacKay also found that on average workers in the highest wage plant were paid approximately 60–80 per cent more than those employed in the lowest paying establishments. Confirmation of these findings was provided by data collected in subsequent years and reinforced by the results of a similar study in Birmingham. Although these quite substantial differences can be partly explained by imperfections on the demand side, in many cases employers were extremely ignorant of the pay offered by competitors, such considerable variations in wage rates are not easily accounted for.

The previous section explained inter-urban wage differences in terms of the costs (including social costs) of removal to the highest-income area and the possible ignorance of workers as to relative wage rates between various cities. In a similar way, intra-urban wage differentials have been explained by Leon Moses [1962] in terms of commuting costs between home and work; he assumes the residential location has already been determined. He argued that 'Labour is not perfectly mobile since the time, money cost and dis-utility of commuting are significant. *As a result the supply of labour is not perfectly elastic to any given point in the urban area*, and the subject of intra-urban differentials cannot be dismissed' (our italics). Moses, therefore, explains intra-urban wages in terms of the shape of the labour-supply curve at different points in the city.

The theory is best explained in terms of a concentric city where all employment is initially assumed to be concentrated within the C.B.D. Further, all households are assumed to be in equilibrium; any move would worsen their level of satisfaction or well-being. Moreover, all workers are paid identical wages, work the same number of hours and undertake an identical number of commuting trips. In these circumstances, the net incomes, after work-trip expenditures, will vary between workers according to the nature of their intra-urban transport costs and the distance between their homes and the C.B.D. Since residential land values will be influenced by their accessibility to the C.B.D., this will act as a compensating mechanism to ensure all urban residents enjoy the same level of satisfaction. People living away from the core will have to pay higher commuting costs, but their land rentals will be correspondingly lower.

In this rather stylised situation, a worker could improve his level of satisfaction by changing the location of his work; ideally, he would like to work at home. To retain equilibrium, he would be willing to sacrifice some income for this move, an amount of income up to the transport costs involved in commuting to the core. In reality, this is just what does happen; workers do accept lower pay in respect of not having to pay travel costs to their places of employment (the actual trade-off being determined by the disutility associated with commuting). Moses maintains that 'the wage differential, positive or negative, a worker is willing to accept is completely determined by the structure of money transport costs'.

In Figure 4.1, let the vertical axis represent the wage rate and the horizontal axis distance from the C.B.D. *OW* will represent the wage paid at the core, the vertical distance *WA'* is the travel cost between *A* (at the very edge of the city) and the C.B.D., and *OA'* the wage rate required to keep an employee living at *A* in his current occupation if he worked at home. The worker is therefore indifferent between earning *OA'* and working at home and receiving *OW* and working at the C.B.D. The curve *WW'* traces out the wage

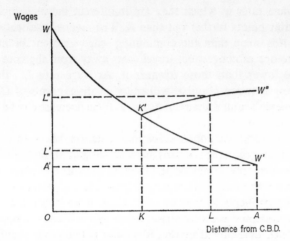

Fig. 4.1 *The spatial supply curve for labour*

rates at which a worker living at *A* would have to be paid to make him indifferent between working at home and at any intermediate site between the C.B.D. and *A*. This is the wage gradient and indicates how wage rates within suburb *A* are likely to vary according to where *within* the city workers are employed. The curve also shows the wage rates at which people living between *A* and the C.B.D. will be indifferent between working at home and at the core. They will require higher wages to work at home than someone living at *A* because of the higher property and land prices nearer the C.B.D., a feature of our initial assumption that households are in equilibrium.

We initially assumed all jobs were located within the C.B.D. and then relaxed this to incorporate jobs between the employee's home and the C.B.D.; we now go further and consider the possibility of 'reverse commuting'. Suppose a firm is located at *L*; to attract local labour from the immediate neighbourhood it will have to offer a wage rate of OL' – workers living between L and A will then be indifferent between employment at L and jobs at the C.B.D. People living nearer the C.B.D. will still commute to work. If the firm finds it requires additional labour, it must increase its wage rate. If workers from as near the core at K are required, a wage of OL'' must be offered to attract them. The curve $K'W'''$ represents the reverse commuting wage gradient for workers living at K and indicates the wage rates at which they are indifferent between jobs at K itself and at points further out than K. The reverse gradient will usually be less steep than the commuting wage gradient because, with the absence of congestion, travel costs away from the core are likely to be lower than those towards it. At wage rate L'', those workers living between L and A will enjoy locational rents of $L'L''$, and for those with homes between K and L rents decrease the nearer they live to K.

In the long term, of course, location rents are likely to cause workers to move into the suburbs between K and A until the increased labour supply brings wages down to the 'normal level' and equilibrium is restored. It is worth noting that the shapes of the various wage gradients cannot be determined by *a priori* methods, but depend upon the actual characteristics of each city's transport system and the local fare structure; it is quite possible, for example, for WW' to be concave to the origin rather than convex as drawn in Figure 4.1.

A similar conclusion to Moses is reached in a study by Richard Muth [1969], although the method employed is slightly different. Muth concentrates much more on residential location and he concludes:

> If locational equilibrium is to prevail for locally employed workers, the wage rate received by any class of worker, defined in terms of the wage received in any given location, must decline with distance from C.B.D. Otherwise locally employed workers at greater distances from the C.B.D. would be better off than those closer to the C.B.D.

The limitations of the Moses–Muth-type approach is its exclusive concentration on the supply side of the equation, the wage gradient forming a spatial supply curve for labour. The demand for labour may also vary at different points within the city. Some areas may offer considerable opportunities for local employment, while others give workers little option but to commute into the C.B.D. In a perfectly competitive and mobile environment, employers would move into areas where local workers would be prepared to accept much lower wages in exchange for less travel, but such conditions are not common. As we have seen earlier, firms have to consider many costs when selecting a location from which to operate and labour costs are simply one of these. A central location may offer advantages offsetting the higher wages required to attract sufficient labour. Also, urban planning frequently prevents industry from establishing in some parts of cities, so as to preserve the local environment, and this distorts the market processes, creating spatial variations in demand.

4.5 The Effects of Trade Unions and National Wage Agreements

In the previous sections we have assumed a perfectly competitive market for labour, with wage rates varying between different locations according to local differences in the supply and demand conditions for workers. In many types of occupation this assumption is not realistic; wage rates are negotiated at the national level. Such a situation occurs in those sectors which are highly unionised or when a large firm has branches or plant in several cities but pays a common wage to all employees irrespective of their place of work. The removal of local wage differentials distorts the workings of local labour markets and frequently leads to either an excess (when national wage rates are too high) or shortage (when the rates are too low) of certain categories of worker in the local labour market.

This problem has occurred in several large cities during the 1960s, especially in public-sector undertakings, and London has been particularly badly affected. Even in national wage negotiations, London is usually treated as a special case and higher rates of pay are generally offered: the so-called London allowances. Despite this recognition of the special problems of the capital, wages have seldom been sufficiently above the national average to cover the high costs associated with living in London and, as a result, there have been periodic shortages of labour in certain sectors.

In order to circumvent the straitjacket of national wage rates, employers in many cities offer non-pecuniary rewards to their workers. In many cases these 'perks' are quite clearly defined, often including subsidised canteen meals, luncheon vouchers or cheap travel facilities, but in other instances they are not so immediately apparent. One very common incentive offered by urban public undertakings is job security – the freedom from redundancy and arbitrary dismissal, which this means, has been found to be of considerable importance in sociological studies of urban labour markets, for example see Dennis Brooks's study of London Transport [1975]. In other cases, for example the Greater London Council, non-pecuniary advantages attached to employment include assistance with mortgages on houses or cheap rented accommodation. Transport undertakings, which tend to be very labour-intensive, have found it particularly difficult to recruit sufficient workers. London Transport attempted to solve its problem of an acute shortage of bus drivers on one occasion by changing the career structure in the sector. By introducing one-man-operated buses in the 1960s, it was possible to pay drivers considerably more because of the dual role of driver and ticket collector they now fulfilled, and in this way the shortage was temporarily overcome.

Where the introduction of collective bargaining has distorted the normal market mechanism and imposed a national wage settlement on a sector of a local economy, the system frequently adapts. Non-pecuniary considerations assume increasing importance. In many cases apparent differences in pay between, and sometimes within, cities are illusory and only apply in monetary terms; when all types of reward are taken into account and we consider *real*-wage rates, such distortions tend to be very much smaller.

However, attempts to actually quantify the importance of non-pecuniary income have been singularly unsuccessful and in many instances produced perverse results (for example see Robinson [1967] and MacKay [1970]). In U.K. studies which have been undertaken, a frequent finding is that, rather than compensating for low monetary incomes, non-pecuniary elements are often greatest where wages are highest. The problem is that non-pecuniary factors tend to be very numerous and, when identifiable, frequently extremely difficult to quantify. Empirical work has thus concentrated on 'fringe benefits' such as pensions, life assurance and sickness schemes which are easily recognisable, but have ignored, for practical reasons, factors such as job satisfaction, security, prospects of rapid internal promotion and motivation. The difficulty is that many non-pecuniary factors are only perceived by the employee and do not fit into conventional economic models. Until survey techniques and statistical analysis are improved, the exact importance of non-pecuniary elements in explaining inter-plant wage differentials in the same city will remain uncertain.

4.6 Discrimination in the Urban Labour Market

Discrimination takes many forms (racial, sexual, social, religious, and so on), and occurs in many spheres of urban activity (housing, education, occupation, health, and so on). In this section we are primarily concerned with discrimination in the labour market and particularly with racial discrimination. Racial discrimination can take place at any one of three stages within the workings of the local labour market. It may occur in the search for jobs when prospective employers explicitly exclude certain ethnic groups in their advertising or, if this is illegal, advertise in areas where only preferred racial groups live. Second, discrimination may occur at the selection stage where applicants are interviewed and vetted. Finally, there may be discrimination at the place of work itself; certain groups may only be permitted to undertake lower-grade work or they may find it more difficult to gain promotion.

A common pattern has been illustrated by a case study of the Yorkshire woollen industry (Cohen and Jenner [1968]). Here it was found that coloured workers were only taken into the labour force as the production day lengthened, when shift working was introduced or in other circumstances where companies found it difficult to recruit labour at the going rate. In other instances we find coloured workers excluded from highly paid manual jobs in the car industry unless, because of their negative non-monetary attributes, these jobs were shunned by white workers.

The analytical literature on this aspect of the urban labour market is almost exclusively American: racial problems being one of the major issues in the United States, mainly because of the relatively large coloured population in most large cities and because of the social, as well as economic, problems created by the diverse ethnic mixture that constitutes the American people. In 1966, for example, Stanley Friedlander [1972] found the ratios of non-white to white unemployed (male and female) was 4·4 and 4·3 in Pittsburgh and San Antonio respectively, and he concluded that 'racial discrimination in employment is a major contributor to the high rates of unemployment among non-whites and slum dwellers'. In the United

Kingdom, the situation is different and, as a consequence, the associated economic problems are not so pronounced. In the past there has been a steady stream of immigrants into the country, the most recent being the European refugees of the immediate pre-war and post-war periods and the inflow of New Commonwealth citizens as former colonies have been given independence. Past tides of immigrants have successfully integrated into society and each successive wave has worked its way up the social ladder and been incorporated into the economic system. At present the New Commonwealth immigrants seem to be causing some concern however. Firm evidence has been produced to show that even the well-qualified immigrants are being discriminated against in local labour markets (Political and Economic Planning [1967]) and it is equally apparent that there is discrimination in the urban housing market (Haddon [1975]).

These immigrants are concentrated in several of our larger cities and conurbations, especially in the industrial area of the North and Midlands, and in a limited range of jobs, notably in foundries, textiles, clothing, bakeries and bus transport. In some cases, especially with respect to the West Indian community of London, they were initially recruited as labour to fill jobs at times of labour shortages – this was certainly true of London Transport. More recent groups have come over in the expectation of finding work or because they are refugees. The existence of established immigrant communities naturally results in new immigrants gravitating to the larger urban centres. Despite the fact that no black ghettos, in the American sense, have yet emerged, considerable problems have arisen as the result of the increasing concentration of coloured immigrants in a limited number of areas (see, for example, Deakin and Ungerson [1973]).

Although in the United States the large cities have exhibited consistently high rates of unemployment amongst the coloured population over the years, the situation in the United Kingdom is less dramatic. In the most extensive study of this problem yet carried out, Rose [1969] found that, 'when the national trend of unemployment rises, the proportion of immigrants among the total unemployed also rises; thus in times of rising unemployment Commonwealth immigrants tend to be harder hit than the general population'. A more detailed look at Greater London reveals that although in 1971 the coloured male immigrant population constituted only 5·3 per cent of the resident work force, it accounted for 6·9 per cent of the unemployed (Lomas [1973]).

Where racial discrimination does occur, it reduces the efficiency of the local economy: it implies that labour selection is based upon criteria other than the productivity of the worker. Since discrimination implies inefficiency, the best workers not necessarily being employed, other firms not discriminating will be able to produce at lower unit costs and hence be more profitable and the discriminators will be driven out of business. In a perfectly competitive world, therefore, discrimination would soon disappear. In practice, there are a number of imperfections which slow down the workings of this mechanism, although, judging by past experience, it does seem to work in the very long term.

The labour market is not perfect and employers cannot simply hire and fire at a moment's notice; this is partly due to the unionisation of the work force, but is also a feature of most firms' cost functions. Irrespective of a worker's ability, training and previous experience, it takes time for him to become fully efficient in a new firm; he must become familiar with its own particular methods and routine. In these circumstances there is a tendency for firms to hold on to their labour force rather than pay the cost of continually taking on new workers, even if in the longer term they are more productive. Because this 'tooling-up cost' tends to be higher for more skilled jobs, one would anticipate that labour turnover would be even slower at management levels (see Oi [1962]). Clearly in this environment it will take time for new immigrant groups to work their way up through the various strata, even when there is no discrimination. In the meantime they do low-paid work and are susceptible to unemployment during recessions in the economy.

We have so far assumed that immigrants are as well-trained and educated as the indigenous work force; in practice this is seldom true. Second- and third-generation immigrants (if the term 'immigrant' still applies) should theoretically have a better chance of gaining employment and a job commensurable with their abilities because they will have become more familiar with the local labour market and will have been brought up and educated in an urban environment related to local employment opportunities. However, the degree to which immigrants segregate themselves from the rest of the urban population and live in areas where educational facilities are sub-standard will slow down this mechanism. Indeed, there is empirical evidence that a degree of discrimination against coloured school leavers still continues partly for this reason even for second-generation immigrants (Political and Economic Planning [1967]). Related to this, Werner Hirsch [1973] has isolated a vicious circle in American cities which tends to reinforce racial inequalities rather than reduce them:

> The disadvantage is increased as a result of the interdependence of actors and the market in the system. If a man receives less income as a result of being black, then his children are likely to receive less education as a result of their parent's smaller wealth; this is in addition to the difference in education that would result purely from the fact they are black. The smaller educational attainment of the children will lead to expectation of less income, which is further reduced by the same discrimination which applied to their father.

The situation is not yet this extreme in the United Kingdom, but, nevertheless, a 'dual labour market' does seem to be evolving to some extent (Bosanquet and Doeringer [1973]), and the low initial income levels of immigrants is likely to prevent them enjoying the full benefits of state education and training which might otherwise enable them to move into the 'primary' or high-wage sector. If the full potential of the immigrant work force is to be realised, this dualism must be removed.

4.7 Summary and Conclusions

Urban wage rates differ for a multiplicity of reasons. Traditionally, variations in these rates serve the important function of encouraging labour to move into those occupations where it will be most productive and to live in the city where it will be most useful. In the intra-urban context, spatial wage differences may be seen as a counter-vailing mechanism to compensate workers for the travel they must undertake in order to reach their places of employment. Since workers consider factors other than income in their locational and occupational decisions, this mechanism is somewhat diluted. In particular, one needs to look at the other facilities a particular location offers besides a high income and the other benefits a specific occupation confers besides a wage. Large differences in earnings may also occur because of imperfections on the demand side of the urban labour market. Employers, for example, are frequently ill-informed about rates being offered by similar firms in the city. In other cases there may be 'anti-pirating agreements' whereby firms do not take workers from one another or there may be institutional bargaining arrangements. In all these examples, competitive pressures will be felt but their effects will be restricted. As MacKay [1970] has said, 'the simple mechanistic model based on the "economic man" provides only a partial explanation of labour market behaviour'.

Despite the complexity of the labour market, its central position in the workings of the urban economy demands that efforts should be made to gain a full understanding of its intricacies. It is lamentable that this is one of the more neglected fields of urban economics, in terms of the theoretical and empirical studies which have been made of it.

References

N. BOSANQUET and P. B. DOERINGER [1973], 'Is there a Dual Labour Market in Great Britain?', *Economic Journal* (June) pp. 421–35.

S. BOWLES [1970], 'Migration as Investment: Empirical Tests of the Human Investment Approach to Geographical Mobility', *Review of Economics and Statistics*, pp. 356–62.

D. BROOKS [1975], *Race and Labour in London Transport* (Oxford University Press).

K. BUCKLEY [1969], 'Intra-occupational Wage Dispersion in Metropolitan Areas 1967–8', *Monthly Labour Review* (September).

B. G. COHEN and P. J. JENNER [1968], 'The Employment of Immigrants: a Case Study within the Wool Industry', *Race* (July) pp. 41–56.

N. DEAKIN and C. UNGERSON [1973], 'Beyond the Ghetto: the Illusion of Choice', in *London: Urban Patterns, Problems and Policies*, ed. D. Donnison and D. Eversley (London: Heinemann).

S. L. FRIEDLANDER [1972], *Unemployment in the Urban Core* (New York: Praeger).

J. F. B. GOODMAN [1973], 'The Definition and Analysis of Local Labour Markets: Some Empirical Problems', *British Journal of Industrial Relations*, pp. 179–96.

R. HADDON [1975], 'The Location of West Indians in the London Housing Market', in *Cities in Modern Britain*, ed. C. Lambert and D. Weir (Glasgow: Fontana).

W. HIRSCH [1973], *Urban Economic Analysis* (New York: McGraw-Hill).

L. C. HUNTER and G. L. REID [1968], *Urban Worker Mobility* (Paris: O.E.C.D.).

E. C. ISBELL [1944], 'Internal Migration in Sweden and Intervening Opportunities', *American Sociological Review*, pp. 627–39.

J. E. KING [1972], *Labour Economics* (London: Macmillan).

G. LOMAS [1973], 'Labour and Life in London', in *London: Urban Patterns, Problems and Policies*, ed. D. Donnison and D. Eversley (London: Heinemann).

I. LOWRY [1966], *Migration and Metropolitan Growth: Two Analytical Models* (San Francisco: Chandler).

D. I. MACKAY [1970], 'Wages and Labour Turnover', in *Local Labour Markets and Wage Structures*, ed. D. Robinson (London: Gower Press).

L. N. MOSES [1962] 'Towards a Theory of Intra-Urban Wage Differentials and their Influence on Travel Patterns', *Papers of the Regional Science Association*, pp. 53–63.

R. F. MUTH [1969], *Cities and Housing* (University of Chicago Press).

W. OI [1962] 'Labour as a Quasi-fixed Factor', *Journal of Political Economy* (December) pp. 538–55.

Political and Economic Planning [1967], *Racial Discrimination* (London: P.E.P.).

W. J. REILLY [1929], 'Methods for Study of Retail Relationships', *University of Texas Bulletin*, 2944.

D. ROBINSON [1967], 'Myths of the Local Labour Market', *Personnel* (November) pp. 36–9.

E. J. B. ROSE and Associates [1969], *Colour and Citizenship: a Report on British Race Relations* (Oxford University Press).

A. SMITH [1776], *An Inquiry into the Nature and Causes of the Wealth of Nations* (London: Strahan & Cadell).

W. R. THOMPSON [1965], *A Preface to Urban Economics* (Baltimore: Johns Hopkins Press).

5 THE DYNAMIC URBAN ECONOMY

5.1 Introduction

In the previous three chapters we have concentrated on micro-economic theory, discussing in particular the location and production decisions of firms and of individuals. We now turn to look at the urban macroeconomy and specifically at the mechanisms underlying economic growth. The models we consider tend to assume a free market with no government direction and control and perfect mobility of both people and factors of production; unfortunately for economists these conditions are less common today than they were a century or so ago. The advent of urban planning has meant that many towns and cities expanded and developed in a semi-controlled environment, under the influence of either local or central government. The New Towns of the twentieth century are a classic example of urban centres developing in previously small villages offering little natural growth potential in the traditional sense – their growth has been induced by deliberate policy. Does this mean that the theories outlined below are of only academic interest? The answer is a firm no. Urban economic-growth models are important if we are to understand how cities developed in the past and they are still of use to planners and economists today. When planners decide to either alter the land usage in an existing city or to develop an entirely new centre, they need theories of growth to enable them to predict the effects of their actions in the longer term, for the urban centre itself, but also for its surrounding hinterland. It is no use founding a new town if it is incapable of surviving once government support is withdrawn. Moreover, planning in one city can affect the economies of others and, in particular, their own growth rates. Information of likely spillover effects of this kind is therefore necessary if planning is to be successful.

In many texts, urban growth is simply assumed and urban problems are automatically treated in a growth framework. Where growth is explicitly mentioned, it is in the context of changing structures of economic activity rather than the expansion of the urban economy *per se*. We do not adopt this approach but concentrate on growth in its own right – the dynamic structural form of urban economies is explicit in our discussions of location theory and in the following chapter on city size. To simply take urban growth for granted seems a rather naive approach; its validity depends upon how growth is measured and the time horizon assumed. Certainly some writers would argue that cities, like people, have a life cycle; they grow to their prime, prosper for a time and then fade away. Growth is simply one phase of a much longer cycle, and to understand the workings of urban economies we need to understand the underlying mechanisms of this cycle.

The difficulty at present is not any shortage of growth theory to account for the current urban expansion but rather an abundance. Even if we ignore those models which are not strictly of an economic nature (which is not intended to cast any aspersions on their quality), the remainder constitute an impressive list. We concentrate only on the more important of these theories and the ones which seem to have gained the widest acceptance. These models can be divided into those which are demand-orientated and those which are supply-based. The former, of which the export-base and input–output approaches are considered in detail, assume growth is stimulated by some predetermined exogenous increase in the demand for goods produced within the urban economy. (The central-place theory, discussed in Chapter 3 and outlined in more detail later in the book, is another case of a demand-induced growth model.) Supply-based theories take the opposite approach and argue that the supply of facilities and amenities within the city attracts workers, capital and business to the area, and this in turn generates growth. Whichever stance is adopted, empirical verification has proved almost impossible, mainly due to the limited data available and the complexity of tracing out causal linkages.

In the remainder of the chapter, the general problems of explaining urban growth are discussed in more detail and a critical account is presented of the attributes and limitations of the various theories which have been advanced up to the present time.

5.2 Economics and Urban Growth

It should be stated at once that economists are not very good at explaining why some cities grow faster than others. This is because it is far more difficult to build and test an urban growth model than one for an entire country. In part this stems from the infancy of the subject – there are not yet adequate techniques to adapt national growth models to the urban level of disaggregation (always assuming such disaggregation is legitimate and appropriate) – but there are also a number of other reasons why disaggregation is difficult. National growth models ignore the effects of scale and agglomeration, being based on so-called 'linear homogeneous production functions', yet these are the characteristics of an urban economy. Cities are also very open economies – they supply each other with inputs into industry, labour moves freely between them and products are traded – but little information on inter-city trade is collected. A city also has space constraints, its supply of land being far more limited than that of a country. Urban economies are complex and vary considerably in their natures, frequently differing in their stage of development and racial composition. Finally, cities are created for reasons much wider than the simple objective of income maximisation and actions are frequently trade-offs between more rapid economic growth in the narrow pecuniary sense and the provision of cultural, social and leisure facilities. All of these factors make it difficult to apply national growth models in an urban context; they either need considerable modification or entirely new models must be devised.

An intrinsic problem of urban-growth analysis is how to actually measure the economic growth of a city. Strictly, one is attempting to analyse changes in the economic well-being of the community living within the urban area, but this leaves the problem of defining some proxy for well-being or welfare. In national-income accounting, *per capita* income is used as a surrogate for welfare, although such a measuring rod tends to ignore a wide range of other important factors – the state of the environment, the standard of public services and the range of social amenities for example. Although many theoretical models employ *per capita* income as the indicator of growth, in empirical work it is of limited use because of the inadequacy of income statistics at the urban level. As a consequence of this, demographic variables tend to be used in practical investigation, population size being the standard proxy in which to measure urban growth. Clearly this is very much a second (or even third) best choice, population size frequently bearing little relation to the welfare enjoyed by a city's inhabitants. Indeed, as we see in a later chapter, an expanding population tends to increase certain negative aspects of urban living, especially pollution and congestion. In these circumstances it is conceivable that, after a certain level, population size may actually be negatively related to people's welfare. A further variable sometimes used in urban-growth models (although more frequently found in regional analysis) is the rate of unemployment; a city's economy is considered to be growing if unemployment falls. The limitation with this approach is that it only relates to short-term growth, while there are surplus factors in the economy, and is of little use over a period of years as the size of the total labour force varies. Even in the short term, it is a poor indicator of a city's prosperity because the level of unemployment is influenced by a great number of other things besides the growth rate, for example local activity rates and the method of registration. Its one advantage is the ready availability of data.

A common weakness of all these variables is their attempt to measure aggregate welfare without considering the spread or distribution of welfare across the urban population. Many cities may be experiencing rapid economic growth in the aggregate sense of a rapidly rising level of *per capita* income but the distribution of this increase may so favour the wealthier sections of the community that the poorer are actually becoming worse off. This is a problem being experienced in several developing countries, especially where there is considerable differences in the skills and abilities of various groups within the community, but is less common in Western countries where initial income differences are narrower and education standards generally much higher. Nevertheless, as urban growth occurs, different groups do tend to benefit to different degrees, although everyone's standard of living may rise to some extent.

The difficulty of defining an operational variable to act as a yardstick against which urban growth may be measured has tended to limit the amount of empirical work done in this field, and as a consequence our knowledge of actual growth processes lags a long way behind the theoretical models which have been devised (and these are still very weak). Because the basic features of the urban macroeconomy bears some resemblance to those of the national economy, there has been a tendency for analysts to adapt and modify national growth models to fit the peculiar characteristics of city economies. This has been done with varying degrees of success. We now take a critical look at these models, consider the validity of their underlying assumptions and assess their ability to simulate the real world. It should be borne in mind, however, that many of these models have been developed for specific uses and, although often open to adverse comments of a general nature, frequently serve the limited purposes for which they were originally intended.

5.3 Keynesian Growth Models

Ever since the publication of his *General Theory of Employment, Interest and Money* in the 1930s, the economic ideas of John Maynard Keynes [1936] have played a significant part in the formulation of macroeconomic theories of growth. It comes as no surprise, therefore, that growth models of the urban economy have been developed along the basic approach contained in *The General Theory*. The most widely used adaptation of the Keynesian approach is the economic-base model of urban growth (developed from the regional growth models of Hoyt [1949] and others). This theory assumes the urban economy can be divided into two distinct sectors: the basic sector and the services or non-basic sector. The former is the only source of growth in these models; the service sector is seen simply as a supplier of local wants, and demand for its products is derived from the activities of the basic sector.

The most common form of this model is the export-base approach which relies upon the common characteristic of most urban economies that they sell, or export, a considerable proportion of their production outside their boundaries. Industries engaged in exporting form the basic sector in our dichotomy. The demand for any city's exports is considered independent of any actions of the city; hence the level of exports is treated as exogenously determined. Urban models which attempt to relate a city's income, rate of employment or production growth to the level of its exports are defined as being of the export-base type.

Keynesian growth theorists using these models point to the wide repercussions external sales can have within the urban economy. The sale of goods to outside markets brings income into a city which will in turn be spent within the local service sector generating further incomes and employment. The process should go on indefinitely, successive waves of economic expansion vibrating around the economy for ever, but there are constraints on the mechanism. Those people receiving the initial incomes from sales outside the city will not spend all of this money within the local service sector; some of it they will save, some will be spent on goods produced in other cities and some will be taken by government in the form of taxation. These leakages will then apply at each successive round of the multiplier process until no additional income is generated.

A simple numerical example demonstrates the basis of the model. If we assume that there is an exogenous increase in the demand for a city's exports amounting to £100, then this will initially provide an additional income of the same amount to those involved in the export sector. These people will, in turn, spend some of this money in the non-basic sector – but not all of it. Let us assume they save a tenth of their income, that a further tenth is spent on imports from outside the city and that the government taxes away another two-tenths. This means that £60 is spent in the non-basic sector and will, in turn, create incomes of an equal amount. Assuming those in the service sector have identical propensities to save, import and be taxed as those in basic industries, only £36 of this £60 is spent locally in the service sector. This process continues with ever-decreasing amounts of income being generated in each successive cycle until the impact of the export expansion is exhausted. If we sum the successive rounds of income, they will total £250; in other words, the initial export income has multiplied 2·5 times. An export-base multiplier therefore indicates by how many times an increase in export incomes will be magnified in additional economic activity within the urban economy. Of course, the example only shows a once-for-all expansion; for continued growth it is necessary for export demand to rise through time.

Attempts to estimate sub-national multipliers in the United Kingdom have usually been at the regional rather than urban level (for example Steele [1969]), but it is clear from the openness of urban economies that their multipliers will be low; probably below the 1·2–1·6 level calculated for U.K. regions. Indeed, it is possible that the export-base multiplier may be negligible in some instances where a large proportion of generated income is spent on goods and services produced elsewhere. In theory, multipliers may be calculated for a city as a whole, although data limitations make this difficult, or for specific industries located within in. Studies of the latter kind have been made of a pulp and paper mill (Grieg [1971]) and a new university (Brownrigg [1973]) but they have not been explicitly of the export-base type nor have they restricted themselves to purely local effects. The problem of calibrating a meaningful export-base model is not simply one of inadequate official data but rather involves the conceptual problem of measuring the export base. Initially one must draw fairly definite economic boundaries to the urban economy itself, political boundaries being poor indicators of the confines of local activity. Assuming one can make approximation as to the physical confines of the urban economy (perhaps in terms of the labour-catchment area or retail-trading area), one still has to classify local activities into basic and non-basic sectors. Although labels can be attached fairly easily to some firms (for example local government, medical and legal services are non-basic, while mineral extraction is basic) as the urban economy expands, and interdependencies become more complex, the divisions become increasingly blurred. For this reason, empirical tests of the export-base model have been very limited.

Even if the practical problems associated with calibrating an urban export-base model could be satisfactorily circumvented, the theory itself is open to criticism. Especially weak are the underlying assumptions of the approach. The model assumes that all investment in any urban economy is either directly or indirectly induced by exporting activities. This is simply not the case. Much investment is entirely autonomous, frequently speculative and on occasions induced by the quality of the local service sector rather than by the size of the export base. The urban public sector and central government are large investors, especially in infrastructure, and their actions are usually motivated by social considerations unrelated to inter-city trade. Second, the export-base theory assumes that the propensity to consume within a city remains constant, irrespective of the level of income. Implicitly this implies an unchanging distribution of income. This assumption is not supported by historical fact; as the general level of incomes has risen through time, disparities in distribution have tended to narrow. A consequence of this is that, as an urban economy grows, the propensity to consume, which is generally regarded to decline at higher-income levels, will fall rather than remain constant. Finally, the model assumes that the proportion of income spent in the service sector remains the same through time. Empirical evidence suggests that, on the contrary, as growth proceeds an increasing percentage of income goes on non-basic services which in turn will, via multiplier effects, further stimulate demand in this sector. This is important because many of the goods imported into a city may have a 'threshold' level of demand beyond which it is economical for the city to provide them itself. When import substitution does occur, by reducing the propensity to import, it increases the size of the export-base multiplier – and hence leads to faster growth.

In summary, the export-base model is a useful indicator of possible urban economic expansion in the short period when production techniques, industrial mix and the income distribution remain fairly constant, but in the longer run its underlying assumptions prove unrealistic and severely limit its forecasting potential.

5.4   Input–Output Models

Input–output models were initially designed as aids to planners in centrally controlled economies, but they are now widely accepted as useful in the study of free-market economies. An input–output model describes the interrelationships among producers and final consumers in an economy and, although usually employed at the national level, can be applied at any level of aggregation including the urban. The matrix developed shows how the output of each sector in a city's economy is distributed amongst all other sectors and the final consumers (final demand). The latter group will include not just households but also sales for investment, export and to the public sector. The approach is, therefore, at a more disaggregated level than export-base analysis, and investigates the level and mix of economic activity within the city by tracing out relationships between buyers and sellers.

A simplified input–output matrix will illustrate the main features of the technique. We assume the city has only two sectors, although in practice models are built with several hundred, which we designate A and B. We can then draw up a hypothetical input–output table (see Table 5.1). This table shows that sector A sells £20 of its output to itself (intra-sector trade between firms in the same sector), £40 to sector B and £40 to final demand. Row 2 gives a similar breakdown of the sales from sector B. Row 3 indicates the value added; this is the value added to output other than through intermediate goods (for example imports and payments to factors of production). The majority of value added is usually payment to labour and hence may be considered as constituting a third sector, services provided by households. The bottom row simply shows the total gross input into each sector.

TABLE 5.1

Purchases from (£)	Sector A	Sales to (£) Sector B	Final demand	Total gross output
Sector A	20	40	40	100
Sector B	30	80	90	200
Value added	50	80		
Total gross input	100	200		300

SOURCE: adapted from Miernyk [1965].

So far the model has been purely descriptive, showing the various flows of goods within the city, but it can be turned into a predictive growth model if a number of assumptions are made, namely:

(1) all output is consumed during the time period it is produced;
(2) inputs are entirely determined by the outputs of each sector;
(3) technology and methods of production are constant; and
(4) supply equals demand in all markets within the urban economy.

We say more about these assumptions later. If we accept them at present, then we can calculate the direct input coefficient showing the input requirements per £ of output produced in each sector. The direct coefficients in the example are found to be:

	Sector A	Sector B
Sector A	0·2	0·2
Sector B	0·3	0·4
Value added	0·5	0·4

In other words, if sector A sells another £10 worth of its product to final demand, its own output would rise by a *further* £2 (that is in addition to the £10) and that of sector B by £3. Clearly there will now be a further set of indirect effects because the additional £2 of output in sector A and the £3 worth in sector B will themselves require inputs from other sectors. Input–output analysis incorporates these indirect effects alongside the direct ones by manipulating the above matrix; the reader might like to think of this as analogous to the summation of the direct effects of several rounds of increased sales. The combined effects in the example, indicating the total input requirements for a £'s worth of goods for final demand, are:

	Sector A	Sector B
Sector A	1·43	1·48
Sector B	0·71	1·90

The intra-industry trade coefficients exceed unity because in this table, unlike the last, the initial sale to final demand is included. If we subtract the direct effects calculated above (and the initial sale to final demand in the case of intra-industry sales), we are left with the indirect effects. Hence an extra £'s worth of output from sector A sold to final demand involves the production of that unit, plus £0·2 worth of A's output as the direct effect and another £0·23 worth as the indirect effect. There is no *a priori* reason for the direct effect to exceed the indirect in this type of calculation.

The input–output matrix is capable of showing the detailed transactions which take place within the complex framework and this information in turn helps the economist gain a better understanding of the growth process. The table indicates where the greatest potential for growth lies and provides the detail necessary for policymakers to assess the effects of stimulating specific sectors in order to achieve growth. In some senses, the input–output technique is a development of the export-base model since it can indicate the degree of interdependence between urban economies and, by introducing a sub-matrix of external trade coefficients, it enables the economist to trace out the effects on individual sectors within an urban economy of an exogenous expansion in export demand.

Input–output analysis at the urban level is an extremely useful way of studying a local economy, but it is not yet widely used. Certainly a number of models have been calibrated for the United States – for example by Miernyk [1967] and Dolenc [1968] – but little empirical work has been attempted for the United Kingdom. The main problem with the technique is its enormous appetite for data. A relatively small model with only 50 sectors and no inter-urban trade requires sufficient information to enable reliable estimates of 2500 input–output coefficients to be estimated. The necessary data are not available from official sources, as they are at the national level, and to collect them by surveying local firms and businesses is extremely expensive. The American studies have tended to rely on national coefficients, adjusted where additional information is available of local peculiarities, but these are usually poor proxies for the actual transactions structure in any single urban economy. National figures are particularly poor in the context of inter-urban sales and when sectors are not of very specialised nature, and hence, are likely to vary considerably between cities.

The assumptions underlying the use of input–output models also face a number of major criticisms. The assumption of a constant technology implies that the input–output coefficients remain fixed over time. This may be valid in the short term, but as growth proceeds this is likely to encourage innovation as some factors of production become scarce and more expensive. As labour supplies become fully utilised, it seems reasonable to assume firms will seek less labour-intensive methods of production; new techniques of production will be invented or existing ones, previously impractical, will become viable. This means the coefficients are likely to change over time. It seems equally unrealistic to assume that output is consumed during the period it is produced. As economic growth occurs, there is a tendency for individuals and producers to become cautious and to refrain from consuming their total output immediately; inventories build up. Finally, there are often considerable lags in different markets as they adjust to changes in demand or supply conditions and this may violate the assumption of equilibrium in all markets.

5.5 Supply-Orientated Models

The majority of urban-growth models concentrate on the demand for a city's output but, in the longer term, supply considerations become increasingly important. An urban economy is often capable of quite rapid growth in the short period when the indigenous supply of factors of production and raw materials may be assumed fairly elastic but as growth proceeds these supplies become exhausted and the city's capacity for further expansion is increasingly constrained. Demand-orientated models may therefore provide quite adequate explanations of urban growth in the short or medium term, but an approach incorporating supply considerations is necessary to account for long-term growth patterns.

The importance of supply constraints is particularly relevant to highly industrialised economies where resources are approaching full employment. When over-all resource utilisation is high, scope for growth in any city is limited by its ability to attract additional factors of production from other urban areas. Supply in the urban-growth context, therefore, refers not simply to the physical resources controlled by a city at any moment in time, but also to the city's capacity to attract additional factors from elsewhere when necessary. In this sense, growth potential is dependent upon a city's locational advantages and its relative attractiveness to skilled manpower, management, investors and specialised services. There may also be scope for a limited amount of internal growth; this will depend upon the local rate of population increase, the level of investment and the degree of technical progress (including education, training, innovation and managerial organisation). In summary, the supply approach states that urban growth ultimately depends upon the initial stock of resources held by a city and its capacity to act as a magnet for mobile factors within the wider national economy. (This is somewhat more complex than national supply-orientated growth models where factor mobility between countries is generally treated as negligible.)

Traditional neoclassical economic theory would seem to suggest that cities ought to grow at roughly the same rate over the long period. If one city lags behind, it will accumulate a pool of unused resources, particularly labour, which will force local production costs and wages down, making its output more attractive to other cities and its economy more profitable for investors. Unfortunately, this approach is much too simple and just does not correspond to reality. There is a tendency for the largest and most prosperous cities to attract investment – not areas with surplus capacity in their economy. The attraction of these large cities is partly explained in terms of agglomeration and scale economies.

Perhaps the most explicit supply model of urban growth is the theory of 'circular and cumulative causation'. This was first advanced by Gunnar Myrdal in an attempt to explain growth in underdeveloped countries, but it is equally applicable in the urban context. According to Myrdal:

Contrary to what the equilibrium theory of international trade would seem to suggest, the play of the market forces does not work towards equality in the remunerations of factors of production, and consequently incomes. If left to take its own course, economic development is a process of circular and cumulative causation which tends to award its favours to those who are already well endowed and even to thwart the efforts of those who happen to live in regions that are lagging behind (Myrdal [1956]).

In other words, momentum tends to be the driving force behind urban growth; people and factors move to cities because their economies are prospering. In particular, there is a tendency for the more dynamic and ambitious people to move to thriving economies, leaving those with less initiative in cities with sluggish economies.

Associated with the theory of cumulative causation are two important neighbourhood effects on the area immediately adjacent to the expanding urban economy. These are likely to be 'spread effects', as the expanding urban economy stimulates the production of raw materials and other inputs into the growth process; this may set off chain reactions in secondary centres and create a process of cumulative causation in these other areas. At the same time there will also be 'backwash effects', as labour, capital and other resources are sucked into the large urban centre, depriving the secondary cities of their services. The output of the major centre may also flood into these secondary markets, depressing local business and industry. In this way the cumulative causation process can either generate further urban growth in other centres or it may depress such growth. The outcome will depend upon the relative strengths of the two effects – Goodall [1972] suggests the spread effects are more likely to dominate, the more developed the national economy, although there is little hard evidence to support this.

Of course there are constraints on the growth of any city's economy. In the shorter term there are clear geographical constraints imposed by the city's legal boundaries. Although it is usually possible for some continued expansion, even in the most crowded city, by using land more efficiently, there are limitations to this, and eventually it may impair the efficiency of individual production units. In the longer term, this constraint is usually less severe and city limits are forced outwards (there are exceptions when it is physically impossible to extend boundaries, as is the case for Hong Kong). Second, as cities grow they tend to generate increasing harmful external effects which make them less attractive to potential immigrants. The exact importance of this constraint is difficult to determine but it would appear to be very weak, at least until cities reach the metropolitan scale. A final constraint, which is of increasing importance, is the attitude of local planners. Physical planning affects not just land-use patterns but can also determine the attractiveness of an urban area to outsiders. Frequently, planners consciously plan for a predetermined population size and land-use mix which is deliberately designed to minimise inward flows of migrants. The objective of such a policy is to safeguard the living standards and economic viability of those already in the city rather than to attract fresh enterprise and enlarge the population (see the following chapter).

The idea that urban growth is a self-perpetuating process concentrated in the largest centres has its attractions, but it also has its theoretical weaknesses. In particular, the theory of cumulative causation tells us nothing about how the growth process is initiated; it is purely an account of how growth is likely to continue once set in motion. This is itself useful to planners working in established and growing urban centres intent on further expansion, but offers little help to authorities responsible for depressed urban areas.

Ideally, the supply-orientated approach needs to be married to a demand-based model. It seems reasonable that the forces of demand create the initial stimulus to growth but that supply factors are the determinants of the speed and duration of the expansion. It is inappropriate to simply concentrate on one aspect of the urban economy: growth is determined by the interactions of supply and demand.

5.6 Economic Stability

Urban growth does not simply vary between cities, but also fluctuates over time for any given city. Economists are therefore not only concerned with the long-term rate of growth but also with the temporal stability of the growth process. This interest extends to urban planners who are responsible for developing policies to ensure growth at some predetermined pace. The speed and stability of urban growth is as important as the growth itself, as Wilbur Thompson has said:

> To grow too slowly is to invite chronic unemployment and poverty, the symptoms of which are slums, blight and crime. To

grow too fast is to invite the capital shortages that lead to the irritating delays and expensive congestion that can be just as damaging to the quality of urban life (Thompson [1965] p. 2).

Moreover, uneven economic growth introduces a degree of uncertainty into the investment decision, making the city less attractive to businessmen and occasionally leading to an outward migration of workers.

The models already outlined in the previous three sections provide some insight into factors influencing the stability of the growth rate, but additional influences also have a bearing. The growth models need supplementing with extra inputs and outside calculations if they are to be really useful guides to potential stability. The export-base model, for example, must include details of national economic performance over time if long-term export growth is going to be forecast accurately.

Three major determinants of the stability of the urban growth rate are the dependence of the city's economy on the national business cycle, the industries the city specialises in and the flexibility of the local economy.

The degree to which any urban economy will be sensitive to fluctuations in the over-all level of business activity within the national economy depends upon the similarity of its industrial mix to that of the rest of the country. The greater the similarity of economic structure, the greater the interdependence of the urban and national economies. Of course, cities are never exact replicas of the parent state, and if an urban economy has an above-average proportion of thriving industries, then this may offset any downturn in the national growth rate. This was a feature of many Midland cities during the 1930s, when their economies continued to expand because of the buoyancy of the motor-car industry despite national economic depression.

There is a second point with respect to specialisation. If a city's primary export is a commodity with a high income elasticity of demand, then over time its exports will rise faster than the growth in national income. This is a short-term stability factor, however, and, because elasticity is a relative concept, it is quite conceivable that once the market becomes saturated with the commodity, export sales will become more difficult.

Stability also depends upon the flexibility of the local economy and its responsiveness to innovation and changes in demand patterns. Steady growth is more likely if a city is capable of substituting dynamic for declining industry as economic conditions require. To some extent the ability of any urban area to change with varying demand patterns will depend upon the degree of diversification within the local economy; excessive specialisation makes change very difficult, due to inertia in the capital and labour markets and the reluctance of businessmen to write off large amounts of obsolete, but mechanically sound, capital. Where there is diversification, the amount of equipment becoming obsolete at any one time is likely to be small and the retraining and placement of labour are much easier.

In addition to these three general influences on the stability of the growth rate, a more specific force may be the size of city involved. A large city may be able to sustain growth more easily than a smaller one. Wilbur Thompson [1965] has argued that there is a minimum size (about 250,000 inhabitants) above which growth will probably take place and economic decline becomes impossible. The 'urban-growth ratchet' permits step-like growth over time but never any retardation and is the result of the natural characteristics of large cities, in particular:

(*a*) extensive industrial diversification,

(*b*) greater local political influence at the national level,

(*c*) considerable amount of social infrastructure, sufficient to keep basic industry in the area,

(*d*) an increasingly large service sector as growth proceeds, and

(*e*) increased chances of innovation and the development of new industry resulting from sheer size.

The difficulty is that not all cities reach this critical size, and it may not be desirable for them to do so for reasons of efficiency in management and production as well as for social-welfare reasons. Moreover, there are forces which tend to slow growth at larger population sizes and higher income levels which are likely to make each successive step on the growth ladder smaller than the previous one. In terms of an economic-base model, people's marginal propensities to consume tend to decrease with rising income, making increasingly large stimuli necessary if growth is to proceed at an even pace. Thompson's assertion that the relative size of the service sector increases as growth proceeds also leads to difficulties. As Douglas Brown [1974] has illustrated, this can only support the ratchet theory if resources are allocated to the service sector at a rate exceeding the inevitable increases in cost in that sector (for an explanation of the causes of these rises see Chapter 10). If this condition is not met, then economic decline *is* possible. Finally, empirical evidence to support Thompson's hypothesis is scant, but recent problems in some large American cities, highly dependent on the motor-car industry, cast a shadow over the ratchet theory.

5.7 National Urban-Growth Policy

Large conurbations tend to play a leading role in regional and, in some instances, national economies, and because of this their influence can extend well beyond the welfare of local inhabitants. The government, therefore, has a vested interest in watching, and at times influencing, the patterns of growth in the main urban centres. The actual policy concerns of the authorities are numerous and varied, being reflected in the different levels, mixes and rates of growth of economic activities found in urban areas (Friedly [1974]). Differing rates of economic growth between urban centres will not simply be reflected in variations in productivity (and, *ipso facto*, in wage levels) but also in the economic structures of the cities and the degree to which they suffer from pollution and congestion. To the extent that market imperfections will prevent such variations being automatically smoothed out over time, the government may decide to intervene in order to maximise the long-term welfare of the country as a whole.

In the United Kingdom, urban-growth policy has never been an explicit official objective (with the possible exception of London). As Harry Richardson [1973] has put it, there is only a 'skeleton framework of national urban policy, except in the very loose sense of the term'. There are several reasons for this. First, the country is very highly urbanised, and hence any form of urban-growth policy must involve considerable movements of population and wealth from one city to another rather than a move from a rural to an urban situation. The repercussions of policies in this environment are wide-ranging and difficult to forecast with any degree of certainty. Second, the economic activity of the country is geared to the existing framework of transport networks and urban centres, making any attempt by government to alter regional or urban imbalances very difficult and, by necessity, long term. Finally, there is a natural reluctance for people to relocate or take a cut in living standards as part of any official policy. This puts in doubt the political expediency of any urban-growth policy which would result in the decline of some areas so that others may prosper.

Where urban-growth policy has been attempted, it has generally been part of a much larger regional plan or policy package. Since the 1930s there have been debates over the desirability of reducing the size of London so that the south-eastern region as a whole may enjoy more rapid growth, and a policy of encouraging outward migration of workers and industry has been pursued throughout the post-war era. London is atypical, however, and is dealt with in much more detail in the final chapter of the book.

In more general terms, an urban area has been encouraged to grow if it has been deemed necessary for the economy of the surrounding area to expand. Over the post-war period, various incentives, in the form of grants, loans, building permits, and so on, have been offered to industry if it would locate in such areas. Although one objective of this type of policy has been to generate faster growth in these areas, including local urban centres, frequently a much more urgent criterion has been job creation. However, as we have indicated in the theoretical sections of this chapter, increases in employment are not necessarily a good indication of genuine economic growth and may well result in some actual long-term decline in welfare. The difficulty really goes back to a point made earlier: the government is too often committed to short-term policies and hence prevented from taking the most desirable long-term action. In the case of some of the older northern cities, for example, it would be preferable to attract a much wider industrial base to the areas rather than take the short-term approach of encouraging firms offering immediate employment irrespective of longer-term potential. In order to achieve the demand objective, the infrastructure of these cities, both economic and social, should be replaced and modernised. Such a course of action has been suggested in the past, notably by the Hunt Committee (Department of Economic Affairs [1969]) with regards to the Intermediate Areas, but, because of short-term economic crises, has never been acted upon.

Whereas U.K. urban-growth policy has been minimal, there have been quite large-scale exercises in controlling city growth in some other countries. In particular, both Spain and Canada, and to a lesser extent the United States, have attempted to encourage migration from congested urban areas to less developed regions of the country. The situation in these countries is different to that in the United Kingdom; effectively they have 'dual economies' with growth concentrated in confined geographical urban belts, with under-utilised or unexploited natural resources in the remainder of the country. Spain's urbanisation, for example, has tended to concentrate in the north-east, leaving a vast area of virtually uninhabited land in the centre of the country; while in Canada there is a rapid population increase and considerable reserves of natural resources to be utilised. Both of these countries are employing, to a greater or lesser extent, a growth-centre strategy in their national urban policy. The idea is to promote the development of certain urban centres until they reach a sufficient size to become self-sufficient or meet some other objective (which may involve wider regional questions). The actual size at which growth becomes self-sustaining is open to debate (as mentioned earlier) but in Canada there appears to be an attempt to encourage the development of urban centres with a minimum population of 15,000–20,000. The critical minimum size to be aimed for, however, is likely to depend both upon local conditions and the underlying objective of the exercise, for example in some cases self-sufficiency may not be considered essent: l by the authorities because it may damage the growth potential of competing centres. Policies of this kind have proved relatively successful in developing economies which are not fully industrialised and where an established pattern of urbanisation has not developed, but in a country such as the United Kingdom the existing hierarchical urban structure, combined with a stable population size, suggest a growth-centre policy would meet with considerable natural resistance.

References

D. M. Brown [1974], *Introduction to Urban Economics* (New York: Academic Press).

M. Brownrigg [1973], 'The Economic Impact of a New University', *Scottish Journal of Political Economy* (June) pp. 123–93.

Department of Economic Affairs [1969], *The Intermediate Areas*, Cmnd. 3998 (London: H.M.S.O.).

M. Dolenc [1968], 'The Buck County Inter-regional Input-Output Study', *Papers of the Regional Science Association*, pp. 43–53.

P. H. FRIEDLY [1974], *National Policy Responses to Urban Growth* (Farnborough: Saxon House).

B. GOODALL [1972], *The Economics of Urban Areas* (Oxford: Pergamon).

M. A. GREIG [1971], 'The Regional Income and Employment Effects of a Pulp and Paper Mill', *Scottish Journal of Political Economy* (February) pp. 31–48.

H. HOYT [1949], *The Economic Base of the Brockton, Massachusetts, Area* (Arlington: Homer Hoyt Associates).

J. M. KEYNES [1936], *The General Theory of Employment, Interest and Money* (London: Macmillan).

W. H. MIERNYK [1965], *The Elements of Input–Output Analysis* (New York: Random House).

W. H. MIERNYK et al. [1967], *Impact of the Space Program on a Local Economy: An Input–Output Analysis* (Morgantown: West Virginia Library).

G. MYRDAL [1956], *Development and Underdevelopment*, 50th Anniversary Commemoration Lectures (Cairo: National Bank of Egypt).

H. W. RICHARDSON [1973], *The Economics of Urban Size* (Farnborough: Saxon House).

D. B. STEELE [1969], 'Regional Multipliers in Great Britain', *Oxford Economic Papers* (July) pp. 268–92.

W. R. THOMPSON [1965], *A Preface to Urban Economics* (Baltimore: Johns Hopkins Press).

6 THE THEORY OF CITY SIZE AND SPACING

6.1 Introduction

The theory of city size has attracted a great deal of attention in recent years. The literature has concentrated on two distinct but nevertheless related issues. The first of these involves the definition of the most desirable 'optimal' city size. Discussion of this question has been far-ranging, involving not just economists but also sociologists, town planners, social psychologists and ecologists to name but a few. In a purely practical sense it is particularly difficult to reach any firm conclusion in this area because of the lack of really relevant information and the immense difficulty of quantifying many of the considerations important to the debate. These are problems additional to the theoretical difficulties involved, but the lack of a solution in the short term suggests it is unlikely that any of the various theories of optimality which have been advanced will be empirically substantiated in the foreseeable future. These practical and theoretical problems often distract from the far more important question of whether an optimum size of city can ever be defined satisfactorily or, indeed, whether it is important to attempt such a definition. The general argument to justify work in this area is that local authorities need some idea of the optimal-size population they should encourage to settle in their cities but, as we shall see later, this can lead to various conflicts of interest. A further reason for interest is that many people are concerned with the present state of the environment in cities and consider this is partly the result of their excessive size – this would imply some implicit recognition of an optimal city on their part.

The second issue concerns the empirical fact that the vast majority of industrialised countries exhibit remarkably regular size distributions of cities and towns. This is a phenomenon that has interested a great number of economists and social statisticians alike in recent years, although, as Tinbergen [(1968] p. 65) has correctly pointed out, 'No scientific explanation worthy of that name has been advanced so far.' This chapter does not attempt to explore all of the work in this field or to present a comprehensive synopsis of the numerous different theories, many of which are highly specialised and involve a considerable degree of mathematical sophistication, but instead an attempt is made to pinpoint the main economic forces at work underlying the common hierarchical structure of urban centres. It should be emphasised at the outset that economics alone cannot provide a complete explanation but it does offer a framework around which more realistic models may be constructed.

The two issues of city size and the distribution of sizes are not altogether unconnected. As we see later, it appears quite probable that there is no such thing as the optimum city size *per se* but rather a series of optimum sizes, each determined by the physical and social characteristics of the economy under consideration. In this context, von Boventer [1973] has argued that 'city system parameters are dependent on the speed of economic development, on the sectoral structure of the economy, on the quantity and quality of the country's international economic relationships, on the spatial distribution of the raw material sites, on the political decisions and planning processes, and a host of other things'. Clearly this is a long list. Despite this obvious link between the concept of an optimal city size and the nature of the economy, it is still useful to begin by discussing the theory of the optimum in some detail.

6.2 The Optimum City Size

Historically the movement towards a more urbanised society has produced both more cities and larger cities. Accompanying this trend has been a steady migration of people from the countryside into these expanding urban settlements. As the urbanisation process has proceeded and accelerated so ideas of the ideal city size have been developed and modified. In classical times Plato voiced the opinion that a city's population should not exceed that which could fill a forum, in the days of Greek City States this amounted to 5040 citizens. Although Plato excluded slaves from his calculations, it seems unlikely that his ideal met the military and economic needs of even his time – already many of the great cities of antiquity had populations of perhaps 100,000 or more. Today, modern forms of transport and communications, together with improvements in the other prerequisites of urban life, make Plato's optima appear unrealistically small.

(a) The Administrative Optima

Plato's criteria were political in character but much of the more recent work in the field has been concerned with organisational efficiency, and in particular with minimising the *per capita* costs of urban government services. The costs of these services have been observed to initially fall as a city begins to expand, but after reaching some minimum level they start to increase again, a typical 'U-shaped cost curve'. By finding the bottom point of this curve it is theoretically possible to determine the least-cost, and hence optimum, city size from an administrative viewpoint. A number of studies using this technique have been attempted in both this country and the United States. Table 6.1 gives a summary of the most efficient population sizes derived in these pieces of work.

TABLE 6.1 *Estimates of the optimum administrative population of cities*

Study	Optimum population (thousands)
Baker [1910]	90
Barnett House Survey Committee [1938]	100–250
Lomax [1943]	100–150
Clark [1945]	100–200
Duncan [1956]	500–1000
Hirsch [1959]	50–100
Royal Commission of Local Government in Greater London [1960]	100–250
SVIMEZ [1967]	30–250
Royal Commission on Local Government in England [1969]	250–1000

We can see from the table that no consensus view has emerged from these studies but this is hardly surprising considering the widely differing types of local government examined. The studies make no allowance for varying degrees of urban government mix in the cities studied although this tends to differ from one country to another, for example some authorities may concentrate expenditure on public transport while others prefer to finance education. Similarly, there is no allowance for the expenditure mix changing over time. These factors make direct comparisons between the different estimates almost impossible.

In addition to the practical problems involved with this approach, Richardson [1972] has raised a number of theoretical criticisms. The cost-minimisation method implicitly assumes that the range of local government services remains invariate with respect to the size of the city. In fact as the urban area expands there is a complementary expansion in the number and types of service provided by the local authority. This makes it almost impossible to trace out a cost curve for a homogeneous package of services, as the approach requires. Second, many of the services performed by the local authority do not involve genuine costs but represent transfer payments between different groups within the community. Because administrative structures tend to differ, and are in any case seldom well-defined, it is generally impossible to separate actual real-resource costs from transfer payments in local authority accounts, clearly this further complicates the construction of local government cost curves. Perhaps the strongest criticism which can be laid against this type of approach, however, is its exclusive reliance on the efficiency of the urban public sector as a guide to the optimum city size. Local government expenditure usually represents only a very small proportion of total expenditure within any community, the lion's share coming from private purses. It has been used as a proxy for the over-all costs incurred in urban living simply because there is little conclusive evidence available on the relationship between private urban costs and benefits as perceived by individuals and firms. It is this latter relationship which is important in the determination of the optimum city size, however.

(b)   The Individual's Idea of the Optimal City Size
Very little work has been carried out to see how private costs and benefits vary with city size, and consequently the amount of firm evidence available is negligible. For this reason much of what follows must, by necessity, be rather inconclusive and lacking in a firm empirical foundation. Nevertheless, it is important to try and establish some idea of the various factors instrumental in determining the patterns of private cost and benefit curves with respect to city size, and to tentatively attempt an interpretation of their relevance in the optimum-size debate. Initially we look at how these costs and benefits can vary for the individual citizen.

There is a considerable amount of evidence that productivity (output *per capita*) increases with city size, at least for smaller cities. This increase is the result of agglomeration economies possible in large urban areas (see Chapter 2) and applies not only to private firms but also to public undertakings, notably in education, police services, communications and a variety of public utilities. Traditional economic theory therefore suggests that this higher productivity in larger centres should be reflected in higher incomes for those people who are employed in them, a fact that tends to be borne out by the available data. It seems probable, though, that after a certain size these agglomeration economies are more than offset by increasing congestion and other costs and that in the largest cities productivity actually begins to fall. This suggests that the appropriate productivity (and consequently *per capita* income) curve takes an inverted U-shape, initially rising with city size but eventually levelling off and finally, at the biggest city sizes, actually declining.

Individuals do not only derive benefits from their monetary incomes but also from the wide range of facilities which a city can offer them. Social amenities, such as public transport, shops, theatres, eating places, clubs, sports facilities and cultural activities, usually increase with the size of the urban concentration. Duncan [1959] summed up this phenomena in the American context thus: 'Whereas shoeshine parlours, hat cleaning shops and fur repair shops appear in cities above 25,000 population, diaper services appear only in cities above 50,000.' These particular types of benefit tend to increase positively with city size but they do so at a decreasing rate; it seems unlikely, though, that there is any actual decline in *per capita* benefits after some maximum city size has been reached; instead the 'social-benefit' curve is likely to simply flatten out.

By combining the pecuniary with the social benefits of urban living it is possible to develop a graphical picture of the way total individual benefits vary with the size of the city lived in. Figure 6.1 offers just such an illustration. The combined average-benefit curve (*AB*) indicates the initial rapid rise in average *per capita* benefits derived from increasing city size; these eventually taper and finally decline. The marginal curve (*MB*) reflects the benefits accruing to each additional member of the urban community. The exact shapes of these curves is open to some conjecture; A. J. Brown [1972], for example, feels that there is no eventual decline in the *AB* curve and that it simply tends towards an asymptote without ever falling. (The effects of adopting Brown's assumption should not prove too difficult for the reader to trace out.)

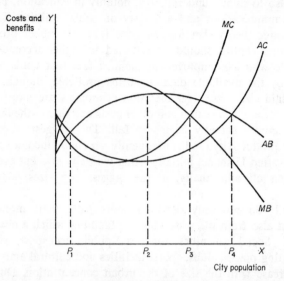

FIG. 6.1 *The costs and benefits to individuals associated with city size*

Having considered the benefit side of the equation, we now need to discuss how costs vary with city size. There is a considerable degree of general agreement on this aspect of the problem. The average cost (*AC*) of living in a city tends to rise with the size of the urban area (although there may be some initial fall for the very smallest population sizes). A number of factors contribute to this. Large cities frequently imply long journeys to work and considerable traffic congestion at peak times. This clearly imposes costs on individuals, and any attempt to minimise these by choosing accommodation near the place of employment will usually be offset by higher rents and house prices. In addition, it becomes increasingly difficult to gain access to the countryside or other open spaces as city boundaries expand outwards. At the same time, the larger the city the higher the prevailing noise levels and the greater the degree of pollution which has to be tolerated. There are also indications that psychological pressures increase with city size, manifesting themselves in high crime rates, greater mental illness and more suicides in the largest urban centres. In general, therefore, it is true that the 'quality' of the urban environment is inversely related to a city's size. Consequently, the basic shape of the *AC* curve is upwards as in Figure 6.1, although specific characteristics are slightly more difficult to define. Brown suggests that costs rise only slowly in smaller centres but accelerate at higher population levels; he admits, though, that these ideas are very speculative.

Figure 6.1 illustrates the various cost and benefit curves although it represents little more than an educated guess as to their exact configurations. As a measure of city size we use population although this is not without its limitations. Many of the costs and benefits associated with living in cities vary not with population size but with the density of the population or with the size of the geographical area involved. In addition, one also needs to consider the physical lay-out and characteristics of the city which are themselves in turn partly related to the historical development and age of the urban area. We are also simplifying the analysis by ignoring the proximity and characteristics of other urban centres which can exert a considerable influence over the shapes of the cost and benefit curves. However, it is necessary to accept these limitations at this stage if we are to derive any general principles at all.

The diagram reveals several city sizes which are of interest to the economist (for a more detailed discussion see Richardson [1973b] pp. 11–14). We can define the minimum economic size for a city as that population where the average-benefit curve cuts the average-cost curve from below. In Figure 6.1 this population is P_1; cities below this size do not offer benefits which exceed the cost of living in them. As we shall see, this minimum economic size may not correspond to the least-cost city, where *AC* is minimised. The least-cost population may or may not exceed that for the minimum economic size; this will depend upon the exact shapes of the relevant curves. To obtain the city size which maximises the net benefit of urban life *per capita*, one needs to consider that population where average cost diverges most from average benefits; this would be P_2 in the diagram. Although this is the city size which confers the maximum net benefit on each existing urban resident, it is not a stable equilibrium. The marginal benefit of moving into the city considerably exceeds the cost of doing so at this point, and consequently there will be a tendency for migrants to be drawn to the urban area. It is in the interests of the existing inhabitants to resist this inward movement of population which can only force down their own net surplus and reduce their welfare.

If market forces prevail and existing residents cannot prevent the city's population increasing beyond P_2, then, with perfect competition, the city will grow until it has a population of P_4. Only at this stage will the benefits derived from living in the urban area be equated with the average cost of doing so. This population is in excess of the social optimum however. It is only with a population of P_3 that the *total* net benefit obtained from urbanisation is maximised; each additional inhabitant beyond this level creates more cost (in the form of congestion and so on) than he receives in benefits – the reason being that the MC curve is above the MB curve after this point. However, people tend to consider, not the marginal benefits of urban living nor the additional costs they create by moving into a city, but rather look at the average benefits. Consequently, they will continue to be drawn to the urban area until the AC and AB curves converge, unless prevented from doing so by local authorities. Since both the total and the *per capita* net benefits associated with being resident in the city are greater with a population of P_3 than with one of P_4 there will tend to be political pressure from existing inhabitants on the local authority to adopt measures which constrain further immigration.

Clearly, looked at from the individual's point of view, there is no single optimum size of city but rather several optima depending upon whether the person is a local councillor (who would prefer P_3), an existing inhabitant (who would favour P_2) or a potential migrant (favouring P_4). The picture is complicated further if we consider the preferences of another party, namely the businessman or entrepreneur, who may well prefer an entirely different city size.

(c)   The Optimum Urban Population Size for Industry
The ways in which firms view city size depend upon both their objectives and the type of good that they produce. If we consider the motivations of firms first, then we can develop a further diagram. In Figure 6.2 the vertical axis represents the costs and revenues associated with producing a given bundle of goods in cities of different size. We assume the price of goods is invariate with respect to population size – this is not unrealistic but even if the assumption

is relaxed it does not affect the validity of the argument. Consequently, the total revenue (TR), regardless of city size, is constant and the TR curve horizontal. The cost of producing the bundle will tend to fall as the population increases and agglomeration economies are reaped but eventually congestion will begin to offset these initial advantages. The over-all pattern of costs is thus U-shaped. Empirical evidence provided by Evans [1972] suggests that the total cost (TC) curve is a shallow U which is not so steep as the individual's cost curves depicted in Figure 6.1.

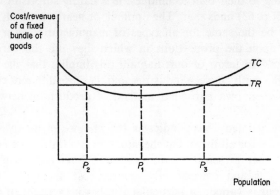

FIG. 6.2 *The costs and revenues associated with different city sizes*

If a firm is intent on profit maximisation it will consider a population size P_1 as optimal; a city of this size offers the maximum excess of revenue over cost. A study by Neutze [1965] suggested this point falls in the population range 200,000–1,000,000 inhabitants. Because we have assumed the TR curve to be horizontal this is also the optimum city size for cost-minimising firms, the TC curve being at its lowest point. (If, as some empirical evidence suggests, prices rise with city size, the TR curve will be upward-sloping and the optimum population for a profit maximiser will be larger than for a cost minimiser.) A revenue maximiser has no reason for preferring P_1 and will be indifferent between populations in the range P_2–P_3 – cities either larger or smaller than this will involve him in actual loss. A further type of entrepreneur is the sales maximiser; he will have another idea of the optimum city size although this is impossible to identify in a diagram concerned with a fixed output of goods.

Just as there is no reason for firms with different objectives to view city size in the same way, there is no reason for firms in different industries to have the same concept of optimality. Evans, in his work, has found that the cost curves for each individual factor of production have their own particular characteristics. Although the *TC* curve is U-shaped, the costs of floor space and labour tend to rise with city size, the cost of business services to fall while that of capital is fairly constant. As different products require particular mixes of these factors, and individual firms will combine them according to their own techniques, it is hardly surprising that Evans ([1972] p. 63) finds that 'The optimal, or nearly optimal, city size will not be the same for all types of manufacturing firm but will depend upon the proportions in which they use the various kinds of input.' In terms of our diagram this implies that the *TC* curve will differ both between industries and, because different companies adopt their own particular method of production, between firms.

The picture painted above indicates the absence of an over-all optimal city size for all firms, but the situation is a little more complicated than that presented so far. Figure 6.2 refers to a given bundle of goods and consequently ignores cost fluctuation that occurs if output is varied; in particular it takes no account of cost economies that accompany increased output. If this latter factor is taken into account, optimality will depend not only on objectives and the type of output but also on the level of production.

6.3 The Validity of the Optimal-City Concept

It becomes apparent from what we have said in previous paragraphs that there is no such thing as *the* optimum-size city; instead there are a number of optima which may be considered important to different groups of individuals or firms. Local government sees the city in a different way to residents, whose attitudes in turn differ from possible migrants or businessmen. Each of these categories has its own views of what determines the optimum-city-population size. In general we can define four distinct types of optima, namely the city sizes which correspond to the following alternative criteria:

(1) minimises local authority expenditure;
(2) maximises the net benefit enjoyed by existing residents;

(3) exhausts all the possible net benefits for potential inward migrants; and

(4) fulfils the objectives of various types of private firm.

In the event, a city is unlikely to fulfil any of these criteria; this is not only because they clearly conflict with one another but also because the basis of the static model outlined above is inappropriate. Although it is true that the general shapes of the cost and benefit curves depicted above are fairly realistic for any moment in time, the dynamic nature of the urban economy means that they are continually moving over time. The urban economy is not static but continually changing and with changes in technology, social aspirations, life styles, and so on, come new ideas of what the optimum city size should be. What is required is a dynamic urban-growth model which incorporates not just the features of the city itself but also its relationships with other parts of the national economy. The basic problem has been succinctly put by Harry Richardson ([1972] p. 32):

> There is a close degree of kinship between the concepts of optimum city size and optimum national population. No serious economist would use the optimum population concept nowadays, and it is paradoxical that urban economists, supposedly extending the frontiers of a new field, should find themselves chasing, if only in an analogous form, such an ancient will-o'-the-wisp.

Despite the rather elusive nature of the optimal-size concept, the idea of the ideal city size implicitly underlies much of the recent debate on the urban environment. Economists such as E. J. Mishan ([1967] pp. 106–7) argue that many cities are now too large, being consequently detrimental to human welfare; he feels that 'There is an asymmetry in the forces at work which tends to make the city too large. The economics of large-scale productions are apparent and there is every incentive for their exploitation by private and public companies.' In other words, cities may be optimal in the sense of minimising costs of production but their sizes are only achieved by a population growth in excess of the social optimum. This is a very static type of argument and many cities are now a great deal larger than they were a century ago, yet simple observation suggests the standard of life for inhabitants has improved considerably (see Chapter 7). To borrow Wilfred Beckerman's terminology [1974], the 'ecodoomsters' ignore the dynamic elements which have brought about shifts in both the cost and benefit (or revenue) curves. It is this dynamic consideration which makes the optimal-size city such a slippery concept.

Given the obvious conceptual and practical problems associated with defining the optimum city size, many economists have turned instead to consider the existing distribution of city sizes. This is a movement away from attempting to achieve optimality in the size of a single city towards the problem of obtaining the optimum urban system. By accepting the possibility of different optima in different places and circumstances, one must immediately begin to bring in wider considerations and to look at cities in the larger framework of the national economy and start to incorporate considerably more dynamic influences into the analysis.

6.4 The Distribution of City Sizes

For many years geographers and statisticians have shown a keen interest in the distribution of city sizes. Work in the 1930s and 1940s suggested that countries all exhibit similar distributions of city size; specifically it was claimed that the urban hierarchy corresponded to the 'rank-size distribution' where the rank of a city times its size always yields a constant product (Evans [1972] p. 65). This view has been questioned more recently by Berry [1961] who, in an examination of urban hierarchies in thirty-eight countries, found only thirteen which exhibited any approximation to the rank-size distribution. The remainder, although having fewer cities in each of the successive stata of the hierarchy (that is all the distributions were positively skewed in statistical terms), showed few other common characteristics. Statisticians continue to argue over the possibility of a universal distribution and its possible shape. A detailed survey of this work is presented in a paper by Richardson [1973a] and it is quite apparent from the types of statistical functions employed that the alternative models being advocated are so similar that, with the data currently available, it is unlikely that any dominant distribution will be isolated. For this reason we will give little space to the attempts being made to explain the exact shape of the urban hierarchy and concentrate instead on examining why such a hierarchy should exist at all.

Two basic approaches have been adopted by economists when working on differences in city sizes. The first of these, systems theories, is an extension of the statistical approach and uses mathematical models to explain regularities in urban hierarchies in terms of the most probable distribution under a number of set conditions. Little more will be said about these theories, partly because they describe the existing situation rather than explain it and are consequently only of academic interest, and partly because they are based on the quite untenable implicit assumption that there is no correlation between city size and growth in city size; all available empirical evidence refutes this.

The 'central-place' approaches to urban hierarchies are of much more significance. These theories try to explain differences in city sizes in terms of a hierarchy of market areas; these stem directly from the work of Losch [1954] on location theory (see Chapter 3). Generally, the larger the city the greater the range of goods and services it will provide and the larger will be its marketing hinterland. It is assumed that a hierarchy of cities exists because it is possible to provide some goods and services, especially those for a local market, more efficiently and cheaply in a small city while others can be more economically provided by larger cities. The majority of work using this technique has concentrated on regional hierarchies and has specifically been concerned with intra-regiona! phenomena – it is, none the less, a useful way of explaining the national distribution of city sizes. Empirical evidence suggests that central-place theory can provide a fairly accurate account of the distribution of retailing and other services but tends to be less helpful when considering manufacturing industry. This is not altogether surprising since manufacturers tend to serve an international rather than national market, and consequently it is inappropriate to define their market areas in terms of national political boundaries.

Central-place theory applied to the national distribution of cities states that the urban area that can capture the largest share of the national (or international) market, and at the same time retain its own local markets, will dominate the hierarchy. Other cities will supply regional, as well as local, markets and will consequently form the next stratum while smaller centres, which have little economic significance outside their own boundaries, will come further down the ladder. The position of any city in the hierarchy will therefore be determined by the particular type of industry it can attract. This then leads back to the question, 'why do firms locate in certain cities?' A more detailed consideration of this question was presented in Chapter 2 but it is generally true to say that firms catering for a national (or international) market prefer to establish their main offices in the largest city because of the agglomeration economies that is offered there.

This tendency for head offices of national firms to concentrate in the largest cities has been empirically verified by Evans [1973] in an examination of the largest companies in the United Kingdom. Considering the 1000 biggest companies quoted on the Stock Exchange for 1970-1 he found that of the twenty-five largest some 88 per cent had their headquarters in London while only 22 per cent of the 200 smallest companies in the sample did so. In summary he found that 'although Central London is very attractive as the location of the headquarters of the very largest companies, this attraction declines rapidly and continuously and is comparatively slight for the small companies on the list' (p. 387). Presumably many of the smaller companies locate in the regional centres because of the more localised markets they serve.

The urban hierarchy may be seen as a reflection of the needs and wishes of both individuals and firms. In the case of the former, many people prefer to live in large cities because of the wide range of amenities which are available while others prefer the relatively less-hectic pace of smaller centres. Brown [1972] has suggested that the differing values which individuals place on city size has a reinforcing effect on the existing hierarchy. People's tastes are, at least partly, determined by their environment, and consequently those born in large cities tend to remain there but people familiar with the quieter life in a small town tend to move out if it expands too rapidly and re-settle in a smaller village. In this way, larger cities tend to continue their expansion while smaller ones require considerable inflows of migrants to enlarge their populations. Taken alone, however, this phenomenon could never explain the common pattern of urban hierarchies observed in industrial countries (unless, of course, they have identical proportions of 'urbanities' and 'ruralities') but it may be a factor contributing to it.

Urban hierachies are important to large firms and corporations which themselves have hierarchical structures of management, marketing and production. Firms tend to have head offices in the largest centre while regional and sub-regional branches are located further down the hierarchy. If the concern is national in character, it is usually based in the largest city within its marketing area. (To some extent a similar organisational structure can be observed in governmental control.) The need to contact and deal with other firms at similar levels in the managerial hierarchy means that there are decided advantages to be gained in locating in centres which already contain offices of rival and complementary firms of like importance. Head offices enjoy external benefits by being in the same city as the head offices of other firms, while regional offices of the various concerns tend to concentrate at the largest city in the region. Because regions differ in their geographical size and physical characteristics, they attract differing numbers of industries and branches of varying importance; the exact composition will be determined by the nature of the local market and the relative predominance of the region. Consequently, the leading city within each region is likely to attract a different number of branch offices which will themselves be of varying importance. Additionally, the local firms operating from these centres and catering purely for the regional market will differ in size and number depending on the peculiarities of the region. In this way a hierarchy of regional centres is built up. Similarly at the sub-regional level this process will create further strata in the city hierarchy, the size of urban centres further down the ladder being dependent upon their importance in the national, regional and local markets. In this way, central-place theory can explain the existing distribution of city sizes; it is a distribution favoured by industry and commerce because it provides a wider choice of location for new plant and permits them to operate more efficiently.

The public sector tends to reinforce the city-size distribution created by industry. The largest cities in Western Europe are, with a few exceptions, also the seats of national governments – this is not a pattern found in other continents, for example North America – while regional centres tend to be the location of district authorities. The large number of people associated with the efficient functioning of each strata in the administrative hierarchy swells the population in these cities, for example London is not just the heart of the national government but is also an administrative centre for the South-east as well as its immediate surrounding area. In addition, the public services supplied in cities are usually a function of their size, and as the city grows there is a corresponding expansion in the manpower required to provide such things as public transport, sewage-disposal facilities, postal services, and so on. If one extends central-place theory to include the public sector, this is as one would expect.

6.5 Conclusions

Harry Richardson [1973b] has described the search for an optimal city as 'almost as idle as the quest for the philosopher's stone'. This certainly seems to be the case if the analyst is seeking a universal optimum size of urban population but is less so if the objective is to define the optimal city given a set of constraints. These constraints – the availability of raw materials, ease of access to national markets, the size of the adjacent hinterland, and so on – mean that a series of optima will appear and that a hierarchy of city sizes may emerge as the optimum urban system. In terms of the analysis presented in Section 6.2, this implies that the urban cost and benefit curves do not only have different shapes and meaning for the various interested parties but also that they vary from city to city dependent upon the prevailing constraints. Basically the idea of a universal optima is replaced by a series of optimal city sizes, each corresponding to their rank in the national hierarchy. This approach corresponds to much of the work done on urban-growth theory and introduces a degree of continuity into the debate on urban dynamics.

References

C. A. BAKER [1910], 'Population and Costs in Relation to City Management', *Journal of the Royal Statistical Society* (December) pp. 73–9.

Barnett House Survey Committee [1938], *Survey of the Social Services in the Oxford District* (Oxford: Survey Committee of Barnett House).

W. BECKERMAN [1974], *In Defense of Economic Growth* (London: Jonathan Cape).

B. J. L. BERRY [1961], 'City Size Distributions and Economic Development', *Economic Development and Cultural Change*, pp. 573–88.

E. VON BOVENTER [1973], 'City Size Systems: Theoretical Issues, Empirical Regularities and Planning Guides', *Urban Studies* (June) pp. 145–62.

A. J. BROWN [1972], *The Framework of Regional Economics in the United Kingdom* (Cambridge University Press).

C. CLARK [1945], 'The Economic Functions of a City in Relation to its Size', *Econometrica* (April) pp. 97–113.

O. D. DUNCAN [1956], 'The Optimum Size of Cities', in *Demographic Analysis*, ed. J. J. Spengler and O. D. Duncan (New York: Free Press).

O. D. DUNCAN [1959], 'Service Industries and the Urban Hierarchy', *Papers and Proceedings of the Regional Science Association*, pp. 105–35.

A. W. EVANS [1972], 'The Pure Theory of City Size in an Industrial Economy', *Urban Studies* (February) pp. 49–77.

A. W. EVANS [1973], 'The Location of the Headquarters of Industrial Companies', *Urban Studies* (October) pp. 387–95.

W. HIRSCH [1959], 'Central Place Theory and Regional Urban Hierarchies: An Empirical Note', *Review of Economics and Statistics*, pp. 232–41.

K. S. LOMAX [1943], 'Expenditure Per Head and Size of Population', *Journal of the Royal Statistical Society*, pp. 51–9.

A. LOSCH [1954], *The Economics of Location* (Yale University Press).

E. J. MISHAN [1967], *The Costs of Economic Growth* (Harmondsworth: Penguin).

G. M. NEUTZE [1965], *Economic Policy and the Size of Cities* (Canberra: Australian National University).

H. W. RICHARDSON [1972], 'Optimality in City Size, Systems of Cities and Urban Policy: a Sceptic's Views', *Urban Studies* (February), pp. 29–48.

H. W. RICHARDSON [1973a], 'Theory of the Distribution of City Sizes: Review and Prospects', *Regional Studies*, pp. 239–51.

H. W. RICHARDSON [1973b], *The Economics of Urban Size* (Farnborough: Saxon House).

Royal Commission of Local Government in Greater London [1960], *Report*, Cmnd. 1164 (London: H.M.S.O.).

Royal Commission on Local Government in England [1969], *Report*, Cmnd. 4040 (London: H.M.S.O.).

SVIMEZ [1967], *Ricerca sin Coste d'Insediamento*, cited by G. C. Cameron [1970], 'Growth Areas, Growth Centres and Regional Conversion', *Scottish Journal of Political Economy* (February) pp. 19–38.

J. TINBERGEN [1968], 'The Hierarchy Model of the Size Distribution of Centres', *Papers and Proceedings of the Regional Science Association*, pp. 65–8.

7 THE URBAN ENVIRONMENT

7.1 Interest in the Urban Environment

Public and specialist concern with the urban environment has grown again in recent years and increasingly economists are being drawn into the new debate. There are two main issues being raised: have urban environmental standards declined to unacceptable levels and, assuming they have, how should improvements be achieved? A very clear, and apparently irreconcilable, dichotomy of opinion has emerged within the economic profession over both the gravity of the situation and the appropriate economic action required. Members of one school talk of the dereliction of the city and advocate the abandonment of traditional economic principles and the adoption of more direct controls to alleviate urban pollution and congestion. The alternative view, held primarily by Professor Wilfred Beckerman in the United Kingdom and Edwin Mills in the United States, is that any sub-optimality in urban environmental standards is the result of distortions within various economic markets and that the situation can easily be rectified if the pricing mechanism is correctly adjusted.

It may seem rather strange that interest in the urban environment should emerge as such a controversial topic in the 1960s and 1970s. Clearly, conditions in the major cities of Western Europe are infinitely better than they were a century or so ago during the main phase of the Industrial Revolution (or indeed during the days of the Roman Empire, judging by some of Juvenal's writings). The late eighteenth century witnessed urban expansion at an unprecedented rate as industrial demands for labour grew. Technology was not sufficiently advanced to provide transport capable of permitting a suburban pattern of life, which, combined with the high concentration of industry in particular areas, led to densely packed working-class estates. These communities were forced to live directly adjacent to factories and to endure the effluence that was pumped into the atmosphere and rivers around them. Local government in this period was neither equipped nor designed to cope with the massive influx of immigrants from the countryside, and proved incapable of meeting the bare minimum standards of sanitation required for health and well-being. Environmental problems existed in cities before this period but the inflow of workers during the eighteenth century greatly increased their magnitude and the number of people affected.

By today's standards the conditions prevailing in the cities of the Industrial Revolution were appalling, with filth and overcrowding the rule rather than the exception. One contemporary report from the middle of the last century by the Health of Towns Association summarised the conditions in our main cities thus: 'Bolton – very bad indeed; Bristol – decidedly bad; the mortality is very great; Hull – some parts as bad as can be conceived; many districts very filthy; with a few exceptions, the town and coast drainage extremely bad; great overcrowding and want of ventilation generally.' This does not paint a very commendable picture of urban life at that time but it is in no way atypical; a statement in the House of Lords in 1842 concerning Greenock, for example, went:

> In one part of Market Street is a dunghill . . . it contains a hundred cubic yards of impure filth . . . it is the stock-in-trade of a person who deals in dung; he retails it by cartfuls. This collection is fronting the public street; it is enclosed in front by a wall; the height of the wall is almost twelve feet; and the dung overtops it; the malarious moisture oozes through the wall, and runs over the pavement.

The urban environment during the Industrial Revolution was unquestionably squalid and is incomparable with anything existing in the United Kingdom today. Over the last fifty years urban conditions have improved steadily; simply comparing 1971 with the situation a decade before shows the average smoke concentration in cities to have fallen by 60 per cent and the sulphur-dioxide concentrations by 30 per cent. These figures include all areas; looking just at those where the Clean Air Acts have been enforced, one finds that the improvements in our main industrial cities have been even more pronounced (Beckerman [1973a] p. 498).

Despite the obvious improvement, there is still a feeling that all is not well: in a rather dramatic statement Mishan ([1967] p. 121) expresses a sentiment felt by many: 'The city as a centre point of civilisation, as a place of human concourse and life and gaiety, is becoming a thing of the past. Hoarse beneath the fumes emitted by an endless swarm of crawling vehicles, today's city bears close resemblance to some gigantic and clamorous arsenal.' Disregarding the sentimental and emotive content of the statement, it is worth pausing to consider why people should be so concerned with the state of our cities at this particular time.

Accepting that the urban environment is still not perfect, one is left to explain why the clamour for further improvements should occur during this particular period which, in its historical context, is one of relative and growing prosperity. The comparative affluence of modern society itself provides at least part of the answer. People no longer need to devote themselves exclusively to procuring the necessities of life but can now afford to spend more time on improving their everyday surroundings (Richardson [1971a]). Although it is possible to explain the growth of the environmentalist lobby partly in terms of these higher material living standards, this is not the entire answer.

Advances in techniques for quantifying and measuring the components which together make up the urban environment mean people now have a clearer and more objective assessment of phenomena, many of which they have always been aware but formerly could only express in qualitative and rather imprecise terms. Pronouncements that the lead content in London's atmosphere is x per cent, for example, tends, because of its apparent scientific exactitude to have a profound effect on the local population, although few have any idea of the significance of this particular level. In some ways connected with this is the fact that the type of environmental problem has changed since the beginning of the century; no longer are there smogs or belching chimneys, which are clear signs of pollution, but instead we have invisible and odourless pollutants which are, nevertheless, equally harmful to health and well-being. It is the invisible and apparently insidious nature of the problem which has generated much of the current public uneasiness. This has been coupled with a general international concern about the impact of increased economic activity on the ecological structure of the planet as a whole.

One topic which is now arousing increasing concern is the environmental damage being caused to our cities by the motor-car. In many ways this particular problem typifies the type of situation which is emerging – the significant environmental effects which transport has in all aspects of urban life is considerable. A list of the damage caused by motor vehicles will include (Foster [1974]): noise, vibration, air pollution, dirt, visual intrusion, loss of privacy, changes in the amount of light, neighbourhood severance, relocation, disruption during planning and construction, accidents, pedestrian inconvenience, and general congestion. With one particular aspect of urban life having such a profound effect on the environment, it is hardly surprising that people are becoming concerned about the situation.

7.2 The Economic Causes of Urban Pollution

Economists have been fully aware of the pollution and congestion that can accompany economic development for a great number of years. Indeed, the classical economist, Alfred Marshall ([1920] p. 804), suggested a 'fresh air levy' on property-owners, which was to be spent by local authorities on air quality control. The problem is seen as a malfunctioning of the normal economic processes where the consumption of any scarce resource (such as a clean environment) is determined by the forces of supply and demand. Although the first important comments by an economist on pollution can be found in the work of Alfred Marshall, written at the turn of the century, it was Arthur Pigou who really laid the foundations of modern environmental economics. In developing the theory of welfare economics, Pigou defined and discussed the negative aspects of 'externalities'.

Traditionally, economics has been involved with goods and services which 'can be brought directly or indirectly into relation with the measuring rod of money' (Pigou [1920]), but this has not prevented the recognition of other categories of costs and benefits which do not directly enter the market process and consequently have no money value attached to them: these are externalities. An externality was defined in Chapter 2 as either a cost or benefit experienced by an individual or group of individuals as a byproduct of action by a different individual or group for which there has been no contract or trade.

External costs have two basic characteristics: they are unpriced, and consequently outside the control of the market mechanism, and are imposed upon the recipient without his consent. We can usefully distinguish three broad categories of external cost.

(a) *Producer-upon-producer externalities.* This type of externality exists when the productive activities of one firm or plant interferes with other firms or plant. The classic example of an external cost of this type is when the activities of a dye firm dirties river water and hence increases the production costs of producers downstream who have to clean the water before using it in their processes. Producer-upon-producer externalities are important in industrial-location decisions (see Chapters 2 and 3) and in selecting the appropriate production technology but they only have minimal effects on the urban environment, possibly influencing the conditions under which the local labour force works.

(b) *Producer-upon-consumer externalities* (sometimes called user-upon-non-user). It was this type of external cost that caused the appalling urban conditions of the Industrial Revolution. Factories often generate smoke, dirt and noise which inconveniences and distresses people living around them, but are not recorded in firms' accounts – except possibly indirectly inasmuch as they impair the health and eventually the efficiency of the labour force. These activities are, nevertheless, costs to society and are borne by the people afflicted. The classic example of this category of external cost was provided by Pigou ([1920] p. 184) when he wrote that 'smoke in large towns inflicts a heavy uncharged loss on the community, in injury to buildings and vegetables, expenses for washing clothes and cleaning rooms, expenses for the provision of extra artificial light and in many other ways'.

Today the situation has changed slightly; pollution is not so immediately apparent as it was a century or even a decade ago; there are no longer belching chimneys or smoking steam engines to pollute our cities. The new environmental damage by internal-combustion engines and power stations is of the same basic type however – the activities of one sector of society are imposing uncharged costs on another, passive, sector.

(c) *Consumer-upon-consumer externalities* (sometimes called user-upon-user). Congestion is the commonest form of this category of external cost; people in their quest to pursue some activity impede and hinder others pursuing a similar activity. Traffic congestion is the most familiar example, but there are other consumer-upon-consumer externalities where the consumption patterns of one section of the community affect the utility enjoyed by other sections without any compensation being given or payments received. The specific problem of traffic congestion is considered in detail in the following chapter, but it is worth noting that many of the general principles outlined there are equally applicable in other circumstances where the activities of one group of consumers interfere with those of another.

Urban environmental problems are usually phrased in terms of external costs, but it is a little more complicated than this. In the next section a more detailed discussion of the economic difficulties of reducing pollution and congestion is presented. The economist's solution to the urban environmental problem has not been generally accepted and this has, in part, been due to the lack of any consensus amongst the experts as to the appropriate course of action to pursue. The following is intended to clarify many of the issues which have concerned ecologists and environmentalists in recent years and to vindicate the economist – in this sense it is somewhat subjective.

7.3   The Classical Economic Approach to Pollution Control

Economics is not concerned with removing pollution entirely – this is both an impossible objective and is opposed to the general philosophy of the discipline. Economists are interested in obtaining the optimal level of pollution – the level at which any further reduction imposes greater social costs than the social welfare that it confers (Mills [1966] p. 44). Since it is generally felt that the present rate of effluent discharge is excessive and the environment sub-optimal, this implies that there is currently a need to reduce pollution. In simple terms, the economic mechanism by which this is achieved is that the externalities are *internalised* or given shadow prices reflecting the social costs they impose. With the appropriate price attached to the externality, it may be traded as with any other good and the forces of supply and demand can be left to determine the optimal output. (Road pricing, which is a particular type of shadow price reflecting the social costs of congestion which a motor vehicle creates, is discussed in Chapter 8.)

The problem is a little more complicated than this however. There is the obvious difficulty of deciding the appropriate price to use – this is considered in the following section – but there is also the rather more fundamental problem of deciding who bears the cost of environmental improvement. The difficulty stems from the fact that while an externality may be seen as a cost to one group, it is a benefit to another. As Beckerman ([1974] p. 137) has said: 'Pollution can be analysed either in terms of the *pollutant* – for example, the smoke or the effluent or noise – that is produced as a by-product of some activity, or in terms of the *clean environment* that is destroyed, or "used up" by the pollutant.' Consequently, if we consider Pigou's example of a smoking chimney, this represents an external cost to those who have to endure the dirt and fumes, but to the factory owner and his customers, who enjoy cheap goods, it is an external benefit: they are enjoying the use of a 'free' commodity.

This dual nature of externalities poses the question: should the polluter be made to pay for the external costs he imposes on the rest of the community through his activities, or should they compensate him for reducing the environmental harm he causes and for the consequent benefits they would reap? There is no easy answer. Arguments for the alternatives are usually based either upon moral attitudes or distributional grounds.

Many people feel that it is morally wrong for the polluter to use up the clean environment which is the heritage of all and that he should therefore pay the charge. This ignores the distributional problem. It is usually the less wealthy sections of the community who actually benefit from much of the environmental damage done to our cities. They are less concerned with the aesthetic things of life but appreciate the cheap everyday necessities modern industry can offer. Is it morally right that they should bear the incidence of a pollution charge by having to pay higher prices for their goods so that richer people can live in cleaner cities? The question of who should be liable to pay the price of pollution is therefore not easily settled by looking simply at the moral issues involved.

On pure efficiency grounds, however, there is much to be said in favour of the polluter bearing the charge – a price on all pollution he creates would encourage the development of new production techniques which do less environmental damage. If the polluted compensate those contaminating the urban environment for curtailing their activities, there is no incentive for the introduction of cleaner technologies; the polluters would quite happily continue to collect their compensation *ad infinitum*.

Although a great deal has been written about the merits of charges *vis-à-vis* compensation, the whole problem has probably been magnified out of all proportion. Certainly there are instances where there is no objective way of selecting the correct approach but these are perhaps less widespread than is sometimes thought. In many cases a common-sense solution provides the answer – one should charge whoever is using up a scarce resource. Take clean water as an example: suppose a factory dirties river water in its processes, it is using a scarce resource and should be charged the appropriate shadow price, but if someone drinks water they are also consuming a scarce resource and must also be charged.

In many ways related to this problem of who should be made responsible for the urban environment is the need to make any system of economic control comprehensive. If the polluter is charged for the damage he causes, there is an incentive not only for him to develop new methods of production, but also to change the character of the pollution he is generating. In the transport field, for example, 'the use of barriers in the urban environment might ease the noise problem at the expense of creating a visual intrusion problem' (Foster and Mackie [1970]). Consequently, it is necessary that any approach embraces all types of environmental considerations.

7.4   Environmental Prices or Standards?

So far we have just considered the possibility of putting a price on pollution, but there is an alternative: namely, the setting of environmental standards. This latter method has been favoured in recent official policies which have set down legal constraints on the amounts of certain pollutants which may be discharged. In many ways this does form a very crude pricing system since the usual penalty for exceeding the prescribed discharge is a fine which, in a broad sense, may be conceived as a charge for creating excessive pollution.

There is a clear relationship between the setting of prices and the establishment of standards, which we can illustrate with the aid of Figure 7.1. In this diagram D_1D_2 represents urban society's demand curve for a cleaner environment – the fact the curve slopes down indicates that, although great value is attached to initial improvements, once pollution has been reduced, further reductions yield less and less welfare. It is also assumed, not unreasonably, that the costs of reducing pollution increase with each successive unit removed – this results in the upward-sloping cost curve, C_1C_2.

A policy of making polluters pay the full costs of their activities would result in them paying a price of P for each unit of effluence discharged. With this levy, 'pollution should be reduced to the point where the costs of doing so are covered by the benefits from

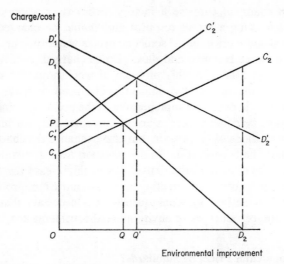

FIG. 7.1   *The optimum urban environmental improvement*

the reduction in pollution', the criteria for optimal environmental improvements set by the Royal Commission on Environmental Pollution ([1972] para. 20). This charge would improve the urban situation by an amount OQ by either making the polluter reduce his output or by encouraging him to adopt a 'cleaner technology'. Any environmental improvement beyond Q is unjustified since the marginal costs of achieving it will exceed the social benefits it confers.

The alternative approach, that of setting standards, will superficially produce the same result if applied correctly. The authorities would set a standard requiring the environment to be improved by an amount OQ; no price is set or charge made, but polluters are legally compelled to comply with the regulation. (It is worth noting at this stage that the standard should *not* require an improvement of OD_2, which implies all environmentally damaging activities are banned. The reason for this is that the total social cost of such a move is $C_1C_2D_2O$, while the social benefit is D_1D_2O – there is no *a priori* reason why the former should exceed the latter. The standard should be set so the social cost of improving the urban environment by the next increment exceeds the benefit generated.)

The appropriate charge or standard will not be identical for all cities. This may sound strange when one is familiar with legislation setting national environmental standards but, in fact, it is unlikely that the demand and cost curves associated with pollution will be identical in all situations. As Peltzman and Tideman [1972] have shown, the optimal environment is at least partly determined by city size. The people who benefit from pollution abatement are individuals, and consequently the demand curve for improvement is the aggregate of numerous private individual demand curves. It is therefore clear that the larger the city the greater the demand. Similarly, the costs of reducing pollution are borne by individuals and again a community's cost curve must be the summation of the numerous personal curves. Consequently, the aggregate cost curve for reducing pollution will be higher for large rather than small cities.

Returning to Figure 7.1, if we assume C_1C_2 and D_1D_2 to be the cost and demand curves for a small city, we can show the corresponding curves for a large city as $C'_1C'_2$ and $D'_1D'_2$. Although empirical evidence suggests that the urban environment is worst in our larger cities, the diagram indicates the largest city to be in need of greatest environmental improvement, OQ' – the current situation in this case would appear far from optimal. (Of course, there is no *a priori* reason why the improvement should necessarily be more, less or exactly the same for the larger city than the small; it depends on the actual empirical relationships of the different curves.) The example demonstrates the need to set appropriate and, in many cases, different charges or standards for each city. They should be determined locally to meet the particular needs of individual centres.

Although superficially pricing and standards appear identical in their effects, there are in fact several reasons for preferring the pricing technique on economic grounds (see Victor [1972] pp. 38–43 and Royal Commission on Environmental Pollution [1972] pp. 74–85).

(i) The effect on long-term economic efficiency. Pollution charges, by putting a price on environmental damage, encourage firms to develop techniques which reduce pollution at all levels of output – in other words, there is an incentive for them to try to push the C_1C_2 curve in Figure 7.1 down and to the right. This long-term effect does not occur with standards where polluters are only required to curtail their activities to the current optimum without providing any encouragement for them to reduce their discharges further. In dynamic terms, pricing is therefore preferable.

(ii) The determination of the shadow price or standard. Many opponents of pollution charges point to the difficulty of calculating the correct price to levy and hence advocate the use of standards on practical grounds. This is hardly a valid argument however. First, as Harry Richardson ([1971b] p. 162) has pointed out, standards are not normally determined by economic criteria but are frequently set for ease of enforcement and political acceptability, and consequently are unlikely to produce the optimum for this very reason. Second, as Wilfred Beckerman [1974] argues, prices are simply the converse of standards – it is impossible to determine one without knowledge of the other. As he says, 'Whatever can be controlled must be measurable; if it isn't measurable it is an illusion to believe it is being controlled. And if it is measurable it can be taxed.'

(iii) It is sometimes claimed that very exact knowledge of the optimal degree of pollution is required if charging is employed, whilst environmental standards can be 'rough and ready'. This criticism of pricing can be refuted in the same way as the previous one: namely, if you can use a rough-and-ready approach to determine the appropriate standard, there is no reason why the same procedure cannot be applied to charges. In terms of Figure 7.1, prices set slightly above or below P will have exactly the same effect on the urban environment as standards slightly above or below Q. The point is that both prices and standards would need to be adjusted to (*a*) initially find the optimal level and (*b*) later to correct for changes in this optimum as the demand and cost curves move. Indeed, one could argue that prices are preferable for this purpose. First, firms and other polluters are familiar with frequent price changes and make allowances for them in their forward planning. Second, the pricing system has the advantage that it permits a gradual movement to the optimum. Firms retain financial reserves to meet changing price levels of raw materials (of which the environment is a particular one) and consequently when pollution charges increase, they have the options of either immediately reducing their discharge or temporarily paying more and gradually modifying their production processes. In terms of over-all social welfare, it may be preferable for the firm to gradually change its methods of production and in the meantime compensate those who have to continue living in a polluted environment.

(iv) The distributional consequences of pricing are not always progressive. Some people object to pricing *per se* on the grounds that it means the less well-off are penalised because of their lower incomes. It is argued, for example, that to put a tax on smoking domestic chimneys will unfairly hit the poorer sections of the community who will no longer be able to afford sufficient heating. On the other hand, the standard can be regulated, it is claimed, to ensure that the weaker sections of society do not suffer as the result of environmental improvements. Again, these arguments can easily be questioned: the economist is primarily concerned with efficiency; it is the politician's job to determine the most desirable distribution of income – if it is decided some people will suffer unduly, subsidies may be given. Just as it is possible to vary standards for distributional reasons, it is possible to adjust the pollution charge on the same basis.

(v) Charges are far more flexible than centrally determined environmental standards. Edwin Mills [1966] gives this as the primary reason for preferring pollution charges, but this is one argument which is not altogether convincing. There is some truth in the idea that standards tend to be cumbersome and inflexible, but this is also true of many prices, especially those set by central government. One might more legitimately argue that people expect price changes from time to time to respond to them; they are less familiar with variable standards and consequently these may be less acceptable. However, the arguments on this point are by no means conclusive.

There are, therefore, a number of grounds for referring the use of environmental charges to standards – certainly there are few strong arguments to the contrary. (For an interesting statement in support of environmental standards, however, see Burrows [1974].) The reason why prices have not been used in this context stems partly from political decisions and partly from the attempts of town planners and others in the past to build some Utopia where the problem of pollution is just whisked away. Where pollution charges have been introduced, they appear to have been very successful.

One of the most effective methods of reducing the load caused by trade effluents is to make a charge for their treatment which is based on a sliding scale in accordance with their volume and strength. . . .Some remarkable results have been achieved in this way with profit to the trader, and with greater advantage to sewage works operation, and with considerable resulting contribution to the national economy (from a memorandum of the Institute of Sewage Purification, 1952).

7.5   Urban Environmental Policy

Local and central government have been actively engaged in reducing urban environmental damage for well over a century – the first Alkali Act, for example, was passed in 1863. Despite this long interest in the problem, it has only been in the post-war period that their policies have really had any significant impact.

The policies that have been pursued can be divided into three broad categories. First, there are the regulations and standards which have been introduced to curtail the activities of polluters – the Clean Air Act of 1956 is perhaps the best known of these. Second, there have been public expenditures to provide the necessary economic infrastructure for a clean environment – notable amongst these are sewerage plants, refuse collections and supplies of fresh water. Third, local authorities have attempted to improve the urban environment by taking upon themselves far wider planning powers – the New Towns, where the emphasis is on space and the segregation of noisy and dirty activities from residential areas, are extreme examples of this.

Before considering the economic implications of these policies, it is worth mentioning that, although the general approach which has been adopted is open to criticism, the results have on occasions been spectacular. For example, 'It is not generally appreciated that, despite the recognised continuance of a number of "hard-core" problems . . . the record of the U.K. in regard to clean air is one which commands widespread respect and admiration in other countries' (Department of Environment [1974]). These improvements do not, however, mean an optimum has yet been reached; indeed, Mishan's statement quoted earlier combined with the continued existence of 'hard-core problems' suggest that there is still a long way to go.

The emphasis placed on the different types of policy has changed over the years. The late nineteenth century saw extensive public expenditures on various social projects, many of which had important environmental implications – the main sewers in our major cities, for example, were laid in the 1870s. Public schemes like this are a necessary part of urban improvement, but need to be accompanied by appropriate pricing policies to ensure optimal usage. If facilities are unpriced, then polluters will pass on the environmental costs they impose to the ratepayers and taxpayers who are effectively paying for the treatment and disposal of the polluter's effluence. More recently, legislation has been passed to enable local authorities to place the financial burden of discharging industrial waste into the sewage system on the firms responsible (for example the Public Health (Drainage of Trade Premises) Act, 1937, and the Public Health Act, 1961).

In this century there has been an increase in the direct control of environmental pollution: this is a trend which began with the first Alkali Acts to control industrial pollution; these powers were then extended to domestic discharges and, more recently, there have been attempts to regulate motor-car nuisances. Some of these measures, especially the post-war clean air regulations, have been remarkably effective, but in the main they have proved to be 'blunt and inefficient instruments' (Richardson [1971b] p. 165). Part of the weakness of the legislation is that it has tried to impose national standards rather than allowing for different local circumstances. It is unfortunate that many of the more recent proposals for controlling the most harmful emissions from internal-combustion engines have been postponed, not on grounds of economic efficiency, but for political and macroeconomic reasons, especially the extra oil costs involved. (There is no *a priori* way in which one can decide whether the social cost – including foreign-exchange costs – of reducing the lead content in petrol exceeds the environmental benefits, only a full *cost – benefit appraisal* can do this and the outcome is by no means obvious.) To date many of the standards set have been below the optimum and consequently they have not been as effective as one would wish.

Town planning is a more recent innovation, which can be traced back to the Town Planning Act of 1909. The early legislation in this field was permissive rather than obligatory and town planning did not play an important role in urban improvement until the inter-war period. These years witnessed the acceptance of Ebenezer Howard's ideas with the completion of Welwyn Garden City and Letchworth, and a rapid expansion in suburbia. The planning of this time had the disadvantage that it was primarily concerned with moving people from the old congested city centres into periphery housing estates: there was no attempt to provide out-of-town employment or shopping facilities. This aspect of planning, combined with the increase in car ownership at the time, resulted in little improvement at the urban core and contributed to the increased traffic congestion that was experienced.

In existing towns, planners have attempted to improve the general environment by separating different types of activity in their redevelopment programmes; the emphasis in planning being to keep environmentally intrusive activities, industrial estates and main roads for example, away from residential areas. Where the environmental areas do come into contact with industry or heavy transport, attempts are made to provide some form of barrier, a green area or some other form of separation. Many older towns are attempting to improve their central areas by restricting traffic movements, and several of our major cities (for example Leeds, Norwich and Nottingham) now have 'pedestrian precincts' where traffic is completely banned during most of the day. Other cities are discouraging people from bringing vehicles into the core by traffic-management policies, combined with the provision of high-quality public-transport facilities.

Much of the town planning in the post-war era has concentrated on the construction of New Towns which are self-sufficient economic units. Eight such towns were designated around London between 1946 and 1949 and many more have been built since (for example Milton Keynes, Northampton and Haverhill). Initially intended to take overspill from the capital, they have now become an important part of national population planning.

Moving people from the old cities to the New Towns is not a simple solution to the environmental problem. The New Towns must have a real economic role to fulfil – the early ones were far too near London to meet this requirement. It is only socially desirable to encourage moves from the old centres to New Towns when the benefits from doing so, including the environmental benefits, exceed the costs – costs in terms of building the New Town, moving the population, the breaking of community ties and the loss of agglomeration economies to industry which is forced to locate at the new centre rather than the old. Again, environmental improvements can only be achieved at some considerable cost and before embarking on New Town development the economist should consider whether this is the best way of achieving the desired improvement.

7.6 Conclusion

The urban environment is considerably better in the 1970s than it was a century earlier, but nevertheless there is genuine concern about the remaining pollution and congestion in our towns and cities. Attempts to alleviate the problem have had some successes but the prevailing situation is still by no means optimal.

The problem is economic – pollution and congestion result from the existence of externalities for which those responsible are not currently being charged – and consequently the solution is also economic: namely, to make the polluters pay for the full costs of their activities. To date, the authorities have been reluctant to adopt this approach, relying instead on direct controls and town planning, but recent legislation permitting local authorities to charge for the discharge of effluence into the sewage system may indicate a slight change in attitude. Until an economic approach to charging or standards is adopted, the urban environment is likely to remain suboptimal with high social costs being imposed on those living in our towns.

References

W. BECKERMAN [1973a], 'Economic Growth and Welfare', *Minerva* (October) pp. 495–515.

W. BECKERMAN [1973b], 'Growthmania Revisited' *New Statesman* (October) pp. 550–2.

W. BECKERMAN [1974], *In Defence of Economic Growth* (London: Jonathan Cape).

P. BURROWS [1974], 'Pricing versus Regulations for Environmental Protection', in *Economic Policies and Social Goals*, ed. A. J. Culyer (London: Martin Robertson).

Department of the Environment [1974], *Clean Air Today* (London: H.M.S.O.).

C. D. FOSTER [1974], 'Transport and the Urban Environment', in

Transport and the Urban Environment, ed. J. G. Rothenberg and I. G. Heggie (London: Macmillan).

C. D. FOSTER and P. J. MACKIE [1970], 'Noise: Economic Aspects of Choice', *Urban Studies* (June) pp. 123–35.

A. MARSHALL [1920], *Principles of Economics*, 8th edn (London: Macmillan).

E. S. MILLS [1966], 'Economic Incentives in Air Pollution Control', in *The Economics of Air Pollution, a Symposium*, ed. H. Wolozin (New York: Norton).

E. J. MISHAN [1967], *The Costs of Economic Growth* (Harmondsworth: Penguin).

S. PELTZMAN and T. N. TIDEMAN [1972], 'Local versus National Pollution Control: Note', *American Economic Review* (December) pp. 959–63.

A. C. PIGOU [1920], *The Economics of Welfare* (London: Macmillan).

H. W. RICHARDSON [1971a], 'Economics and the Environment', *National Westminster Bank Quarterly Review* (May) pp. 43–52.

H. W. RICHARDSON [1971b], *Urban Economics* (Harmondsworth: Penguin).

Royal Commission on Environmental Pollution [1972], *First Report* (London: H.M.S.O.).

P. A. VICTOR [1972], *Economics of Pollution* (London: Macmillan).

8 THE URBAN TRANSPORT PROBLEM

8.1 The Problem

The last fifty years have witnessed a rapid and accelerating increase in private motor-car ownership throughout the developed world. The advantage the car affords, in terms of greater mobility, convenience and flexibility, provide undoubted benefits to many members of society but, at the same time, the rapid expansion in vehicle ownership has had serious repercussions on the urban economy. The several benefits derived from car ownership, combined with the importance of the motor-manufacturing industry in the macroeconomic sense (it has been estimated that somewhere in the region of 20 per cent of the U.S. economy is either directly or indirectly dependent upon the industry) suggests that it is a mode of transport which is likely to remain with us for some considerable time to come. In this situation it is important to consider the automobile's role in the urban economy and to consider ways in which it can play its part in urban development without generating excessive social costs to be paid by those living in our cities.

The greater mobility afforded by the growth in car ownership has encouraged and enabled the development of urban sprawl and the expansion in suburban living which has been characteristic of urban change over the last fifty years. The compact industrial centres common in the nineteenth century have expanded into the present conurbations precisely because improved transport now enables workers to live some distance from their place of employment. The trend was initially set in motion during the final decades of the last century with the advent of efficient public-transport systems and was accelerated after the First World War by the increasing availability of private transport. This quite radical change in urban structure, the appendage of large residential areas to our traditional radial cities, has created a number of problems, not the least of which is that caused by urban transport itself.

The advent of public transport initially produced problems of air pollution, noise and such like, but these were relatively minor when compared with the social costs currently generated by private motor-cars. Individual motorists are responsible for the generation of two significant external effects for which they are not at present fully accountable. The first externality is that of congestion. When a motor-car owner is deciding whether to make a journey he only considers his own private marginal cost (the cost of petrol and time consumed in undertaking the trip) and ignores the congestion he imposes on road users in the existing flow of traffic. In economic jargon this is a 'user-on-user externality'. The second category of external cost is the 'user-on-non-user externality'; this refers to the environmental and amenity costs imposed on the non-traveller by the motorist in the form of noise, air pollution, dirt, visual blight, and so on. While congestion is confined almost exclusively to the urban situation, the environmental costs of motoring tend to be much more widespread, as people living near motorways are always quick to point out. In this chapter we are primarily concerned with the first of these two categories of externality since this has the greatest effect on the efficient working of the urban economy, congestion slowing and hindering the movement of goods and people in our cities.

8.2 The Economic Theory of Traffic Congestion

Congestion is the product of motorists' defective economic vision. Drivers do not perceive the full cost of their journeys (or, if they do, refuse to adjust their activities accordingly), but instead ignore the fact that the presence in a traffic stream slows the flow for *all* other vehicles in that stream. When the individual motorist undertakes a journey, he assesses only his private marginal cost and takes no account of the increased costs he imposes on other motorists by creating additional congestion. Motorists will keep joining a stream of traffic while the additional private benefit they derive from trip-making exceeds the cost (cost in terms of both money and time). In other words, the costs perceived by a motorist joining a traffic flow, the marginal private cost (*MPC*) as it is known, is below the actual cost of the additional vehicle to other road users, the marginal social cost (*MSC*). Hence the *MSC* is composed of the *MPC* of travel plus the cost of congestion on other road users, marginal social cost in this context referring exclusively to road users and not to society in general.

A simple algebraic example illustrates this divergence more clearly. If the average social cost of a journey on a congested road with n vehicles on it is c then an additional car, by virtue of it slowing the existing flow, will increase this to $c + \triangle c$. The car expands the flow of traffic to $n + 1$ vehicles and the *MSC* of the nth$+1$ vehicle now becomes $(n+1)(c+\triangle c)-nc=c+\triangle c+n\triangle c$. Therefore the *MSC* exceeds the *ASC* by $n\triangle c$. To the motorist, however, his *MPC* is equal to the perceived cost of his journey and this will be the same as that for all the other drivers in the increased traffic stream, namely $c + \triangle c$. Hence we also find that the *MPC* of a trip equals the *ASC*; in this case they both amount to $c + \triangle c$. (See Sharp [1966].)

This divergence between the *MPC* and *MSC* produces a situation where the amount of traffic actually using any urban road may be in excess of the optimal flow when full account is taken of the costs created by excessive congestion. Figure 8.1 illustrates this point; the optimal flow, given the traditional negatively inclined demand curve for trip-making, *DD*, is indicated by Q_o but, if drivers take no account of their effect on other traffic, the actual number of vehicles on the road will be Q_a.

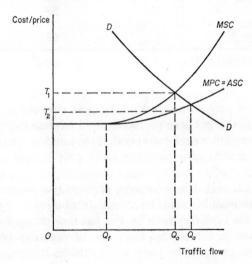

FIG. 8.1   *The optimal flow of traffic and road pricing*

The divergence between *MPC* and *MSC* only becomes important after a certain number of vehicles have entered a road; before this point (Q_I in the diagram) is reached there is no interaction between vehicles, and consequently problems of congestion do not arise. It is for this reason that congestion is almost unique to urban areas and, due to the daily peaks in travel to and from work, to certain times of the day. It is not often that the flow reaches the critical level either on inter-urban roads or during the mid-morning and afternoon periods in towns. Congestion during the peaks is dependent not so much on the number of commuters as on the number of cars; private vehicles create congestion out of all proportion to their carrying capacity. If we look at the figures for commuters travelling to work by car in our major cities we find they form only a small proportion of the total peak-hour traffic – see Table 8.1 – yet they manage to reduce speeds to below 20 m.p.h. for all road users.

TABLE 8.1   *Commuting to city centres in Britain, 1966*

| City | Percentage of commuters using | | | |
	Private car	Rail	Bus	Other
London	11	66	18	5
Birmingham	25	7	61	6
Liverpool	17	15	59	9
Manchester	21	14	59	6
Newcastle	21	8	63	9

SOURCE: Hall [1969] p. 411.

The urban traffic-congestion problem therefore stems from the excessive use of private transport during peak commuting periods. An exception to this has been the recent rapid increase in congestion between the commuter peak-travel periods in London. The requirements of the central area have expanded considerably and with them the number of service vehicles required to bring in goods. It is estimated that each Londoner now requires two juggernauts of goods a year to meet his needs and, since distribution in the capital is mainly by small delivery vehicles, this has now changed the congestion problem in the capital from one of excessive commuter demands to one produced by commercial vehicles demanding more road space.

8.3 'Road Pricing'

The problem confronting economists is that of reducing the flow of traffic to the socially optimum level, Q_o. Traditionally, economists have advocated the internalisation of the externality by the imposition of 'road pricing'. (See Walters [1961], Hewitt [1964] and Lennon [1972].) This approach involves altering the price structure in the market for road space by introducing a 'tax' on each motorist contributing to congestion equal to an amount T_1T_2 in Figure 8.1. This amount equates the post-tax perceived cost of trip-making to the corresponding MSC and consequently will reduce the traffic flow from Q_a to Q_o. The tax each vehicle will have to pay will depend upon its size, speed and the area it is being used in, these being the factors determining the amount of congestion it creates (Beesley [1968]). Strictly speaking, although economists talk of 'road pricing', the charge is a tax because the government is obtaining the benefit from the scheme – in the form of greater revenue – rather than the motoring public who, because of the loss of consumer surplus to those priced off the road, are, in aggregate, worse off. What the remaining motorists gain in having less congested roads they lose in having to pay higher prices to use them. Provided the increase in government revenue exceeds the sum of lost consumer surpluses to excluded travellers and to remaining motorists, the scheme produces a net benefit to *society*, which can then spend the revenue as it wishes (or at least the government can).

Road pricing has not yet been applied in this country but it does provide a theoretically ideal economic solution to the urban congestion problem provided that (*a*) it is physically possible to implement and not prohibitively expensive to impose and enforce, and (*b*) society is prepared to accept the social and economic implications of such a measure. On the first point the Smeed Committee (Ministry of Transport [1964]), which looked into the theoretical and technical possibilities of road pricing in the early 1960s, reported that road pricing is both practically possible and that certain forms would not prove excessively expensive to introduce and thereafter maintain and enforce. The main difficulty in devising a road-pricing scheme, which is both practical and reasonably sensitive to prevailing traffic conditions, is that it proves impossible for motorists to be made aware of the exact cost of making a journey until their destination is reached. Ticket systems have been suggested (including one for Central London), and even introduced in Singapore, which would provide the driver with the necessary information on the cost of travelling through the urban area, but they tend to be rather insensitive to local traffic conditions unless frequent boundaries are drawn, and this becomes impractical, expensive and, because of the queuing to purchase tickets, could easily add to congestion. The alternative of using a meter in each vehicle recording the cost as journeys take place is far more sensitive to the level of congestion if the rate charged can be varied with traffic conditions but does not indicate the cost before the driver actually embarks on his trip. It is of course arguable that motorists would soon learn by experience the approximate cost of driving in different urban conditions and that similar retrospective pricing policies are used in other sectors of the economy (for example in the provision of gas and electricity) but this is no guarantee that anything like an optimal allocation of traffic between alternative routes would materialise. Imperfect knowledge combined with the interdependence of trip-making means that motorists face a situation where they have to make guesses about the likely routes other road users will select before being able to assess their own costs and subsequently decide upon their own journeys.

The social and economic implications of road pricing have been a subject for wide discussion and debate in the academic literature (for a summary see Thomson [1974] pp. 142–54). The strongest argument against road pricing is that, because it is based upon the price mechanism, its implementation could possibly produce a situation where motoring becomes the privilege of the wealthy. William Vickrey [1968] has contested this argument, pointing to the fact that only 10–20 per cent of traffic needs removing from the road and that the majority of this would comprise of 'second-car' trip-makers and middle-class commuters both of whom could easily switch to public transport. He also criticised conventional restraint policy which he thinks *is* regressive and illustrates this by reference to the parking policy employed in Manhattan which, he maintained, has made motoring the privilege of the rich there. Vickrey's argument is not conclusive, for, although he demonstrates that the poor need not suffer as a result of road pricing, he does not prove that the system of charging would be strictly progressive. A more accurate assessment of a road-pricing scheme applied only to motorists is presented by Harry Richardson [1974] who advances the thesis 'that a large middle income group loses most (the relatively low-income motorists) while gains or minimum losses accrue to both the poor (non-motorists) and the rich (wealthy motorists)'. He argues further that congestion is the most equitable method of sharing out road space because everyone has an equal amount of time to 'spend'. In so far as the less wealthy, non-motorists, are likely to enjoy faster and more reliable public-transport facilities with reduced congestion, and the rich are quite prepared to pay the additional amount for easier motoring, this theory is probably true but it does not destroy the argument for road pricing. Road pricing is desirable on efficiency grounds alone; the fact that it may produce undesirable distributional anomalies is coincidental and outside of the control of the urban-transport economist. If one accepts that road pricing should not be introduced because it is based upon the price system, then there are strong arguments for abandoning the price mechanism altogether and resorting to a controlled economy. As it happens, the continuing existence of the market economy in the United Kingdom suggests that both it and the accompanying price mechanism are acceptable methods of resource allocation for the majority of people. Hence road pricing cannot be rejected simply because pricing is undesirable *per se*.

A rather more serious criticism of road pricing has been advanced by Clifford Sharp [1966] who is concerned about the uses to which the government puts the revenue from any pricing scheme. Any of the revenue which is returned to the excluded motorists in the form of reduced taxation elsewhere will induce a 'buy-back effect' enabling these people to purchase back some road space; the degree to which this will negate the effect of road pricing depends upon the amount of revenue being returned to former motorists and the extent to which they decide to use this to buy urban road space rather than other goods. How the revenue is disposed of is therefore important; to use it to reduce other motoring taxes would clearly reduce the effectiveness of road pricing considerably. The Smeed Report examined the desirability of road pricing under the assumption that the returns from the scheme would be used to improve the quality of the transport infrastructure (roads, traffic lights, and so on) but the size of investments in this kind of capital should be determined by other and wider economic considerations than simply the magnitude of the revenue from a road-pricing scheme. A more practical suggestion is that the revenue should be used to subsidise and improve urban public transport. At present 'there are fundamental reasons why public transport cannot compete in speed, frequency and convenience with the private car if competition is on equal terms' (Reynolds [1966] p. 82), and, as we shall see later, official policy has done little to improve the position. Subsidies alone will not attract car users to public transport; the non-financial benefits of the private car tend to outweigh any small financial cost disadvantages. Road pricing would, however, push the price of motor travel up and the price differential between modes would be widened considerably if the revenue from the tax was directed to public transport. At this higher price for motoring, subsidised public transport could well become a realistic substitute (Button [1975]).

A high rate of subsidy given to public transport would also reduce the semi-regressive nature of road pricing for the middle-income range by making attractive an alternative mode of travel to them. An interesting point related to this is that if road pricing was applied to both private and public transport, then it is likely that automatic subsidies (negative taxes) would be given to the latter by virtue of the fact that, over the lengths of cost curves considered, the *MSC* of public transport is probably *less* than the *MPC* (Tyson [1972]).

Despite the theoretical difficulties and practical problems involved with implementing an efficient road-pricing policy, the reason one has not been introduced in this country is almost certainly political. The 'motoring lobby' is extremely powerful and any threat to curtail the private motorist produces widespread and noisy objections. Allied to this is the fact that each motorist is personally reluctant to abandon his vehicle unless he is sure that others will join him and that an adequate alternative is available.

An interesting hypothetical illustration of this latter problem is provided by E. J. Mishan [1969] in his book, *The Costs of Economic Growth*. He takes the example of a radial city where initially a commuter uses public transport, averaging ten minutes per journey to work. Then this commuter buys a car and reduces his travel time to five minutes and, provided he is the only vehicle owner, the speed of public transport for others is unaffected. However, the demonstration effect is likely to encourage others to buy cars, and eventually congestion will result with the commuter now taking fifteen minutes to reach his job and the only alternative, public transport, now taking twenty-five minutes. Eventually one would suspect the public-transport system would be closed down completely.

The point is that at each stage the individual commuter benefits by his decision to have a car but this does not mean social welfare is maximised or that resources are efficiently allocated; clearly everyone would benefit it they *all* returned to public transport but this must be a community decision – there is no incentive for the individual 'to go it alone'. At present there is no satisfactory alternative public-transport system available to induce society to make such a decision.

8.4 Investment in Urban Roads

Since urban roads are frequently overloaded in our major cities, a case can be put forward that the only solution to the congestion problem is for the supply of road space to be increased. The implications and effects of such an idea on both the urban form and the urban environment are discussed elsewhere; here we are simply concerned with the basic economics of the proposal. There is certainly a case to be made for selective and, in some cases, quite extensive pieces of urban road construction being undertaken, but the proposals for widespread building of urban highways and motorways need careful examination. The present situation, where the low perceived cost of motoring creates excessive traffic, could easily lead to a clamour for over-investment in urban roads.

The Buchanan Commission (Ministry of Transport [1963]) was established in the early 1960s 'to study the long term development of roads and traffic in urban areas' and concluded that the urban transport problem could only be solved by a massive dose of investment. The Report, however, paid scant attention to the economic aspects of the problem, ignoring the quite unacceptable cost of their investment proposals which, according to one later calculation, would have amounted to an investment of some £18,000 million (at 1963 prices) spread over forty years. Buchanan simply assumed the benefits of this investment would be infinite and ignored the reality that existing roads were being used in a sub-optimal fashion and that the social gain from expanding the road network further to meet the unrestrained demands of potential travellers was limited.

The high cost associated with completely reconstructing our urban road systems to meet the increasing numbers of cars suggests that investment can never supply the complete answer to the urban transport problem. Our older cities were not designed for motor traffic and cannot easily and cheaply be adapted. In some instances, however, investment in new roads may be desirable and beneficial; it is this piecemeal investment which concerns the economist. The appropriate method of assessing the worth of such investments is social cost–benefit analysis; this technique provides

> a useful framework for identifying and clarifying the crucial issues in what at first sight often appears to be an impenetrable tangle of conflicting facts, opinions, judgements and assertions. By marshalling data systematically, putting it in quantifiable terms wherever appropriate, and rendering it as commensurable as possible, it lays bare the considerations relevant to a complex decision in a manner which provides policy-makers with a much more intelligible and comprehensive view of the situation than is possible by any other means (Walsh and Williams [1969]).

More details of how this appraisal method is employed are presented when we discuss urban planning and the Greater London Development Plan in particular. Clearly, however, the durability of urban roads, and the diversity of their impact, requires that a comprehensive technique of this kind be used when assessing the merits of expanding our cities' road systems.

To demonstrate the danger of inappropriate investment procedures, it is worth considering the relative benefits to be enjoyed from investing in road improvements when (*a*) traffic is free to enter as it pleases, and (*b*) when entry is restricted by the imposition of an appropriate road-pricing scheme. Figure 8.2 depicts the two situations; both the *MPC* and *MSC* of travel curves are shown to fall once the investment project has been completed, the pre-improvement costs being indicated by the subscript 1 and the post-investment costs by the subscript 2. The benefits resulting from the improvement if road pricing is not operative are represented by the area P_1ABP_2 in the diagram, but with road pricing the benefits would amount to T_1WXYZT_2. Thomson [1970] has shown that the latter area represents a smaller social gain from the investment if road pricing is operative than if unregulated congestion is allowed to occur, although the difference is unlikely to exceed 25 per cent. One would expect this; if the pre-investment congestion level is optimal, further expansions of the road system will not produce such large social benefits as when congestion is excessive. It does explain, though, why many urban transport investment projects appear to offer such high returns in the current situation where traffic congestion is widespread.

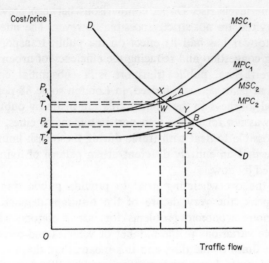

FIG. 8.2 *The benefits of urban road investment with and without road pricing*

In practice, road investments are not appraised in a strictly economic manner. Urban transport planning has concentrated primarily upon changes which will reduce congestion and paid little attention to producing an optimum solution. The general practice is to forecast the future unrestrained traffic flows over the urban transport network and then attempt to provide facilities to meet this demand, proposing various *ad hoc* constraints where flows could still prove excessive. The economist's role in this procedure is to assess the relative costs and benefits of the alternative proposals advanced by the planners and to select those which offer the highest social return; he is seldom given the opportunity of altering the pricing mechanism on the existing network which may prove even more beneficial.

8.5   The Public-Transport Problem

The horse-drawn system of urban public transport, developed in the last century as a means of moving the middle classes around our cities, has now changed into a service used primarily by lower-income groups. Public transport is therefore in many ways a classic example of an inferior good with travellers transferring out of it as their income levels rise. Direct comparisons between previous and present services are not strictly possible however. The intervention of the motor-car has had its effect on the public-transport system by creating congestion and reducing the efficiency of urban bus services. Nevertheless, public transport is a substantial carrier of passengers at peak periods; indeed, in London some 88 per cent of peak-period journeys to the central area are made by public transport. If it was not for public transport in our major cities, it would prove impossible to deal with traffic during these rush hours and it is probable that an entirely different urban pattern of living would have evolved by now.

Despite the overwhelming need to provide public transport to meet the peak, the very nature of the resultant demand pattern creates serious economic problems for bus operators. There are considerable variations in the number of vehicles and crew needed at different times of the day, and this means that, due to the need to meet the peak, buses and men are under-utilised much of the time. In Manchester it was found (1966) that while 1090 buses were required to meet the peaks only 400 could meet the mid-day demand; similar figures for Birmingham's requirements were 1356 and 350 respectively (*Bus and Coach*, November 1967).

In economic terms, public-transport operators should equate their prices to their marginal costs; this would ensure economic efficiency. When there are peaks in demand, operators should charge off-peak users only the operating costs associated with the service and load all capital costs on peak-period travellers (Victor Morgan [1974]). In practice the tendency is for fares to be uniform throughout the day irrespective of demand. This leads to peak traffic being subsidised from the revenues obtained from other travellers, a fact substantiated in empirical work undertaken by Tyson [1970] of the activities of a small bus company and, more recently, by studies of municipal bus operations in Bradford by the local authority.

A further form of cross-subsidisation occurs when revenues on profitable services are employed to subsidise other routes. In the past the Road Traffic Act (1930) actively encouraged this type of activity by favouring the granting of licences to operators willing to mix unprofitable services with profitable ones. Besides being inefficient, encouraging travel at peak times and on congested routes, cross-subsidisation is also inequitable, there being no reason why one group of public-transport users should finance the journeys of other groups. The dwindling number of profitable services means, however, that cross-subsidisation is no longer a practical method of financing urban transport activities – in 1969–70, 23 of the 68 municipal bus fleets were making over-all losses – and since the late 1960s the trend has been to finance unremunerative services from either taxes or rate revenues.

The long-term temporal decline in the demand for public transport, and the actual pricing policies pursued by the operators, have only added to the urban transport problem. Rather than attempt to minimise the peaking problem by charging differentiated fares, with a premium added for rush-hour travel, they have offered cut-price season tickets to commuters. In so far as this encourages travellers to switch from private to public transport during the peaks, there is a limited rationale behind this (a bus being capable of carrying fifty passengers but requiring the road space of $2\frac{1}{2}$ cars), but in terms of over-all transport optimisation it is an inappropriate policy. *Both* private- and public-transport users should be charged a premium at peak periods to encourage off-peak travel and the staggering of working hours but, due to the differing relative divergences between *MSC* and *MPC* for the two modes, the premium would probably be larger for the private mode. Without any form of road pricing it seems unlikely, however, that peak-rate differentials for public transport will be introduced by urban authorities.

8.6 Freight Transport in Towns

Passenger-transport problems in cities have received the greatest attention in the literature but the congestion and environmental damage caused by heavy lorries is an increasing nuisance – something like 20 per cent of the vehicle-miles travelled in cities are by lorries. London has been particularly affected by the rising number of goods vehicles but the problem is growing in other urban areas. Road pricing provides an ideal economic solution by charging lorries for the costs they impose but, on the assumption that it is not a politically acceptable measure, a number of alternative proposals have been advocated. Many of these schemes are similar to those suggested for alleviating the passenger-transport problem and so we consider only those particularly designed for freight traffic.

The inter-urban road construction programme in recent years has explicitly included provisions for the building of bypasses and ring roads to take heavy traffic off city streets. Indeed, the primary objective of the inter-urban road programme announced in 1971 was 'to achieve environmental improvements by diverting long distance traffic, and particularly heavy goods vehicles, from a large number of towns and villages' (from a statement in the House of Commons by the Secretary of State for the Environment, 23 June 1971). Unfortunately, unless some complementary attempt is made to actually discourage heavy vehicles from town and city centres, it is unlikely that the bypasses themselves will be attractive enough to encourage drivers to adopt the circumferential routes. The elasticities of demand are such that, in many cases, the generalised costs of urban travel for lorries must actually be increased, as well as alternative facilities being supplied, if goods vehicles are to be discouraged from going through our cities.

The difficulty with much heavy lorry traffic is that it has destinations within the urban area. The problem is then one of optimally allocating goods between vehicles in such a way that (a) the number of lorries employed is minimised, (b) vehicle-miles travelled are reduced, and (c) trips are encouraged at off-peak periods and in areas where they are likely to cause little environmental damage. The adoption of appropriate pricing policies to penalise those who generate the highest social cost would produce the desired result but, as this is not considered a viable proposal at the moment, some practical, if imperfect, alternative is required. A number of *ad hoc* second-best solutions have been suggested which may reduce the magnitude of the problem without removing it entirely.

Direct controls could prove useful in preventing vehicles loading and unloading during periods of peak demand for road space. Objections to this approach centre around problems of enforcement and the implicit assumption, underlying the proposal, that goods vehicles have a lower demand for road usage during these times than other road users. In addition, measures of this kind, as with any terminal controls, tend to encourage vehicles to cruise around adding to congestion until they are free to unload.

A more reasonable approach is the provision of 'bulk-breaking' depots at the periphery of urban areas where incoming loads may be split and reloaded on to smaller vehicles more suited to urban conditions. This scheme has the advantage that it would rationalise deliveries in cities by putting all goods going to a particular destination on a single lorry. The idea has many advocates, but in terms of economic merit one must ask whether the high costs of the scheme, in terms of initial capital outlays, increased delivery times and manpower demands, exceed the benefits it confers in the form of reduced traffic congestion and an improved environment. There is a need for a comprehensive cost–benefit study to be carried out on each individual bulk-breaking project but it seems probable that in many cases a positive return will be offered.

8.7 Urban Transport Policy

The official approach to the urban transport problem has changed quite considerably over the last decade. The early 1960s were characterised by a period of urban construction and improvement; policy had a definite private-transport bias. Up until 1966 it was official policy in London, for example, only to permit commercial developments if adequate parking facilities for staff were also constructed as part of the scheme. This general approach was typified by the Buchanan Report, *Traffic in Towns* (Ministry of Transport [1963]) which advocated vast expenditure on urban motor and express ways to alleviate urban congestion and was continued into the late 1960s by the Greater London Development Plan with its extensive urban motorway proposals. Although this type of approach may provide an ideal engineering solution to the urban problem, the physical composition and nature of U.K. cities, a legacy of past planners and developers, makes its adoption prohibitively expensive and impracticable. M. E. Beesley and J. F. Kain [1964] have gone further and questioned whether the benefits derivable from 'motorising our cities' actually outweigh the costs, both social and financial, involved in the operation. The Buchanan Report presented a very one-sided picture of what might be done without really considering whether it could, or indeed should, be done. The current trend is therefore towards policies biased rather more towards public than private transport.

The present system of controlling and regulating urban transport stems directly from the 1968 Transport Act. The basic problem was set out in a White Paper preceding the legislation where it was said:

Our cities and towns developed on the pattern set by radial public transport systems – buses, trams, surface and underground railways. The growing use of private transport, brought about by rising prosperity, has now fundamentally altered the situation. The motor-car, allowing much more diverse patterns of movement, gives people greater freedom of choice in both their living and their working places. Goods vehicles, catering for the growing needs of urban living, help to fill the streets (Ministry of Transport [1966] p. 11.)

In an attempt to deal with the urban transport problem the 1968 Act placed the public-transport systems of the four major U.K. conurbations under the control of Passenger Transport Authorities (P.T.A.s) which were responsible for the over-all policies pursued, and Passenger Transport Executives, which looked after the day-to-day operation of the urban transport system. The 1969 Transport (London) Act, by denationalising London Transport, fulfilled the same role for the capital. At the same time, the 1968 Act also gave local authorities far greater powers of traffic management and parking control with the intention that they should regulate the use of private transport. Unfortunately this dual administrative arrangement did not produce the desired co-ordination of urban transport nor did it alleviate congestion.

Additional to the problems created by the lack of a central co-ordinating body was the unsuitability of the policies pursued by both the P.T.A.s and local authorities. Public transport was subsidised on a financial rather than economic basis, with sums provided to cover shortfalls in revenue below costs. The P.T.A.s had the power to levy local rates in order to subsidise local bus and suburban rail services and were commanded to provide 'a properly integrated and efficient system of public transport to meet the needs of the area' (1968 Transport Act, Section 9(3)). However, to obtain ar optimal spread of traffic between modes, it is necessary to subsidise further than the P.T.A.s were prepared to go. In many instances, where the *MSC* of public transport is below the financial cost, it is necessary to subsidise already profitable services to enable them to take even more passengers away from private cars. Because marginal-cost pricing is not universally practised throughout the economy, administrators in the public-transport sector should introduce a 'second-best' policy designed to produce a *MSC*/price ratio in their sector similar to that operational for the closest substitute, which in the majority of cases is the private motor-car – the exact relationship between the two ratios being determined by the cross-elasticity of demand – (Tyson [1972]). In many instances this would mean far larger subsidies than were possible under the 1968 Act.

The approach which local authorities adopted towards the private car was half-hearted and inappropriate. Policy revolved around the use of traffic management to direct traffic on to optimal routes within cities, taking much of it away from the congested centres, and the imposition of parking restraints to discourage people taking cars to central areas. Traffic management has had spectacular short-term effects in London and other centres but it is only useful when the initial *pattern* of movement is sub-optimal (Thomson [1968]). By improving the flow of traffic within cities, without restraining the entry of new vehicles, traffic management tends to eventually generate additional traffic with a consequential return of congestion.

Parking policy is widely used to restrain urban traffic and has been extensively employed in London since 1966, but unfortunately for all its advantages of cheapness and political acceptability, it will not solve the urban transport problem. Terminal charges of this kind do not restrain traffic during the peak nor do they reduce through-movements of vehicles. In fact, by limiting the number of local trips into the centre, a restrictive parking policy may actively encourage through-traffic to adopt direct routes via the city rather than circumferential ones. In addition, the general approach adopted by traffic departments has been an administrative one, levying parking charges which just cover the cost of providing the facility plus an amount to finance the long-term land use involved. This has produced parking charges below the economic rate needed to equate the demand for spaces to the available supply, and hence has meant motorists adding to the congestion by driving round seeking non-existent parking places for which they are prepared to pay the artificially low administrative price.

In the only work done comparing the respective advantages of road pricing and an economic parking policy, Thomson [1967] found that the former would offer approximately twice the benefits of the latter if introduced in London. Both the road-pricing and parking policies would act to speed traffic flows, reduce noise and diesel fumes without increasing the number of road accidents, but the effects of the two policies in each of these spheres would be different. In 1966 prices, the road-pricing alternative would confer benefits of between £6 million and £7 million p.a. whilst the economic parking policy could only offer half of this. Consequently, even an economic approach to parking restraint will only provide a partial solution to the urban problem.

In the much longer term, the 1968 Act envisaged that in each of the major urban areas *all* land-use and transport planning should be placed under the direction of a single body, for example we find the White Paper on *Transport Policy* stating 'the right solution seems likely to be found in the establishment in these areas of single authorities with responsibilities covering land use, highways, traffic and public transport'. The P.T.A.s did not fulfil this role, first because their power was restricted solely to public transport, and second because their geographical area of control differed from that of the local authority. To some extent the changes introduced in the Local Government Act (1972) have reduced this problem. Three new P.T.A.s, two in Yorkshire and one in Glasgow, were created to join the original four of Liverpool, Manchester, Newcastle and Birmingham. The seven authorities were integrated into the local government framework as Metropolitan Counties' Passenger Transport Authorities. In other areas, both urban and rural, where the 1968 Act had permitted local authorities to subsidise their public transport, with a 50 per cent reimbursement from central funds in certain approved instances, the new non-metropolitan councils have increased power to assist their public transport and are obliged to develop policies designed to promote the provision of efficient and co-ordinated public transport.

In addition to the reformulated structure of administration, a new concept in urban transport finance is to be introduced. The new system, outlined in the White Paper on *Urban Transport Planning* (Department of the Environment [1973]) divides government support into (*a*) a new transport supplementary grant, and (*b*) additions to the needs element in the rates-support grant. By initially funnelling the majority of funds through transport grants, it is intended that the Department of the Environment will be able to ensure that local authorities pursue a 'suitable and comprehensive policy for their area', making adequate provisions to support public transport and at the same time placing sufficient constraint on the private car. Eventually it is hoped to move the basis of finance to the rates-support grant and to give local authorities greater autonomy in their policy-making.

Combined with the new method of financing urban transport is a fresh approach to transport planning. It is intended under the Local Government Act that the new county and metropolitan councils should take greater responsibility for integrated planning in their areas. The intention is that each authority should devise a suitable 'Transport Policy and Programme' (T.P.P.) setting out their basic strategy and objectives for consideration by the Ministry but that responsibility for detail and implementation should remain at the local level (for details see Department of the Environment Circulars 104/73, 27/74, 60/73). The main shortcoming with this method of administration and decision-making, besides an initial lack of expertise on the part of the local authorities in the relevant fields, is that programmes are to be drawn up at the county level with no automatic reference to the smaller districts. This conflicts with the more localised approach to land-use planning in which both tiers of the hierarchy participate and could well lead to some friction between authorities (Button [1974] pp. 4–11). A second difficulty is that central government has control over the pricing and investment of both suburban rail services and the National Bus Company which, unless the government makes explicit its long-term policies, must lead to an unacceptable degree of uncertainty in local authority planning.

In addition to the changes in transport financing and administration, recent legislation has greatly increased the power of local authorities to control and regulate urban transport. The Road Traffic Bill (1973) is intended to increase the effectiveness of existing parking restraints whilst the Heavy Commercial Vehicles (Controls and Regulations) Act (1973) should provide the basis on which to limit the flow of heavy vehicles through central areas. Similarly, the provision of lorry parks and the passing of new laws enables councils to ban the overnight parking of heavy vehicles in towns and gives them an incentive to enforce such a policy.

8.8 Summary

Congestion is increasing on urban roads and to date no policy has been applied which seems to offer any hope of reducing or even containing the problem. Road pricing offers an effective theoretical tool but it appears to be politically unacceptable and to have social consequences which make its adoption doubtful. Nevertheless, in recent official publications (for example Department of the Environment [1973] there are indications that policy-makers are again reconsidering its potential usefulness and role in future transport policy. In the meantime, the long-term switch from private to public transport continues with the resultant circle of high fares and poor public-transport services accompanying the change. Government attempts to combat the excessive use of motor-cars in our cities with the carrot of subsidies for public transport and the stick of parking restraints on motorists has proved ineffective, this being at least partly due to the reliance on administrative and financial principles rather than economic criteria. Recent changes initiated in the Local Government Act giving local authorities greater power of control over their transport may go some way to solving the problem but it is really a question of political will. The economist can indicate how urban traffic congestion should be alleviated in a market-based situation but can do little when faced with the constraint of political unacceptability.

References

M. E. BEESLEY [1968], 'Technical Possibilities of Special Taxation in Relation to Congestion caused by Private Cars', European Conference of Ministers of Transport, 2nd International Symposium (O.E.C.D.) pp. 389–441.

M. E. BEESLEY and J. F. KAIN [1964], 'Urban Form, Car Ownership and Public Policy: an Appraisal of "Traffic in Towns"', *Urban Studies* (November) pp. 173–204.

K. J. BUTTON [1974], 'Transport Policy in the United Kingdom, 1968–1974', *Three Banks Review* (September) pp. 26–48.

K. J. BUTTON [1975], 'An Economist's Solution to the Urban Transport Problem', *Economics* (Spring) pp. 15–22.

Department of the Environment [1973], *Urban Transport Planning*, Cmnd. 5366 (London: H.M.S.O.).

P. HALL [1969], 'Transportation', *Urban Studies* (November) pp. 408–35.

J. HEWITT [1964], 'The Calculation of Congestion Taxes on Roads', *Economica* (February) pp. 72–81.

L. K. LENNON [1972], 'An Economic Examination of Traffic Congestion in Towns', *Administration* (Summer) pp. 50–61.

Ministry of Transport [1963], *Traffic in Towns* (London: H.M.S.O.).

Ministry of Transport [1964], *Road Pricing: the Economic and Technical Possibilities* (London: H.M.S.O.).

Ministry of Transport [1966], *Transport Policy*, Cmnd. 3057 (London: H.M.S.O.).

E. J. MISHAN [1969], *The Costs of Economic Growth* (Harmondsworth: Penguin).

D. J. REYNOLDS [1966], *Economics, Town Planning and Traffic* (London: Institute of Economic Affairs).

H. W. RICHARDSON [1974], 'A Note on the Distributional Effects of Road Pricing', *Journal of Transport Economics and Policy* (January) pp. 82–5.

C. H. SHARP [1966], 'Congestion and Welfare: an Examination of the Case for a Congestion Tax', *Economic Journal* (December) pp. 806–17.

J. M. THOMSON [1967], 'An Evaluation of Two Proposals for Traffic Restraint in Central London', *Journal of the Royal Statistical Society* (December) pp. 327–77.

J. M. THOMSON [1968], 'The Value of Traffic Management', *Journal of Transport Economics and Policy* (January) pp. 1–30.

J. M. THOMSON [1970], 'Some Aspects of Evaluating Road Improvement in Urban Areas', *Econometrics* (March) pp. 298–310.

J. M. THOMSON [1974], *Modern Transport Economics* (Harmondsworth: Penguin).

W. J. TYSON [1970]), 'A Study of Peak Cost and Pricing in Road Passenger Transport', *Institute of Transport Journal* (November) pp. 19–24.

W. J. TYSON [1972], 'A Critique of Road Passenger Transport Subsidy Policy', *Manchester School* (December) pp. 397–418.

W. VICKREY [1968], 'Congestion Charges and Welfare', *Journal of Transport Economics and Policy* (January) pp. 107–18.

E. VICTOR MORGAN [1974], 'Pricing Investment Decisions and Subsidies in Transport', *Manchester School* (September) pp. 240–58.

H. G. WALSH and A. WILLIAMS [1969], *Current Issues in Cost–Benefit Analysis*, C.A.S. Occasional Paper No. 11 (London: H.M.S.O.).

A. A. WALTERS [1961], 'The Theory of Measurement of Private and Social Cost of Highway Congestion', *Econometrica* (October) pp. 676–99.

9 URBAN HOUSING

9.1 The Housing Problem

As well as representing the centre of numerous economic activities, cities are also residential concentrations. The expansion of urbanisation since the United Kingdom's first industrial revolution has created a series of housing crises, and today the difficulty of providing adequate housing for the 80 per cent of the nation's population living in urban areas is one of the major problems confronting policy-makers. Although the exact nature and scale of the problem varies between urban areas, some common features are apparent.

Circa 1825, concern centred around speculation and public health, and was often of a philanthropic nature; simply providing minimum standards of accommodation for the rapidly expanding urban labour force created immense difficulties. The housing problem of the period constituted a simple deficiency in the aggregate supply of urban dwellings.

By the end of the nineteenth century, significant changes in the demographic structure, notably a decline in family size, produced a new dimension to the housing problem. Increased affluence and smaller family units, combined with a marked reluctance to share accommodation, resulted in a change in the pattern of demand; people wanted newer and better-quality houses. At the same time, the demand for accommodation equipped with running water, gas and, slightly later, electricity, made much of the existing housing stock obsolete. These pressures culminated in the national replacement programmes which characterised inter-war housing policy.

The post-war period has witnessed further changes in the housing problem. The steady increases in real income which have occurred in the post-war era have intensified pressure for a more rapid replacement of the housing stock, but at the same time this has been accompanied by demands for the removal of regional inequalities in housing. Whereas previously areas experiencing net out-migration of population tended to run down their housing stock while new construction was concentrated in the recipient regions, this is no longer acceptable.

Today, therefore, the demands are not just for more houses – indeed, the total number of dwellings (19·4 million) in 1974 exceeded the number of households (18·6 million) – but also for cheaper, better-quality houses, situated in an improved residential environment (Tain [1968]). This is, of course, not to say that some cities do not have an absolute shortage of houses; obviously they do, but rather that this problem is not so widespread as it was and has been superseded in many urban areas by pressures to improve the quality of housing. The basic problems that have arisen are the result of two broad characteristics of the housing market. First, on the demand side, there has been the unprecedented expansion of the urban population in many cities, which has put considerable pressure on their existing housing stock. In the urban context this is not just the result of indigenous increases in the population of each city nor is it a problem caused solely by migration from the countryside into urban centres – rather it partly emanates from inter-city movements. The economic forces which have encouraged migration from the depressed to prosperous regions have also created demands for more homes in the recipient urban areas and reduced the financial capacity of the depressed areas to renew their housing stock. Second, on the supply side, housing has a long but finite life and there is a continuing need to rebuild and replace old and decaying properties with newer modern dwellings. This need to continually replace worn-out stock creates a whole range of social and economic problems (some of which are discussed in Section 9.3 below).

It is clear that the magnitude and characteristics of the urban housing problem have altered over the years, but, as Donnison ([1967] p. 45) has pointed out, 'the most urgent and harrowing housing needs have remained much the same over the last two centuries, appearing in the form of overcrowding, sharing, ill-equipped and insanitary housing, the homelessness'. Therefore, although the details have changed, the fundamental problems remain the same and seem equally as difficult to solve in the short term.

Just as the details, if not the basic character, of the housing problem have varied, so has the organisation of the urban housing sector. Public-sector involvement in the urban housing market has increased considerably both at local and central government levels since the

1920s. Similarly, there has been a marked change in public attitudes towards social responsibility. In the last century, working-class housing was provided either through semi-philanthropic housing societies or by private enterprise, and this created serious problems of control in the major cities, particularly London. Today public involvement influences the conditions of supply by means of rent controls and the provision of local authority 'council housing'. On the demand side, central government has encouraged home ownership by offering tax relief on mortgage interest charges and both local and central government have directly assisted in the provision of home-purchasing funds – for example local authority mortgages and loans to building societies, notably the £500 million central government loan of 1974.

9.2 The Nature of the Urban Housing Market

A house falls into that category of good known as a consumer durable. It is consumed in the sense that people living in it derive satisfaction and well-being from doing so. It is durable in the sense that it confers these benefits for a considerable period of time before it finally becomes obsolete or worn out. In a free market, the prices of all goods, including consumer durables, are determined by the forces of supply and demand. The housing market satisfies some of the criteria of a free market, but it has a number of particular features which create difficulties. It is these latter considerations which are responsible for the urban housing problem and make it so apparently intractable. The peculiarities of the housing market may be illustrated by looking in turn at the supply and demand characteristics associated with urban housing.

(a) Supply Considerations

Housing is not a homogeneous product, but can be sub-divided and categorised in several quite different ways. First, houses may be categorised by type, for example detached, semi-detached, flats, terraced, and so on. Second, houses may be distinguished by the conditions of occupancy, for example rented, owner-occupied, leasehold, and so on. Third, houses are location-specific and hence one can categorise them according to where they are, for example suburban, town centre, and so on. Fourth, houses may be distinguished by their age. Fifth, houses can be sub-divided according to their size or residential capacity, for example bedsitter, one-bedroom, two-bedroomed, and so on. In addition, one can also sub-divide the housing sector between private and public housing, the latter now representing 31 per cent of the total housing stock.

The heterogeneity of the housing supply means that there is no single market for housing but rather a series of quite distinct but nevertheless related markets and sub-markets. The interrelationships result from the high degree of substitutability between the various categories of housing and mean that price changes in one market have a considerable impact on prices in other markets. For purposes of exposition we divide the housing market according to whether property is owner-occupied, private rented accommodation or council housing; this breakdown simplifies the analysis but it should always be borne in mind that it is a simplification and ignores the existence of numerous other sub-markets.

One feature common to all categories of housing is the difficulty of increasing the total physical supply in the short period. The time it takes to design and build new dwellings means that there is an inevitable lag between changes in prices and expansion in the number of houses available. In the short term, supply is thus very inelastic. Since it is the supply of new houses that enables movement in the second-hand housing market (Cullingworth [1969]), any stickiness in the response of the new housing sector is reflected and magnified in the second-hand market. Because only about 2 per cent of the housing stock is replaced each year, this means the supply of housing available for purchase or renting at any time is very sensitive to changes at the margin.

The public sector of the housing market is not directly influenced by market forces and the supply of accommodation is not determined by prevailing prices. Since the supply of publicly owned housing is not influenced by the normal motives of profit maximisation, the traditional idea of a supply curve is not directly applicable. The quantity of new council housing is determined by the availability of funds in the public sector and by the political pressures on local authorities to provide more accommodation.

(b)   Demand Considerations
Buying a house is, in the majority of cases, a family's largest single financial outlay. Despite the high costs of house purchasing, there has been a steady growth in home ownership since the war and now

about half of the houses in the United Kingdom are owner-occupied. In general, house prices are around four times the average annual wage for an industrial worker (Cullingworth [1967]), and consequently a sophisticated financial market dealing in house-buying funds has developed to assist purchases. Most house buyers do not pay directly and at once but take out a mortgage and spread their payments over twenty-five years or so. The availability of funds from this source is an important determinant of the aggregate demand for housing and is influenced both by the flow of funds into building societies and other financial institutions and by the incomes of prospective purchasers who must eventually pay back their loans. This means that macroeconomic conditions have a considerable effect on the aggregate demand for owner-occupied housing.

The demand for particular types of housing is less directly influenced by macroeconomic factors, although there is some relationship. Demographic changes affect the size of house required and so, inasmuch as the trend towards smaller family units is at least partly the result of a higher national income, macroeconomic influences are of indirect importance. The current demand pattern seems to be for more but smaller residences.

Although the majority of housing is demanded for the various amenities which it offers the occupant, there are some exceptions. Property values have, over the long term, tended to keep pace with inflation, and consequently house ownership has been an attractive investment. Related to this is the income that can be obtained by letting property; the higher the potential income from a house, the greater is the attraction to invest in it. In the shorter term, house prices have fluctuated wildly and have presented speculators with the opportunity of large capital gains (as was the case in the early 1970s). The entry of speculators and investors into the housing market has tended to both increase the short-term instability of the sector and widen fluctuations in prices. This has created considerable problems in many large cities where the total supply of privately owned housing is limited and the possibilities of further development exhausted.

Of course, not all housing is privately owned – much of it is supplied by local authorities. This adds a further complication. Local authorities do not react to demand in the traditional economic sense (Cullingworth [1969]). They do not base their estimates of future housing requirements on effective demand but on a rather nebulous idea of 'need' – a social concept completely unrelated to price. (In fact, Williams [1974] defines it as a 'quasi-supply' concept.) Demand, in its conventional economic context, and 'need' are not entirely unconnected however. The price–income situation in a country determines effective demand for housing, but it also conditions the social concept of need to a considerable extent. The more affluent a society, the higher it tends to set the minimum standards of housing which are considered acceptable. The distinction between demand and need is therefore more important at the local level and between different types of housing than when one is concerned with aggregated national issues in the housing field.

Although the criteria used to determine 'need' are seldom made explicit, it is generally considered that local authorities should at least try to:

(1) rehouse those affected by public redevelopment schemes, such as slum clearance;

(2) house people in personal need, such as the sick, those incapable of finding accommodation within the private sector, large families and fatherless families;

(3) rehouse people living in bad conditions, for example living in houses in a poor physical state or where there is excessive overcrowding;

(4) provide accommodation for the homeless;

(5) house the elderly;

(6) provide housing for people who are necessary to meet the needs of the community, notably those involved in education, health, social services, and so on; and

(7) house key industrial workers.

These criteria represent a considerable extension to those used only thirty years ago when council housing was seen simply as subsidised accommodation for lower-income members of the working classes. Clearly, council housing still fulfils that initial role, but the concept of need has been extended to include a much wider set of criteria.

The majority of housing problems are concentrated in long-established urban centres where much of the housing stock is old and frequently of sub-standard quality. The authorities are therefore confronted not only with the need to provide additional housing but also to improve much of the accommodation already available. The importance of this problem demands we look at it in some detail.

9.3 Urban Renewal

An account of the economic implications of urban renewal would fit comfortably into chapters on urban planning or the urban environment. Urban renewal is planning in the sense that it involves central directives and designs and amongst its several objectives is environmental improvement, but it is incorporated in this chapter because most urban-improvement programmes involve the demolition and redevelopment of residential areas.

The term 'urban renewal' is American and has been defined by Weiner and Hoyt [1966] as a construction programme designed to (a) rehabilitate an area by bringing existing buildings up to an acceptable standard, (b) conserve by protecting buildings worth preserving, and (c) demolish and clear those buildings which have become obsolete. Urban renewal, therefore, effectively means the demolition of old and decaying properties and their replacement by the construction of new buildings, streets and parks.

The need for urban renewal is partly the result of the long physical life of much housing but Reynolds [1966] has argued that this need has been increased in the United Kingdom by some of the housing policies which have been pursued, these policies having 'aggravated housing shortages and perpetuated the lives of "twilight" housing'. The people who have benefited most from recent housing policy are council-house tenants – who have enjoyed either subsidised housing or favoured conditions of occupancy (for example, until the Fair Rent legislation, rents have tended to be based on the historical, rather than the market, value of the property) and owner-occupiers – who have enjoyed both large capital gains and tax relief on mortgages. The legislation has therefore tended to place those who can neither afford a mortgage nor obtain a council house in the position of having to remain in old and sub-standard accommodation. This, in turn, has put pressure on older housing and prolonged the life of 'slums' (officially defined as areas about to be cleared and subject to compulsory-purchase orders) and 'twilight housing' (similar in type, age and rateable value to slums but with no compulsory-purchase order in effect) beyond that normally considered socially desirable. Much of this property is in the hands of private landlords who cannot afford improvements or redevelopment themselves. (In other cases there may be little incentive for those with the necessary funds to improve their properties if others in the neighbourhood let theirs decay.) Urban renewal is thus carried out to ensure that the conditions of those living in slums and twilight housing are improved and also to make certain that development occurs in city centres, where housing tends to be poorer, rather than as a continual and undesirable outward expansion of peripheral residential estates.

Renewal may also provide a second range of benefits. Rothenberg [1967] has shown that the existence of slums and twilight areas not only causes social problems but actually results in a sub-optimal distribution of economic resources. Urban renewal can improve resource utilisation by reducing the social costs on both inhabitants and non-inhabitants alike, the quality of neighbourhoods improving with the elimination of adjacent slums. Mao [1966] has demonstrated this improvement in resource allocation by showing that in Stockton (United States) the value of property adjacent to a redevelopment area rose by 5 per cent in real terms after completion of a renewal programme. Renewal also tends to reduce the demands on medical, police and fire services, which, for sociological reasons, are usually greater in slum areas than the rest of the city.

If the benefits of renewal are extensive, so too are the costs. Any redevelopment programme is financially expensive, involving the demolition of large numbers of buildings and the construction of new ones. The cost of renewal is compounded by the necessity for the local authority to buy up existing houses before the programme is started. The availability of funds for redevelopment has been limited in recent years, not just because of an absolute shortage of resources, but also because of the opportunity costs involved. Priorities since the war have been to ensure that the total stock of housing is sufficient to meet demand and, in expanding cities, to provide new housing for those moving into the area. Since renewal seldom increases the total supply of houses, it has languished at the back of the queue for funds.

In addition to the financial costs of renewal, there are also quite considerable social costs. Many of those living in slums suffer a diminution of welfare when forced to move. This loss takes two forms: a breaking of community ties and relationships which have built up, and second the loss of the option of living in poor quality but cheap accommodation – which many people actually prefer. To many individuals these are real costs which should be considered in the economic appraisal of any redevelopment programme.

Even making allowances for the costs involved in urban renewal, it is still rather surprising that so little has taken place. In 1969, there were some 1·8 million slum dwellings and 4·5 million twilight houses according to official statistics (Ministry of Housing and Local Government [1969]) and, although the number of slums has now been reduced to 900,000, the renewal programme has progressed slowly. Besides the general shortage of funds, and the priority given to increasing rather than improving the housing stock, Richardson [1971] has suggested a number of supplementary reasons which have contributed to the slow pace. Local authorities have frequently been hesitant to prepare renewal plans, and where they have been drawn up they have been primarily influenced by financial criteria – often the cheapest plan has been accepted regardless of the possible benefits. This latter feature of the process has often led to extensive local opposition to the official proposals and more time elapses during further replanning. In many cases the planning procedure has proved so cumbersome and slow that private property companies have been able to move into areas scheduled for redevelopment. Plans themselves have tended to be inflexible and impossible to modify in the face of changing circumstances, temporary shortages of funds often preventing the implementation of a renewal programme because the plans involve 'all-or-nothing' construction schedules.

9.4   Rebuilding or Modernisation?

Although policies of urban renewal imply a degree of 'rehabilitation' and renovation, they have tended in the past to concentrate on redevelopment and rebuilding. The main difficulty is to decide when a building justifies modernisation and when it is preferable to couple demolition with replacement. The policies pursued by the U.K. government clearly indicate their recognition of the fact that many houses, although superficially sub-standard, are structurally sound and can be brought up to an acceptable condition by investment in improvements and additional amenities. The problem is therefore one of assessing the costs and benefits of renovation *vis-à-vis* those of complete rebuilding.

The arguments for and against renovation can be divided between the economic and social, although in practice the institutional and legal framework in which the decision is reached and the policy pursued can have an important effect.

The main economic argument in favour of renovation is its comparative cheapness – a study in Skelmersdale (Lean [1971]) indicated rehabilitation costs only about 57 per cent that of redevelopment. Renovation usually requires very few structural changes to the property in question and, because much of the work is interior improvement, costs and delays due to poor weather are minimal. In terms of maintenance, however, annual costs over the remaining life of a renovated house are likely to be higher than for a new one, although empirical evidence on this is scant. The main disadvantage of renovation, in terms of the financial costs involved, is the fact that modernised houses generally have a shorter physical life than new ones and will consequently require replacement much sooner. When looking at the alternatives it is therefore necessary to consider not only the initial capital costs of the two policies but also the future costs of maintenance and eventual renewal.

Socially, renovation has the advantage that it does not involve the complete destruction of established communities as is usually the case with a redevelopment programme. It is generally thought that modernising existing houses does not break neighbourhoods up nor does it damage existing social ties, although of course there may be some short-term disruption while the work is in progress. This rather traditional argument should be treated with some caution, however. There is a tendency to over-emphasise the importance people attach to the community in which they live, and many people, although initially objecting to removal for the sake of redevelopment, find that once rehoused and settled they are far happier – the important thing is to ensure that the new environment into which they have moved is as inviting as the one left behind (John Parker [1973]).

Combined with these social arguments is the fact that rebuilding frequently involves rather more than simply knocking down and re-erecting houses. The complete redevelopment of an urban area generally includes supplementary investments in roads, schools and other amenities and attracts new shops and recreational facilities. Housing renovation offers few of these additional advantages, although attempts have been made to improve the general environment where extensive modernisation is scheduled by closing roads to traffic, planting trees, introducing new street lighting, clearing derelict land, and so forth, but it is seldom possible to carry this to the same level as with complete redevelopment.

In general, there is a feeling that, in terms of administration, there is an advantage in renovation because of the speed at which it can be implemented. Comprehensive rebuilding programmes require legislation, planning and public inquiries, followed by the compulsory purchase of land. The process of approving improvement grants and other renovation measures is much quicker, although it may involve a considerable amount of pressure from local authorities before those affected finally accept the proposals.

The decision of whether it is preferable to invest in the complete redevelopment of an area or simply to improve the existing stock of houses is a complex one. Since most urban areas requiring improvement contain both slums which are beyond renovation and other housing where modernisation is possible, and may be practical, a comprehensive policy is clearly required by each local authority to ensure that available funds are spent in the best possible fashion and split optimally between renovation and rebuilding.

9.5 Housing Policy

Policies attempting to solve the urban housing problem have a long and, in many ways, unfortunate history. The main difficulty when formulating a housing policy is the complex interrelationships which exist between the various housing sub-markets. Combined with this is the interaction that may occur between a change in the flow of one type of housing and the stock of other types. Consequently, if a rent freeze is introduced, keeping rents below the level which would prevail in a free market, this will not only reduce the flow of rented accommodation on to the market but may also increase the stock of owner-occupied houses if landlords sell their property rather than letting it out. A policy designed to influence the flow or stock of accommodation in one market could therefore affect *both* the flow and stock in other markets.

The development of a successful housing policy has been further complicated by the dual form of administration and decision-making that exists. Although many of the recent attempts to improve housing conditions and ownership possibilities (for example rent controls, tenant–landlord legislation, renewal policy, and so on) have been initiated by central government, their implementation has often been left to local authorities. (Central government does not provide housing directly, but regulates the framework within which local authorities and private developers operate.) In some instances these policies have clearly conflicted with the views of the local councillors (for example the local council at Clay Cross refused to implement the 1972 Housing Finance Act's provision that council-house rents should be based on the market value of the property), while in others they have only been executed with reluctance and half-heartedness. In these circumstances, the continued existence of a housing problem is hardly surprising; nevertheless, some progress has been made and we now look at this in a little more detail.

The construction of council housing, which was initially sanctioned as long ago as the 1890s, provides one solution to the problem of housing those people in most immediate need. In a sense, therefore, council housing is gradually filling the role formerly occupied by rented accommodation. The difficulty is that, while council houses may now be the best way of meeting the needs of the lowest-income groups, policies in other sectors have prevented a smooth transition.

As council housing is increased, a free-market situation would see the demand for privately rented accommodation falling and with it the prevailing level of rents. Unfortunately, official policy has tended to try and force rents down at a faster rate than would occur under market conditions. The history of rent controls goes back to 1915, although current policy can be traced more directly to the Second World War – specifically the Interest Restriction Act of 1939. By keeping rents artificially low, the government has attempted to help those actually living in rented accommodation but has, as a consequence, reduced the supply for others seeking such housing. As one committee of inquiry reported (Committee on Housing in Greater London [1965]):

> The governments which have been most successful in surmounting stresses and maintaining order and justice within this sector of the housing market have been those which have accepted and incorporated private rented property among the instruments to be used in meeting housing needs, hence assisting those who build, own or live in, and regulating the price, management and distribution of this housing. Less successful have been those governments – our own among them – which have failed to take effective responsibility for this sector of the housing market, either

subjecting it to severe rent restrictions (without the complementary support and additional controls needed to offset and mitigate the effects of such restrictions) or abandoning control altogether and leaving this sector to escape, haphazard and piecemeal, into a 'freedom' politically insecure and sometimes abused.

If government increases the protection and rights afforded private tenants, as they did under the Rent Acts of 1965, 1968 and 1974, then to ensure the provision of adequate housing, they must also either enlarge the stock of council housing or else increase the incentives for landlords to let accommodation. Failure to take such action will result in an inadequate supply of privately rented housing being offered. In fact, the government has done neither; the rapid expansion of council housing (90 per cent of all post-war building in Newcastle and Hull, for example, have been for the local authorities) has been insufficient to meet the 'need', while rent controls and lack of adequate incentives in the private sector have hardly encouraged landlords to continue letting their property.

The basic difficulty with the government's rent controls can be illustrated with the aid of simple diagrams. Let Figure 9.1(a) refer to the market for privately rented accommodation. In the immediate or 'market' period, the supply of rented accommodation can realistically be assumed fixed or perfectly inelastic – this is shown by the curve S_1 in the diagram. If the demand for rented accommodation is DD in a free market, the fixed number of units for letting will each be rented out at R_1. In 1965, however, the government felt that landlords were making excessive 'economic rent' on their property by charging R_1 and therefore decided to impose a 'fair-rent' level. This was to be determined on two criteria according to the 1965 Act:

(a) the nature of the property, including age, amenities, character, location, and so on; and

(b) the 'normal' level of profit (the transfer earnings) the landlord could expect to make on such property, that is the amount just required to encourage the landlord to continue to rent out the accommodation.

Let us suppose that on these criteria a fair rent level of R_2 was fixed. This would not reduce the immediate supply of rented accommodation if calculations of (b) were accurate, but it would reduce the commercial rent for existing tenants by $R_1 - R_2$. The problem is

that at this rent there will be an excess demand for rented accommodation of H_2-H_1 in Figure 9.1(a) because, although rents have
fallen, no additional accommodation is available for letting.

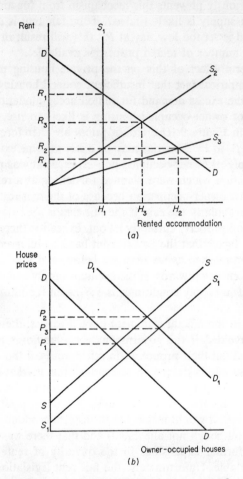

FIG. 9.1   *The effect of rent controls*

In the longer term, without rent controls one would have expected
market rents to have fallen because at the R_1 level landlords were
making considerable economic rents and this would, in time, have
brought more rented accommodation on to the market. Let us suppose the long-run supply curve for rented accommodation is S_2 (this

will pass through the fair-rent level at H_1 because S_2 only includes transfer earnings); then this implies a long-term equilibrium rent of R_3 with some H_3 properties being let out. A fair-rent policy of the 1965 kind obviously prevents this mechanism from functioning and no increase in supply is likely (indeed, if the fair rent is calculated incorrectly and is set too low, say at R_4, this will result in a secular decline in the number of rented properties available).

The long-term effect of this on the private housing market, in view of the empirical fact that insufficient council housing is available to meet the excess demand for rented accommodation, is that the demand for owner-occupied housing is likely to rise, say from DD to D_1D_1 in Figure 9.1(*b*). House prices are therefore likely to increase from P_1 to P_2. This rise may be offset to some extent by an increased supply of owner-occupied houses, especially as properties under construction which were planned for letting at a rent R_1 are now sold off for owner-occupation because of the rent restrictions – this will be particularly the case if the fair rent is set below R_2 and landlords sell off property currently let out. In reality, there has been the additional factor that the government has also intervened in the private housing market, as we shall see below, and this has further pushed the SS curve outwards. If the eventual supply situation, after the adjustment in supply conditions, is S_1S_1, then the ultimate price level will be P_3.

As implied in the official statement quoted earlier, these difficulties may be avoided if the government gives landlords additional incentives to let out their property – in other words, if the long-term conditions of supply in the rented accommodation market are modified. In terms of the diagram, this would mean rotating the long-term supply curve in Figure 9.1(*a*) round until it reached position S_3. If this was achieved, it would mean that short-term economic rent had been reduced (although not alleviated) and that there was sufficient incentive for further expansions in the quantity of rented accommodation available. Unfortunately, the fair-rent legislation has not attempted to do this, as we have indicated above. The criteria for determining fair rent is too harsh on landlords and the necessary incentives and encouragement for them to reappraise their attitudes to letting out property have not been forthcoming (see Cooper and Stafford [1975]). To achieve the necessary change in supply, conditions may actually require some form of direct subsidy to landlords, but this would certainly have to be in excess of that available under the renovation schemes employed to date (see below).

The decline in the supply of rented accommodation has been accelerated by simultaneous policies in the owner-occupied sector. Owner-occupation has risen from 26 per cent of all housing in 1947 to about 52 per cent in 1974 and this has been partly the result of conscious government policy. The majority of houses are purchased on mortgages upon which interest charges are eligible for tax relief (this facility dating back to the first income-tax legislation of 1798). This factor, combined with the general rise in property values, has made house ownership a very attractive proposition for those able to obtain a mortgage.

The tax benefits enjoyed by owner-occupiers were initially pointed out by Adela Nevitt in *Housing, Taxation and Subsidies* [1966], which appeared in the mid-1960s and the argument therein has been adequately supported by recent studies by Harrington [1972] in the United Kingdom and Aaron [1970] in the United States. The advantages enjoyed by those purchasing a house through a mortgage are easily seen in a simple numerical example. Suppose A earns £5000 p.a. and rents a house for £1000 p.a.; if he is entitled to tax allowances of £1000 p.a. and the standard rate of income tax is 30 per cent, then he will pay £1200 in tax (that is 30 per cent of £4000). In other words, his disposable income is £3800, of which £2800 is left after his rent has been paid. If instead, A buys his house for, say, £10,000 on a 100 per cent mortgage, paying interest of 10 per cent, then the situation changes dramatically, because he can now claim tax relief on the interest payments as well as enjoying his £1000 tax allowance. His tax payments fall to £900, making him some £300 better off. Although A will now have to use some of his income to pay off the mortgage, he will be compensated for this by the eventual ownership of a house. The figures we have used are obviously hypothetical, but they do not deviate radically from reality and the empirical studies mentioned above confirm the general impression they convey.

The effect of this policy in the owner-occupied sector has been to increase the supply of, as well as the demand for, housing. The number of houses available for owner-occupation has been increased both by new building and also by landlords selling off formerly rented houses which now, because of their higher capital cost, do not earn a sufficient return to justify their retention as investments.

Despite this expansion of the housing stock, supply has not increased sufficiently to offset the higher demand, and the result has been increased house prices. The over-all consequences of these policies, therefore, is that people in the lower-income brackets find it difficult to acquire rented accommodation but at the same time they cannot afford to buy a house. They must remain in slums or live with relatives, often in overcrowded conditions.

To assist these poorer sections of the urban community, for whom council housing is not available, policies of renewal and renovation have been attempted to improve housing conditions in the slums and twilight areas of our cities. By paying landlords to renovate or improve their properties, the government hopes to encourage them to let them at the legal rent rather than sell them. It also enables people in twilight housing who cannot afford to buy a better house, and have little hope of renting a council property, to enjoy a reasonable standard of living. Assistance with renovation was considerably increased under the 1969 Housing Act, which was intended to enable the modernisation of 'sound older houses'. Empirical evidence collected by Sigsworth and Wilkinson [1972] from ten northern county boroughs suggests that, although considerable use has been made of improvement grants, there are a number of constraints restricting the number given and their over-all effectiveness. To have any significant effect, improvement grants must be incorporated in a package which includes a degree of slum clearance and rebuilding. Indeed, it seems probable that, since the 1969 Act included provisions for grants enabling environmental improvements in designated areas, the central government envisaged parallel schemes of slum clearance where improvement is economically unjustified. Unfortunately, local authorities in the boroughs studied seem to have no co-ordinated improvement programme and instead simply awarded grants 'mechanically and by apparently simple rules of thumb'.

The apparent lack of any over-all strategy found by Sigsworth and Wilkinson in their study suggests that the effectiveness of any government policy regarding the provision of housing ultimately depends upon the attitudes and abilities of local authority planners. (This is perhaps one of the main reasons why housing standards differ so considerably from city to city.) Although it is true that each city has its own particular set of problems, which require local expertise and knowledge to overcome, a common set of objectives, in terms of the number and quality of housing required, should ensure that the differences between urban areas are ultimately smoothed out. In addition, central government intervention in the housing market should be designed to achieve some clear over-all objective rather than being fragmented and aimed at particular groups within the market.

References

H. AARON [1970], 'Income Taxes and Housing', *American Economic Review* (December) pp. 789–806.

Committee on Housing in Greater London [1965], *Report*, Cmnd. 2605 (London: H.M.S.O.).

M. H. COOPER and D. C. STAFFORD [1975]. 'A Note on the Economic Implications of Fair Rents', *Social and Economic Administration* (Spring) pp. 26–9.

J. B. CULLINGWORTH [1967], 'Housing and the State: the Responsibilities of Government', in *The Economic Problems of Housing*, ed. A. A. Nevitt (London: Macmillan).

J. B. CULLINGWORTH [1969], 'Housing Analysis', in *Regional and Urban Studies: A Social Science Approach*, ed. J. B. Cullingworth and S. C. Orr (London: Allen & Unwin).

D. DONNISON [1967], *The Government of Housing* (Harmondsworth: Penguin).

R. HARRINGTON [1972], 'Housing – Supply and Demand', *National Westminster Bank Review* (May) pp. 43–54.

B. JOHN PARKER [1973], 'Some Sociological Implications of Slum Clearance Programmes', in *London: Urban Patterns, Problems and Policies*, ed. D. Donnison and D. Eversley (London: Heinemann).

W. LEAN [1971], 'Housing, Rehabilitation or Redevelopment: the Economic Assessment', *Journal of the Royal Town Planning Institute*, pp. 226–8.

J. C. T. MAO [1966], 'Effluency in Public Renewal Expenditures through Cost–Benefit Analysis', *Journal of the American Institute of Planners* (March) pp. 95–107.

Ministry of Housing and Local Government [1969], *Old Houses into New Homes*, Cmnd. 3062 (London: H.M.S.O.).

A. A. NEVITT [1966], *Housing, Taxation and Subsidies* (London: Nelson).

D. J. REYNOLDS [1966], *Economics, Town Planning and Traffic* (London: Institute of Economic Affairs).

H. W. RICHARDSON [1971], *Urban Economics* (Harmondsworth: Penguin).

J. ROTHENBERG [1967], *Economic Evaluation of Urban Renewal* (Washington: Brookings Institute).

E. M. SIGSWORTH and R. K. WILLIAMS [1972], 'Constraints on the Uptake of Improvement Grants', *Policy and Politics* (December) pp. 131–43.

J. N. TAIN [1968], 'The Housing Problem a Century Ago', *Urban Studies* (November) pp. 290–300.

A. M. WEINER and H. HOYT [1966], *Principles of Real Estate* (Washington: Roland Press).

A. WILLIAMS [1974],'"Need" as a Demand Concept (with special reference to health)', in *Economic Policies and Social Goals*, ed. A. J. Culyer (London: Martin Robertson).

10 THE URBAN PUBLIC ECONOMY

10.1 Introduction

An American observer once stated that:

> Modern urban man is born in a publicly financed hospital, re-
> ceives his education in a publicly supported school and university,
> spends a good part of his life travelling on publicly built trans-
> portation facilities, communicates through the post office or the
> quasi-public telephone system, drinks his public water, disposes
> of his garbage through the public removal system, reads his public
> library books, picnics in his public parks, is protected by his
> public police, fire, and health systems; eventually he dies, again
> in a hospital, and may even be buried in a public cemetery.
> Ideological conservatives notwithstanding, his everyday life is
> inextricably bound up with governmental decisions on these and
> numerous other local public services (Tietz [1968] p. 36).

It is not difficult to see from this quotation why the urban public
sector plays such an important part in everyday life: local government in this country, as in the United States, provides and regulates
a wide range of services which are easily taken for granted by city
dwellers. Just as central government influences the course and
growth of the national economy, so local government influences the
urban economy.

In this and the following chapter, we are concerned with the role
and activities of local government in urban areas and particularly
in our largest cities. Local authority participation in the urban
economy has a long history and is now both fairly extensive (local
authorities employ over two million people) and generally accepted
as a good thing – although there is still disagreement as to the
optimal degree of public involvement. This chapter explains why
there is felt to be a need for an urban public sector and points to
some of the peculiar features of the urban public economy. The
methods used to finance the sector are considered in some detail,
although the 1970s have represented a time of change in this

particular area. In 1972 legislation was passed to reorganise local government, to take effect from 1974, and at the time of writing new methods of controlling and financing urban public expenditure within the reorganised administrative framework are under discussion. For this reason much of Section 10.4, devoted to finance, is speculative rather than definitive.

The administrative changes that have taken place in local government are both outlined and commented upon. This probably goes outside the strict confines of economics into the realms of politics and public administration; nevertheless it is included for two reasons. First, the administrative framework of city government, by defining constraints and stipulating social needs, has an important bearing on the workings of the local public sector. Second, the type of local authority structure in a city determines the type and nature of urban planning possible and this has important consequences for the chapter on urban planning which follows. In fact, the 1972 Local Government Act placed considerably more stress on planning than previous legislation and also divided planning responsibilities between the various tiers of administration in an entirely new way.

10.2 Why an Urban Public Sector?

A large number of the goods and services available within urban areas are supplied by the local authority rather than by private firms. Similarly, a considerable proportion of investment, especially in infrastructure, within cities is carried out by the local public sector. These activities are in addition to those of the national public sector (including the nationalised industries) which also play an important role in urban life. Municipal authorities provide a wide range of goods and services which we might categorise under the following general headings:

(1) *Protection*
   Police
   Fire services
(2) *Utilities*
   Primary and secondary
      education
   Public health
   Cultural activities
   Welfare
   Recreation

(3) *Human-resource developments*
   Sewerage
   Water supplies
   refuse disposal
(4) *General services*
   Administration
   Public transport
   Local roads
   Housing
   Libraries

In this chapter, we are initially concerned with the question of why it is deemed necessary for city authorities in most developed countries to participate to such a large extent in their local economies and to actively intervene in urban markets. Second, we need to consider the policies which local authorities should pursue with regard to their economies and the municipal sector and, in the light of this, to appraise the actual approaches that have been adopted.

Many of the reasons why an extensive urban public sector has developed in most large cities overlap with the more general arguments favouring government intervention in the economy and with the need for urban planning discussed later. Briefly, local government involvement in economic markets can be justified on five broad microeconomic grounds:

(1) Some goods and services are what are known as 'public goods' and would not be available if supply was left to private entrepreneurs;

(2) Certain goods and services are best provided by monopoly agencies, and to prevent the exploitation of consumers local authorities have taken on the role of supplier;

(3) Some goods and services generate negative externalities, and therefore intervention by city authorities is justified to minimise the social costs their production and consumption impose on urban communities;

(4) In some instances it is felt necessary, for welfare reasons, to provide goods and services to the poorer sections of the community at uneconomic rates to offset the low income levels of these groups; and

(5) The decisions made by individuals within urban communities are often made in ignorance of the actions and intentions of others, and consequently are not always in the best interests of the population as a whole. When such interdependence occurs, there may be considerable justification for a degree of local government planning to maximise social welfare; this is discussed in depth in Chapter 11, when urban planning is looked at in detail.

A public good has been defined to exist when 'each individual's consumption of such a good leads to no subtractions from any other individual's consumption of that good' (Samuelson [1958]). National defence is an oft-quoted example of a public good since it makes defence available to the whole population and one person's consumption has no effect on the amount available for other people. Such goods are said to be characterised by 'jointness' or joint consumption. In the urban context, police services, fire protection, local radio stations and, to a lesser extent, urban roads, broadly exhibit this characteristic. The difficulty with these goods is that, although an individual's consumption has no effect on the supply of the good available to others, it is difficult to exclude any individual from consuming the good. Taking a local radio station as an example, it may be technically possible to prevent certain people receiving programmes by scrambling the radio waves, but to do so would be extremely expensive. Jointness, combined with the high exclusion costs of public goods, gives no incentive for private enterprise to enter the market as supplier. Consequently, if members of the community wish to enjoy such goods, they must act collectively. In reality, there are few 'pure' public goods at the local level, but a number of services do exhibit some degree of jointness and it is usually a political decision by the local community whether or not to act as supplier rather than trust that private firms will enter the market.

Some types of urban service are natural monopolies; for example, there is little point in having sewage plants duplicated or large numbers of bus companies serving the same route. When monopolies of this kind occur, the urban authorities can either control them by manipulating the economic framework within which they operate, in order to prevent exploitation of the consumer, or else they can provide the good or service themselves. The choice between these alternatives is political rather than economic in many cases – one school of thought maintaining that private enterprise is more efficient than the public variety, hence favouring monopoly regulation, and the other preferring public-sector ownership.

As we have mentioned in previous chapters, certain urban activities generate negative external effects and it may be necessary for local authority intervention to control them. In some instances this is done by providing services which remove the damage, for example the collection and disposal of refuse. In other cases the authorities supply alternative goods to attract consumers away from those generating undesirable external effects; the provision of public transport to discourage the use of private motor-cars may be cited as an example of this.

Urban public authorities often provide a range of goods and services either at prices below their real cost or else free of charge. It is felt that these goods and services are in some way necessary, and to deprive sections of the community simply because their income is insufficient to permit the purchase of these items would be unjust. In the sense that someone has to pay for these goods and services, and this is usually the tax- and rate-paying section of the population, this policy represents a redistribution of income in favour of the poorer members of the urban community. There are some economic arguments against urban authorities engaging in redistributive activities however. Harry Richardson [1971] feels that subsidies of this kind should come from central government, rather than local authorities, because of its greater knowledge of the full implications of such a policy. Also, local subsidies may prove inequitable between cities: authorities in richer cities being able to redistribute more income in favour of the poorer groups within their boundaries. Counter to these views is the fact that local governments should be better informed of the special needs of their populations than are the central authorities and, consequently, better equipped to deal with them. The division of responsibility between the two levels of government is a complex one and we shall be returning to it in more detail later.

In addition to these microeconomic reasons for the existence of an urban public sector, there is also at least one macroeconomic consideration. By having a substantial public sector, it is possible for a local authority to act as a stabilising agent and to even-out cyclical fluctuations in the city's economy. When local unemployment levels rise, the authority can increase its spending, say on a programme of council-house building or land clearance, and via the local multiplier create more jobs in the area. There are limitations to this sort of policy however. Urban multipliers, as we have seen, tend to be very small because of the openness of the local economy, and the impact of increased public-sector activity is therefore unlikely to be large. Second, the openness of urban economies means that the actions of one authority are likely to affect and possibly destabilise the economies of other cities – there will be 'spatial spillovers'. Finally, central government supplies a considerable amount of local authority finance and may not consider it desirable for stabilisation to be attempted at the sub-national level, especially if it leads to beggar-my-neighbour policies being pursued by authorities trying to maintain full employment in their own area irrespective of the damage it does to the economies of other cities.

10.3   The Size of the Urban Public Sector

The aggregate size of the urban public sector has continually expanded throughout the post-war period both with respect to the national public sector and as a percentage of national output. Whereas in the early 1950s local expenditure amounted to about 10 per cent of the gross national product (G.N.P.), by the mid-1970s this figure had risen to over 19 per cent, and by this time local authority spending accounted for about one-third of all public-sector expenditure. Forecasts suggest that the size of local budgets will increase further in the future. There are two reasons for the increasing expenditures of local government. First, the costs of the services they provide have risen more rapidly than the costs of other goods and services in the economy, and, second, local authorities have extended the services that they provide, both in range and quality, and have improved their methods of identifying those in need, ensuring that they receive appropriate assistance where necessary. We look in detail at each of these two justifications of the rising share of national income going to local authorities.

Many of the services provided by local authorities are for the benefit of certain vulnerable groups in the community which it is deemed necessary to assist, in particular these are the young (for example education, child-welfare services, and so on) and the elderly (for example health services, old people's homes, home helps, and so on). Consequently, as the demographic composition of an urban area changes and a larger proportion of the population falls into these categories, the amount of money needed to simply maintain the existing level of service provided must rise. Over the past twenty years the relative number of young and elderly has risen, and, as a consequence, so has the financial burden on local authorities.

The longer-term problem is that the majority of goods and services provided by the urban public sector are relatively labour-intensive; education, for example, which is very labour-intensive, accounted for over 35 per cent of local authority expenditure in 1971–2. This has important implications for the size of the urban public-sector budget. During periods of wage inflation, the costs of providing labour-intensive services rises relative to that of other services and, consequently, if local authorities are to retain the level of service they provide, their share of national expenditure must go up. Wage inflation has been an important factor in the increased local authority expenditure in the early 1970s. An important contribution to the theory in this field has been provided by William Baumol [1967], who argues that the increase in the share of G.N.P. going to local authorities is inevitable if they are not to reduce the quality of service supplied. He argues that labour-intensive industries have a long-term cost disadvantage compared to capital-intensive ones. Labour-intensive industries offer less scope for technological improvement, and this is particularly the case with the types of service provided by the urban public sector. The importance of this is that increases in wages cannot be offset by the local authority changing the method of supply to incorporate more capital, the industries involved being 'technologically unprogressive'. If teachers, for example, obtain a pay increase, the local authority cannot reduce the number of teachers employed and take on more machines; it must simply accept a higher wage bill. (It may, of course, increase class sizes but this is not an increase in labour productivity, rather it is a reduction in the quality of education being supplied.) Since technical progress does occur in many sectors of the economy, especially manufacturing, this will tend to increase the productivity in these sectors and the wages paid to those working in them. In turn, this will bid up wages in the technologically unprogressive sectors as manufacturers and others attempt to attract more labour. If the urban public sector wishes to retain its work force, it has no option but to pay higher wages; it cannot substitute capital in its place. Baumol therefore feels that the rise in urban public-sector spending is inevitable, even if maximum efficiency is enjoyed and the services provided are left unimproved. As he says, 'this is a trend for which no man and no group should be blamed, for there is nothing that can be done to stop it'.

A further problem is that many of the services supplied by the urban public sector, especially transport, exhibit decreasing costs – the greater the supply, the lower the unit cost of provision. Since the populations of most cities are rising, local authorities must increase the level of service provided just to ensure that everyone remains as well served as before. This tends to push down the incremental cost of decreasing-cost services over time. In many cases these services are owned by the local authority to prevent exploitation by a private supplier, or to prevent duplication and reduced efficiency, and in these instances the authority will be interested in charging the users of the facility an economic price for the service.

The difficulty is that the appropriate price to levy in these circumstances, if efficiency is the objective, equals the marginal or incremental cost of the service and this, because of the relationship between marginal cost and average cost, will fall below the average cost. (It is appropriate to levy a price which equates marginal cost with demand because, if a higher price is charged, it will deter those people from using the service who would gain more from doing so than the costs they impose. Similarly, if a lower price is charged, marginal users will gain less benefit than the costs incurred by providing the additional service needed to meet their demands.) The local authority will therefore make a financial loss on these services which will have to be met by subsidies. Consequently, if marginal-cost pricing is employed for a decreasing-cost service which is being increased in supply, the local public authority will require an increasingly large amount of money to cover the required subsidy. Therefore, as cities grow, the proportion of rates going to finance these types of service will increase relative to income.

So far we have only considered explanations of the rising importance of local authority involvements assuming the *per capita* range and quality of services provided remains unaltered. The existence of decreasing-cost industries, labour-intensity and demographic features can explain a large proportion of G.N.P. currently going to local public expenditure in this situation. Of course, there is the additional fact that the types of services now offered by local authorities are different to those provided twenty years ago and it is this fact that we now consider.

The range and quality of services provided by the urban public sector is frequently thought of as being a purely political decision, and this is particularly the case with public goods. In the early 1950s, Paul Samuelson [1954] demonstrated to his satisfaction that 'no decentralised pricing system can serve to determine optimally' the appropriate level of local authority expenditure on public goods and that some form of 'voting' or 'signalling' was required to replace the traditional economic market mechanism. This essentially politic approach encounters the problem that if members of a community desire greater police protection, and hence vote the 'law-and-order' candidate on to the local council, there is no guarantee he will pursue this policy once elected. Charles Tiebout [1956] has circumvented this and several other problems by reintroducing economic theory into the analysis. Basically, he argues that moving or failing to move replaces the usual market test of willingness to buy a good and reveals the consumer voter's demand for public goods . . . each locality has a revenue and expenditure pattern that reflects the desires of its residents. . . .Spatial mobility provides the local public goods counterpart to the private market's shopping trip.

In short, people 'vote with their feet', and live in the urban area offering the level and mix of local authority involvement in the economy nearest to their ideal. The theory suggests, therefore, that social welfare would be maximised by having the largest possible number of urban communities, each exhibiting a different level of public-sector activity. This would offer the greatest choice to the population. A system of this type also reduces the administrative costs of the authorities because each city would contain a near-homogeneous population and this would minimise decision-making costs. If we accept Tiebout's theory, then the increase in the number of services provided by local authorities (and the increase in taxation and rates required to pay for them) is the result of social pressures, the urban inhabitants desiring the expansion. If this was not the case we would witness population movements to cities with less comprehensive public-sector services, and there is no evidence of this occurring. Empirical support for Tiebout's model has been offered by Wallace Oates [1969] in a detailed examination of property values in a study of the New York metropolitan region. He concludes that his results appear consistent with a model of the Tiebout variety in which rational consumers weigh the benefits from local public services against the cost of their tax liabilities in choosing a community of residence.

Although interesting, Tiebout's model does rely upon a number of rather questionable assumptions to reach its conclusions. He assumes explicitly that movement costs are small and consequently there is little impediment to people 'voting with their feet'. In reality, removal expenses are frequently substantial. Individuals may therefore decide to remain in their current location and accept what they consider a sub-optimal level of local authority participation rather than pay the costs of removing to another city. If relocation does occur, it is often only after considerable time lags, while houses are sold and new employment found. A second problem with Tiebout's theory is that it says little about people who live in suburbs or dormitory towns just outside main cities. These people can enjoy the facilities provided by a city's authorities but, by living outside, do not have to pay for them. If these people were confronted with the same rate demands as those within the city, they may decide to locate elsewhere. Tiebout's model does not deal with this situation in which people can decide separately the rates they wish to pay and the services they wish to enjoy. Finally, the model falls down when local authorities do not differ in the services they provide and there is no preferred public-sector mix for people to move to. Since many urban public services have to be supplied by statute in this country (for example education, police, and so on), the degree of variation between authorities is considerably less than Tiebout envisaged in his theory. Because central government is playing an increasing part in financing and regulating the urban public sector, the freedom for people to 'vote with their feet' is somewhat limited.

We have put forward some of the reasons why an increasing share of G.N.P. is going to the urban public sector but we should not forget that there are some counteracting economic forces controlling this expansion; in particular, certain local authority activities do offer some scope for economies of scale. In particular, we are concerned with services which local authorities provide free of charge; if they attach prices to them, similar problems are encountered to those in services exhibiting decreasing costs, which we discussed earlier.

Economies of scale (or 'scale effects') occur because some factors of production (especially buildings and capital) tend to be 'lumpy' and cannot readily be altered when small changes in demand take place. When these fixed factors are varied then the scale of production changes. If more of the fixed factor lowers the unit cost of providing the good or service, then there are economies of scale. Baumol's thesis outlined above assumes that such economies in the urban public sector are small and cannot offset higher labour costs as output is increased but empirical evidence is not conclusive on this point. Drawing on work done in the United States, Werner Hirsch has summarised the scale effects in urban public-sector undertakings as shown in Table 10.1.

It is noticeable that the scope for economies in the services provided by local authorities in the United Kingdom is very limited compared to that in the United States, partly because of the greater central government commitment in this country. Evidence on scale economies is also less clear, empirical studies frequently finding it difficult to allow for quality variations of service in their calculations. A study by local authority expenditure in Scotland (Hughes [1967]) failed to reveal significant scale economies in the provision of police, health and welfare and cleansing facilities. A more detailed study of the situation in the United Kingdom by Gupta and

TABLE 10.1 *The existence of economies of scale in urban public services: the American experience*

Service	Economies of scale
Police	No
Primary and Secondary Education	No
Refuse collection	No
High-school education	Uncertain
Hospitals	Uncertain
Fire services	Yes (but very minor)
Water	Yes
Sewerage	Yes
Electricity	Yes

* The range of service provided by urban authorities in the United States differs somewhat from the range in the United Kingdom.

SOURCE: Hirsch [1973] p. 332.

Hutton [1968] with respect to housing, highways and health services, and carried out at various levels of disaggregation, both by service and type of local authority, failed to reveal any over-all picture of scale economies, although they were present in some sectors (for example in the provision of housing at the urban-district-council level). In the important field of education, Cumming [1971] has found significant scale economies in relation to the size of primary schools in Scotland, but not for secondary schools. The evidence is therefore somewhat inconclusive with respect to the United Kingdom.

   One point worth noting with reference to the scale of the urban public sector is that size may be a decided advantage in the borrowing of funds. Many of the largest local authorities have been able to finance at least part of their activities in the 1970s by borrowing both within the United Kingdom and on international finance markets. This ability to obtain finance by borrowing has, in the short term at least, permitted far more services to be provided by local authorities than would have been possible if they had relied solely upon their revenues from rates and from the central government.

10.4   The Financing of the Urban Public Sector

The increased expenditure of local authorities in recent years has created considerable problems of revenue-raising. Whilst in 1961–2 local government in the United Kingdom only required a total income of £3437·9 million, by 1967–8 this had risen to £6459·9 million and by 1971–2 to £10,726·2 million. Raising this money has presented difficulties; in particular local revenues have failed to keep pace with expenditures and central government has had to provide an increasing amount of money. This latter problem has been particularly acute in cities where the consumers of public services live outside the local authority boundaries; commuters using the public services in London provide an example of this.

Local authorities have four main sources of finance:

(1) property taxes or rates;
(2) central government grants, principally the Rate Support Grant;
(3) revenues from certain services; and
(4) loans.

We are primarily interested in the first two categories. Loans are generally raised for specific financial purposes or projects and are usually funded by issuing bonds in either the national or international money markets. There has been a tendency in recent years for local authorities to indulge in more borrowing than previously; the total local authority debt in England and Wales has risen quite sharply from less than £6500 million in 1962 to £15,287 million in 1972, and is currently about £25,000 million. (This compares with the National Debt of about £40,000 million in 1975 and building society debts of about £18,000 million.) The difficulty, as London and, more especially, New York discovered in 1975, with financing local authority expenditure by borrowing is that interest charges have to be met and these are usually determined by forces outside the authorities' control. A major cut-back in London's housing programme (£50 million) in April 1975, for example, was the direct result of excessive interest payments on the G.L.C.'s £1600 million debt.

The revenues from public services are self-explanatory and raise few conceptual problems other than deciding which services to charge for and which to provide free. More difficult is the problem of deciding upon the appropriate price to charge. Claims have been made that some urban authority charging policies may lead to a maldistribution of resources – cheap fares for peak-period users of public transport is a clear example of this – and have serious distributional implications (Hepworth [1971]). Wilbur Thompson [1965] also argues that some American authorities over-charge city residents for water and sewage disposal to obtain money from suburban residents who congest city streets and that this further compounds resource misallocation. In general, marginal-cost pricing is to be advocated for achieving optimal resource allocation, although in some cases alternative policies may be justified (see Chapter 8, Section 8.7).

Table 10.2 indicates the various sources of local authority income in the financial year 1972–3. It is clear that the lion's share comes from rates and central government grants. We now look at each of these in turn.

TABLE 10.2 *Income of local authorities for England and Wales, 1972–3*

Source of income		£ thousand	
Loans		2,150,861	
Specific government grants		130,230	
Sales and other sources		562,954	
	Total Capital Receipts		2,844,045
Rates ⎱	Net	2,179,584	
Government grants ⎰	expenditure	3,135,048	
Miscellaneous monies		2,900,205	
	Total Revenue Income		8,214,837
	TOTAL INCOME		11,058,882

(a) Rates

These form the largest source of *local* revenue. They are levied on property within city boundaries and are a tax on the imputed rateable value of property. In the case of domestic residences, this value is calculated on an imputed rental value for the property minus estimated maintenance costs. If the rateable value of a house is, for example, £150 and the local rate (the rate poundage) is 70p, then the householder pays 70p for every £ of rateable value – that is £105 in the example.

There are quite marked differences in the rateable value per head of population between different areas. The Royal Commission on Local Government in England [1969] found the range to be from Hertfordshire's £60·2 to the West Riding's £28·4 for counties, from Brighton's £72·3 to Halifax's £29·6 for county boroughs and from Dunstable's £87·7 to Hendon's £21.0 for boroughs. (Similar ranges will exist under the post-1974 administrative structure.)

The rate poundage also tends to vary between cities. Oliver and Stanyer [1969] attributed these variations to the political composition of the local councils and the different types of hereditament in cities (a city containing a large proportion of houses with high rateable values being able to obtain an identical income from a low poundage as a less well-endowed city can from a much higher local rate). A later study by David King [1973] has elaborated on this, demonstrating that variations can be caused by several factors. There is a tendency for Labour-controlled authorities to levy higher poundages and, although this can partly be explained by the low rateable values of property in these areas, this seems to be mainly due either to them setting higher standards of service or being given inadequate government grants.

The rating system is somewhat antiquated (with a history dating back to a statute of 1601) and is open to a number of criticisms. The system is usually justified on the grounds that the services provided by the urban public sector – police, fire protection, water, and so on – enhance the value of local property, and hence occupiers of this property should be liable for the costs. In fact the rateable values employed are out of date and bear little relation to the market value of property. The rating system is also inequitable in many cases. Although higher-valued properties tend to have higher rateable values and are often occupied by wealthier people, this relationship is far from perfect and the rating system can easily prove to be regressive in its impact. Finally, the rating system may lead to sub-optimal allocation of funds between the local public and private sectors. In many cities, commerce and industry contribute a substantial proportion of local rates but have little to say in the poundage levied. In these circumstances it is possible for householders to vote for a high poundage and divert an excessive amount of money from industry to the urban public sector. This occurs because consumers do not have to pay the full price for the services they enjoy and hence fail to recognise the true costs involved.

Modifications to the rating system in recent years, and the introduction of rate rebates for certain needy groups in the community, have weakened some of these criticisms and it seems unlikely that the system will ever be completely abandoned. It is an easily understood method of revenue collection and enjoys the practical advantage for local authorities that it is independent of central government. Realistically one would expect gradual changes in the rate system over time rather than the introduction of an entirely new method of raising revenues from the local community.

Alternative methods of raising revenue to supplement, rather than replace, the current rate system have been suggested for the United Kingdom and, indeed, some have been introduced in other countries. The most popular suggestion is a local progressive income tax. This would, it is claimed, have few adverse distributional effects and would not lead to the market distortions associated with rates. In a Green (discussion) Paper, *The Future Shape of Local Government Finance* (Department of the Environment [1971]), the level of local tax required to reduce government grants to local authorities from about 60 per cent of local authority revenue to 50 per cent was calculated. The hypothesised objective could be obtained by a three-point increase on the standard rate of income tax. This revenue could either be collected directly by the local authority or, alternatively, the local authority could set the rate, leaving collection in the hands of the Inland Revenue. However, there would be administrative problems with such a tax because the current tax records are kept mainly with reference to the address of the taxpayer's employer rather than his place of residence. There would also be difficulties in allocating profits and other types of non-wage monies. The economic objections mainly relate to the possibility of fluctuations in income, and consequently local revenue, and to the possible time lags in collection. The viability of local income taxes has, however, been demonstrated by the systems used in Sweden, West Germany, Canada and Switzerland.

An alternative scheme involves local sales taxes, for example a local form of value-added tax or purchase tax. These have been used with success in several states in America since the mid-1930s, and the relatively strong financial position of California, in particular, has been attributed to the use of a sales tax. Such taxes are cheap to collect and readily understood but have the serious disadvantage of being regressive in their impact (they tax living standards) and may be inflationary. In the Green Paper mentioned above, the desired reduction in the government grant could be achieved by employing a sales tax of a little over 2 per cent.

motor taxes

A third scheme would be to redirect some of the revenue from motor taxes (vehicle excise duty and fuel tax) directly to local authorities. The present system, whereby local authorities have data on fuel sales needed in the licensing of storage facilities, means the introduction of such a scheme would be relatively easy. Convenience has its problems however. Differential rates of petrol duty between cities would encourage motorists to 'fill up' at the cheapest source, which makes the calculation of probable revenue incomes difficult for the authorities and is wasteful of resources. Despite these difficulties, Ursula Hicks [1969] still feels local motor taxation is 'the most practical new source of autonomous revenue' available for local authorities. In qualitative terms, it would have needed about a third of fuel-duty revenue to be transferred to local control in 1971 to compensate for the reduction in the government grant envisaged in the Green Paper.

(b) Government Grants

The financial support given by central government to the urban public sector amounts to about 60 per cent of the latter's net expenditure; this compares to a figure of 52 per cent in 1962–3. Initially, grants were introduced for specific expenditures but the General Grant System was devised in 1957 to give local authorities more autonomy in their actions. The grants were calculated on the basis of anticipated local authority expenditures on specified items, but once negotiated the individual authorities could spend the money as they wished. The present Rate Support Grant System (R.S.G.) replaced the General Grant System, upon which it was based, in 1967. The R.S.G. is now negotiated annually (an innovation of the 1974 Local Government Finance Act) between the local authorities, the Treasury and the Department of the Environment. The formulae used is based upon the following three specific elements:

(1) *The 'resources element'* – to compensate local authorities with a below-average taxable capacity, that is those containing a disproportionately high percentage of properties with low rateable values. This element constitutes about £1328 million of the total support grant at present (1975–6).

(2) *The 'needs element'* – to compensate authorities with above-average needs, for example those containing an exceptionally large number of schoolchildren. The needs element embraces £2758 million of the total rate support grant and therefore its allocation is of considerable importance.

(3) *The 'domestic element'* – to reduce domestic poundage and therefore ensure a fixed national differential between the rate liability on private homes and on industrial and commercial property. Currently the domestic element amounts to £619 million.

Additional to the R.S.G., the government also gives specific grants which are used to meet the costs of specific investment projects or particular services. For 1975–6 the estimated total of specific grants was £729 million, of which about £250 million was to be for the new Transport Supplementary Grant to embrace former grants towards road works and to support public transport (see Chapter 8).

The R.S.G. system, despite some minor adjustments in 1974, is currently under review by the Committee of Inquiry into Local Government Finance under the chairmanship of Sir Frank Layfield (not to be confused with the inquiry led by the same man discussed in the following chapter). The review has been necessitated both by the shortcomings of the system of government support and by the need for modifications following the local government reorganisations of 1972. The rapid increase in inflation during the 1970s has made reform even more imperative, local authorities finding it difficult to plan their expenditures ahead when uncertain about the speed at which the values of their rate income and support grant will be eroded by inflation over the financial year.

Criticisms of the R.S.G. system have been mainly directed at the method employed for allocating funds between authorities on the needs, resources and domestic elements criteria. Indeed, in a consultative document, the government recognised this and, although the basic support grant system was to be retained, 'certain improvements in the rate support grant are proposed in order to ensure that the varying needs of local authorities are matched more closely, that the resources available to those authorities are more evenly distributed' (Department of the Environment [1973]).

In two papers, a pair of Cambridge economists (Godley [1975] and Godley and Rhodes [1973]) demonstrated that the needs element in particular is biased against London (which, although responsible for 19 per cent of local authority expenditure in 1974–5, only received 13·9 per cent of the pool grant), whilst allocating considerable sums to the richer authorities, and that authorities with a disproportionately large number of children in their area were under-financed. To some extent the 1974 Act removed these anomalies although it is not altogether clear that some bias does not still exist. Godley and Rhodes also argue that, 'while in a general way the formulae for distributing needs and resources elements tend to equalise levels of service and the rate burden, no explicit set of objectives has been set out in terms which make it possible to say how successful they are working' (Godley and Rhodes [1973]). They suggest that an appropriate objective is the compensating of authorities in full for deviations in demographic structures. A formulae for achieving this is presented by them but the objective is itself questionable. A system of this kind could distort the normal economic market mechanisms, for example it would compensate for congestion in an area and hence weaken the incentive for the population to become more dispersed. (Local governments themselves seem to recognise this problem and in 1974 rejected automatic adjustments to their grants for population increases.)

A further difficulty with the present grant system is that of control. There is neither efficient central control of the size of the urban public sector nor sufficient local autonomy over expenditure to make the financing system work efficiently. Although central government theoretically controls the size of the R.S.G., in many cases it bows to political pressure and gives a large settlement simply to remove the threat of 'unacceptable' rate increases. (As Peter Jay said in *The Times* (30 January 1975), 'Local government finance is not the stuff of which best sellers or sensational headlines are made – not, that is, except when huge increases in rate demands are announced (or predicted)'.) At the lower level, central government stipulates the quantity and quality of many local authority services, removing a considerable degree of freedom from the urban authorities (see Page [1975]).

Connected with the problem of control is the question of the appropriate size for the support grant. Local authorities have argued that there are good reasons for reducing the scale of central support and increasing their own revenue-raising activities – hence the Green Paper mentioned above. They are particularly concerned about the loss of civic pride and of local responsibility, which they feel accompanies large support grants, and argue that ratepayers' vigilance is tending to be replaced by bureaucratic supervision (Marshall [1971]). Many authorities would seem to prefer a direct financial nexus with their ratepayers. Counter to this is the need for central government macroeconomic policy on matters such as inflation and national growth to be adequately reflected at the local level. The national government has responsibility for the wider control of the economy, and one way of influencing the level of public expenditure is through the support grant. The exact formula offering local autonomy combined with sufficient central control to achieve co-ordination between local and central government objectives is not easily found. This is why the Layfield Committee is currently seeking a system which would introduce accountability for expenditure and a more rational distribution of the financial burden between the various levels of government.

10.5 Local Government Reforms

In the mid-1960s it was decided that the system of local government in the United Kingdom, which dated back to legislation of 1888 and 1894 when the country's population was less than 28 million, needed reorganisation. A major reform of London's government took place in 1963–5, and in 1966 a Royal Commission on Local Government in England was established under the chairmanship of Lord Redcliffe-Maud to examine the problems of local government in the remainder of the country. The final *Report* (Royal Commission on Local Government in England [1969]) diagnosed the following faults in the existing system:

(1) Local government areas do not fit into the pattern of life and work in modern England;

(2) The fragmentation of the structure of local government has made the proper planning of development and transportation impossible;

(3) The division of responsibility between counties and their

districts means that services which should be in the hands of one authority are in the hands of several;

(4) Many local authorities are too small in size and revenue and, as a result, are short of highly qualified manpower and technical equipment; and

(5) As a result of the above defects, there are serious failings in the relationship of local government to the public and central government.

The Redcliffe-Maud Committee recommended the introduction of unitary authorities to control all local personal services (education, welfare, health and housing) replacing the existing hierarchical structure of district, borough and county authorities. In the three main conurbations – the West Midlands, Merseyside and Greater Manchester – a two-tier system, similar to London's, was suggested. The lower tier was to be responsible for social services, education and housing, while the upper tier was to control environmental and planning matters. The unitary authorities would have a minimum population of 250,000 inhabitants, to enable them to reap scale benefits, while they were not to exceed a million inhabitants, to prevent managerial diseconomies and to permit the full degree of community participation. The *Report* envisaged that these new authorities, both at the metropolitan and the general level, would have a modified system of financial assistance: 'Without such complementary financial reforms, the new local government will be cramped and handicapped as a self-governing institution.'

However, few of the recommendations of the Redcliffe-Maud Committee were accepted, and the eventual reforms introduced in the 1972 Local Government Act differed substantially from those in the *Report*. This was partly the fault of the Committee itself (Jones [1973]) which, by suggesting a two-tier system for the main conurbations, created its own Trojan Horse. It permitted those in favour of this type of local government to argue for a national two-tier structure – 'if it is workable in Manchester why not elsewhere?' The 1972 Act introduced a two-tier system throughout the country; in England and Wales it created forty-seven counties, containing 233 districts, and six metropolitan counties (adding South Yorkshire, Tyne and Wearside and the West Riding to the three proposed by the Committee of Inquiry), containing thirty-six metropolitan districts. If one includes Scotland and Northern Ireland, where similar reforms have taken place, as well as Greater London, this represents a reduction in the total number of local authorities from about 1850 to 547. These new authorities replaced the old ones on 1 April 1974 (16 May 1975 in the case of Scotland).

These reforms have important implications for our large cities. The metropolitan counties are now responsible for strategic planning, and the metropolitan districts for local plans and development controls. This can clearly lead to problems of co-ordinating policies at the two levels, as we noted in the previous chapter in the context of urban transport – the metropolitan counties being responsible for transport planning, while the metropolitan districts provide the actual facilities. However, the problems of co-ordination go further than this, because the personal health service and the water authorities are now separate from local government. If we take sewage as a specific example, the responsibility for its disposal now falls on two sets of shoulders which, as Rhodes [1974] has commented, seems designed to maximise the industrial difficulties of controlling pollution.

The reorganisation also seems to be biased against the smaller urban areas, and those outside of the six metropolitan counties are particularly badly affected. Many important urban centres, such as Southampton, Bristol, Leicester, Derby, Nottingham, Portsmouth and Hull, now fall within basically 'rural counties' where rural dwellers enjoy disproportional representation on local councils. The city authorities have thus lost control of their library, educational and social services and are prevented by the confines of district boundaries from expanding their suburbs. Urban centres have not been linked with their service hinterland nor with their commuting belts by the reorganisations. Jones ([1973] p. 165) summarises this aspect of the situation thus: 'The new local government system marks the end of a long tradition of urban government. County boroughs lose their autonomy.'

The reorganisation of local government boundaries and administration, independent of changes in the methods of financing the urban public sector, is open to criticism. Peter Jay, in *The Times* (30 January 1975), described the policy as being 'as sensible as trying to deploy an army without reference to its armaments and equipment'. Indeed, financial reforms are likely to have more profound effects on local government than changes in geographical boundaries and yet they seem to attract much less attention in the literature. The two reforms must be taken together and viewed as an entity since the success of administrative reorganisation depends critically upon the methods used to finance local authority activities.

References

W. J. BAUMOL [1967], 'Macroeconomics of Unbalanced Growth; the Anatomy of Urban Crisis', *American Economic Review* (June) pp. 415–26.

C. CUMMING [1971], *Studies in Educational Costs* (Edinburgh: Scottish Academic Press).

Department of the Environment [1971], *The Future Shape of Local Government Finance*, Cmnd. 4741 (London: H.M.S.O.).

Department of the Environment [1973], *Local Government Finance in England and Wales: Consultation Paper* (London: H.M.S.O.).

W. A. H. GODLEY [1975], *Reflections on the Control of Local Government Expenditure and its Financing* (Cambridge: Department of Applied Economics).

W. A. H. GODLEY and J. RHODES [1973], 'The Rate Support Grant System', in *Local Government Finance* (London: Institute for Fiscal Studies).

S. P. GUPTA and J. P. HUTTON [1968], 'Economics of Scale in Local Government Services', *Royal Commission on Local Government in England, Research Studies No. 3* (London: H.M.S.O.).

N. HEPWORTH [1971], *The Finance of Local Government* (London: Allen & Unwin).

U. K. HICKS [1969], 'New Revenue Schemes for Local Government', *Local Government Finance* (May) pp. 180–4.

W. Z. HIRSCH [1973], *Urban Economic Analysis* (New York: McGraw-Hill).

J. T. HUGHES [1967], 'Economic Aspects of Local Government', *Scottish Journal of Political Economy* (June) pp. 118–37.

G. W. JONES [1973], 'The Local Government Act 1972 and Redcliffe-Maud Commission', *Political Quarterly* (April–June) pp. 154–66.

D. N. KING [1973], 'Why do Local Authority Rate Poundages Differ?', *Public Administration* (Summer) pp. 165–73.

A. H. MARSHALL [1971], *New Revenues for Local Government*, Fabian Research Series, 295.

W. E. OATES [1969], 'The Effects of Property Taxes and Local

Public Spending on Property Values: an Empirical Study of Tax Capitalisation and the Tiebout Hypothesis', *Journal of Political Economy* (November–December) pp. 957–71.

F. R. OLIVER and J. STANYER [1969], 'Some Aspects of the Financial Behaviour of County Boroughs', *Public Administration* (Summer) pp. 169–84.

H. PAGE [1975], 'Local Government – the Final Phase?', *Three Banks Review* (June) pp. 3–34.

R. A. W. RHODES [1974], 'Local Government Reform – Three Questions – What is Reorganisation, What are the Effects of Reorganisation? Why Reorganisation?', *Social and Economic Administration* (Spring) pp. 6–21.

H. W. RICHARDSON [1971], *Urban Economics* (Harmondsworth: Penguin).

Royal Commission on Local Government in England [1969], *Report*, Cmnd. 4040 (London: H.M.S.O.).

P. A. SAMUELSON [1954], 'The Pure Theory of Public Expenditure', *Review of Economics and Statistics* (November) pp. 387–9.

P. A. SAMUELSON [1958], 'Aspects of Public Expenditure Economics', *Review of Economic Studies* (November) pp. 332–8.

W. R. THOMPSON [1965], *A Preface to Urban Economics* (Baltimore: Johns Hopkins Press).

C. M. TIEBOUT [1956], 'A Pure Theory of Local Expenditures', *Journal of Political Economy* (October) pp. 416–24.

M. B. TIETZ [1968], 'Towards a Theory of Urban Public Facility Location', *Regional Science Association Papers*, pp. 35–51.

11   URBAN PLANNING

11.1   Economics and Urban Planning

Town planning is an extensive subject in its own right and a full discussion of its applications and methodology is beyond the scope of this particular book. (A comprehensive description of the basic techniques is provided by Goodman and Freund [1968].) Here we are concerned primarily with the role of economics in urban planning, although the rather imprecise boundary between physical planning, principles and economic analysis makes it impossible, if not undesirable, to omit some reference to the former.

Modern planning has been defined as 'a continuous process, which works by seeking to devise appropriate ways of controlling the [urban] system conceived, and then by monitoring the effects to see how far the controls have been effective or how far they need subsequent modification' (Hall [1974] p. 269). It is this view of planning with which we are concerned here. It is entirely different to the older traditional approach which literally involved the production of a cartographical plan depicting a future pattern of land use to be created over a given period. The change is recent, occurring in the last fifteen years or so.

It is also only comparatively recently that economics has begun to play an important role in the urban planning procedure; in the past many physical planners have expressed a general mistrust of economic principles and doctrines. The attitude of this group has been aptly summarised by David Donnison [1972]: 'Town Planning was almost wholly non-economic – even anti-economic. Sir Patrick Abercrombie contemptuously dismissed the economist as a "muddler who will talk about the Law of Supply and Demand and the Liberty of the individual".' This dislike of economists stemmed partly from a common misunderstanding among planners who saw economics as a narrow form of arithmetic used in the calculation of cost, rather than a method of allocating resources and as a means of decision-making when confronted with alternative policies. This misunderstanding was hardly helped by the attitude of many economists, who saw planners as meddlers interfering with the natural economic forces of supply and demand.

Economics was not happily married into the planning process until the early 1960s by which time economic, political and social pressures had built up to the extent that the exclusion of economists became impossible. The size and interrelated nature of many urban problems (especially those relating to transport), combined with an increased interaction between the public and private sectors of the urban economy, meant that it was no longer feasible to ignore economic considerations in the preparation of a town plan. The incorporation of economic analysis became even more important after 1968 when local authorities were compelled to produce 'structure plans' stating their planning objectives, the alternative planning strategies and to evaluate the final proposals.

At the same time as planners began to recognise the important role economics has to play in their work, so economists were beginning to view physical planning differently. It became apparent that traditional economic analysis did not apply in an environment of externalities, indivisibilities and monopoly powers, and that the imperfections of the urban economy would prevent an optimal allocation of resources unless there was some degree of direct intervention. Economists realised that the only way the vast number of individual decisions made within the urban economy could be co-ordinated to ensure the greatest welfare for the community was to actively plan much of the city's growth. Resource allocation would not be anything like optimal without a considerable degree of physical planning (although this does not solve the problem of just how much intervention is desirable).

The emergence of an extensive public sector in the urban economy has added another reason for the expansion of urban planning. As we saw in the previous chapter, many of the services provided by local authorities are done so either free of charge (for example education, refuse collection, libraries, and so on) or at prices unrelated to cost (for example swimming pools, council housing, and so on); consequently some method is required to determine the appropriate quantity to supply. Some form of direct planning is clearly needed in these circumstances, although economics is still required to evaluate the alternative planning proposals.

The economist can usefully assist planners in a number of ways. First, he can provide a system of references reflecting the wants of consumers relative to the economic resources available – in this way he can act as a check on over-ambitious plans for which the resources are simply not available. Second, economists have the tools and expertise to tackle specific planning problems, and may in some cases even be able to suggest more efficient economic solutions which would otherwise be overlooked if only physical controls were considered – road pricing as a means of controlling traffic congestion might be cited as an example. Third, economists can assist in the decision-making processes involved; by utilising specialised techniques of investment appraisal, they can help to ensure that the most suitable plan is finally accepted. Last, as Reynolds [1966] has pointed out, the economist acts as a link between those who develop and present the plans and those who are responsible for allocating public funds. By translating physical plans into financial terms, the economist acts as an intermediary between . the two parties.

At present, the principal role of the economist in urban planning is to carry out the final appraisal of the alternative strategies put forward by the planners. He is responsible for selecting the most worthwhile set of investments and policies. Because of the importance of this part of the planning procedure, there has been a tendency to keep the final economic process independent of the remainder of the planning sequence, an economic-appraisal stage being tacked on to the end of the over-all operation. In cases of small schemes this may be justified but in larger urban planning exercises the economist should be present throughout to assist in the elimination of unrealistic options at an early stage and, more generally, to ensure that the planners realise the economic realities of their different schemes.

It is worthwhile noting that planning is very much an interdisciplinary exercise and that there are equally good reasons for introducing sociologists and psychologists at a very early stage in the proceedings to ensure that the social, as well as physical, implications of each plan on the city's inhabitants are fully understood. Any urban plan will necessarily be a trade-off between the ideals of the various disciplines. Sociologists, for example, may not favour large cities with populations exceeding 500,000 but economists may point to the scale advantages of conurbations populated by several million inhabitants; some compromise between the psychological and pecuniary considerations must therefore be sought.

11.2 Cost–Benefit Analysis and Allied Techniques

Any large urban development plan requires the expenditure of a considerable amount of public money. Although the implementation of the plan will confer substantial benefits on the urban community, these will not be adequately reflected in the stream of revenue flowing to the local authority; consequently a technique is required to ensure (*a*) that the over-all benefits of the plan adopted exceed the over-all costs *to the community*, and (*b*) that, where there are alternative plans, the most worthwhile is selected.

Over the years a number of economic techniques have been developed to cope with these problems; of these the best-known and most widely used is social cost–benefit analysis (C.B.A.). This technique was initially developed in the United States to appraise public-sector investment projects but many of its early applications in this country were in the planning field, and in particular in the field of urban transport (for example the pioneering C.B.A. study looking at the implications for London of the Victoria underground railway line (Foster and Beesley [1963])).

The clearest definition of the nature of C.B.A. is provided by Prest and Turvey [1965] in their classic survey article on the subject, namely that

> Cost–Benefit Analysis is a practical way of assessing the desirability of projects, where it is important to take a long view (in the sense of looking at repercussions in the further as well as the nearer future) and a wide view (in the sense of allowing for side effects of many kinds on many persons, industries, regions, etc.), i.e. it implies the enumeration and evaluation of all the relevant costs and benefits.

In urban planning there is a need to take a 'wide view' because any plan will have implications affecting many sectors of the local economy. Also, if the appraisal looked at only the direct financial repercussions, it would omit many important social costs (for example in terms of environmental damage, community disruption, and so on) and benefits (for example increased social amenities, reduced congestion, and so on). Consideration of the 'long view' is important because any major planning exercise will have repercussions into the future and hold implications for generations to come. Indeed, the long-term effects and the durability of the physical changes resulting from a large urban plan are further justifications for ensuring the best plan is finally accepted.

The C.B.A. technique itself involves placing monetary values on all the various attributes and defects of a plan, including those items which do not normally have prices attached to them. In the case of an urban transport plan, this would mean attempting to evaluate travel time savings, changes in accident rates, noise nuisances, air pollution and other items not usually accredited with a money price. Additionally, the economist, by using discounting techniques, must decide how much weight society attaches to costs and benefits occurring today rather than at some future date and make due allowance for this in his calculations.

Conceptually, C.B.A. is relatively easy to understand; it simply involves the consideration of all aspects of a plan as they affect the urban community. In practice, the application of C.B.A. raises a number of problems and the technique has come under considerable criticism in recent years (a fuller discussion of this is contained in Barker and Button [1974]).

At the practical level it is difficult to place monetary values on many of the items which should be included in a full C.B.A. study; how, for example, do you evaluate the loss of community spirit that can accompany an urban-renewal programme? Although economists have developed sophisticated techniques to place 'shadow prices' on intangible items, there is no objective method of judging their accuracy. In addition, many plans are so large that it is difficult to define all the costs and benefits involved and so complicated that it is impossible to trace out their exact repercussions. As a result some items may be accidentally missed from the calculations altogether while others are included more than once (then there is 'double-counting'). There are also problems in deciding how much importance to attach to future costs and benefits relative to current ones, the problem of defining the correct discount rate.

As well as the practical difficulties associated with C.B.A., its application has also been questioned on theoretical grounds. In particular, doubt has been expressed over the justification for comparing the aggregate benefits of each plan with the aggregate costs. This simple comparison could, for example, result in the acceptance of a plan which benefited the wealthier members of the urban community at the expense of the poorer sections. Although more recent innovations in C.B.A. now make it theoretically possible to take the distributional consequences of each plan into consideration, it is difficult to see how they would be incorporated in actual studies.

A second theoretical cloud hanging over C.B.A. concerns one of the implicit assumptions underlying the technique, namely that the project under consideration does not affect the relative price structure in the economy (in economic jargon it is a 'partial-equilibrium approach'). In the case of very large planning exercises – for example the Greater London Development Plan – this assumption does not hold; changes in the price of local land will affect the urban land market elsewhere. For this reason there is much to be said for confining the use of C.B.A. to small-scale plans and to use alternative methods for larger exercises.

One alternative, or set of alternatives, to C.B.A. is the 'cost-effective' approach, although the exact meaning of this term is not always agreed upon (see Foster [1972]). Some of the techniques falling under this umbrella title are of a financial nature, such as cost-minimisation procedures, but a more widely accepted definition is that it is a technique to find the best or most effective way of using a given financial budget. This approach was developed from systems analysis and is the direct reverse of cost minimisation, where the objectives are fixed and costs variable. A development of cost-effectiveness, in its narrow sense, is planning, programming and budgeting (P.P.B.) which has been borrowed from the Defence Department in the United States. This extends cost effectiveness by attempting to measure the output of particular expenditure and, hence, to implicitly introduce non-financial considerations. The difficulty with this family of techniques is that they either concentrate exclusively on financial considerations, which are too narrow for the urban planner, or else, like P.P.B., they reintroduce the C.B.A. problem of having to express intangibles and externalities in some common, frequently monetary, form.

A further alternative is threshold analysis. The technique, which was developed a decade ago in Poland, is based upon the idea that every town has physical limitations to spatial growth, the thresholds of urban development. These thresholds can only be overcome by high capital costs, and the objective of the procedure is to define the appropriate investment combination offering the lowest overhead and operating costs. The thresholds can be specified under three main headings, (*a*) suitability of land for urban development from the physiographic standpoint, (*b*) possibilities of extending the public-utility networks, and (*c*) possibilities of changing the existing land-use patterns (Kozlowski and Hughes [1967 and 1968]). The major limitation of threshold analysis is that, although it considers the relative cost of different investment strategies to overcome thresholds, it does not pay due regard to the benefits of doing so. In this respect the approach is partial and may be seen as little more than a sophisticated cost-minimisation procedure.

An important variation of C.B.A. in the planning context is the 'Planning Balance Sheet', a technique specifically developed for town planning by Nathaniel Lichfield. The planning balance sheet does not involve a definite set of rules but is rather an *ad hoc* procedure, the methodology of which has been developed in a number of case studies – for example of Cambridge (Lichfield [1966a]), Swanley (Lichfield [1966b]), Edgeware (Lichfield and Chapman [1968]), Peterborough (Lichfield [1969]) and Ipswich (Lichfield and Chapman [1970]). Lichfield has summarised the general philosophy of the technique thus:

> Since it would be virtually impossible to evaluate alternatives from the various points of view of a multitude of individuals, the planning balance sheet groups the community into homogeneous sectors distinguished by the kind of operations they wish to perform. It then evaluates the alternatives from the point of view of the advantages (benefits) and disadvantages (costs) accruing to every sector from each alternative, to see which would provide the maximum net advantage (benefit). . . . In order to assist in isolating the myriad of costs and benefits involved in town planning so that they may be measured for each alternative, the planning balance sheet translates the operational demands of the sectors into 'instrumental objectives': the utilities that are sought by each group and the disutilities they try to avoid. Instrumental objectives are the steps by which more widely defined goals are made operational in the sense of their practical application to a specific problem of choice between alternative means towards achieving the goals (Lichfield and Chapman [1970] p. 158).

The principal distinction is that although both C.B.A. and the planning balance sheet method attempt to be comprehensive in their coverage of costs and benefits, the planning balance sheet does not try to translate all the implications of a plan into monetary terms, and, in addition, explicitly shows the incidence of the various costs and benefits. Instead of evaluating the costs and benefits of different plans, except for those items which normally have monetary values attached to them, the various implications are left in physical terms and set out in tabular form indicating the extent to which the various groups within the urban community will be affected. These are then compared to a set of predetermined planning objectives which are intended to reflect the needs of the community. Alternative plans are ranked under each objective heading and the ranks are then added together to produce a ranking of the plans with respect to the objectives taken as a whole – the scheme with the lowest algebraic total being deemed the best.

Lean [1967] has pointed to several fundamental difficulties in this approach. First, it assumes that the ranks accredited to each plan under the various objective headings can sensibly be added together to produce a grand over-all ranking; explicitly this must assume a constant difference in value between each plan. If, for example, we have two alternative schemes each designed to both reduce traffic congestion and improve the urban environment, the ordinal-ranking method would prove incapable of distinguishing between the first plan, which is infinitely better at removing traffic congestion, and the second, which is only marginally superior from the environmental standpoint. The planning balance sheet would accredit them with identical over-all rankings. Only if a plan is superior in *all* respects can it be deemed the best using this method of ranking.

Second, unless value judgements are made it is necessary to assume that the objectives stated in the planning balance sheet are all of equal importance. In reality an urban plan attempts to fulfil a wide variety of objectives, some of which will be given greater priority than others. Unless the local authority states exactly how much weight should be accorded each objective, the economist must either assume they are all equally important or else attach some other set of weights himself. A further alternative is that the economist simply presents the authorities with the matrix of costs and benefits and lets them decide upon the appropriate priorities. This latter approach has much to recommend it.

The main difficulty with cost–benefit analysis and allied techniques is that they are often seen as substitutes for decision-making. In fact, they are aids to the decision-maker and depend very much upon the assumptions incorporated within them; as one economist has warned, 'Cost–benefit analysis is one of the techniques most prone to misunderstanding and misapplication in the hands of the uninitiated (not to mention the unscrupulous!)' (Williams [1972] p. 200). Used carefully, and with an understanding of its limitations, C.B.A. is an extremely useful tool in town planning, but employed indiscriminately, and without due regard for the underlying assumptions, it can add apparently scientific weight to an argument where none exists. C.B.A. has its greatest use in highlighting the pros and cons of alternative plans but ultimately it is up to the decision-maker to evaluate the social implications of these. As Prest and Turvey [1965] have stated, 'cost–benefit analysis is only a technique for making decisions within a framework which has to be decided in advance, and which involves a wide range of considerations, many of them of a political or social character'.

11.3 A Case Study in Urban Planning: The Greater London Development Plan

To illustrate some of the economic implications of urban planning we consider a particular case study, the Greater London Development Plan (G.L.D.P.). The size of the plan makes it slightly atypical but many of the basic problems encountered in planning are highlighted. It reveals clearly the types of economic considerations central to the urban planning process and illustrates many of the basic conflicts which must be resolved if the eventual plan is going to achieve its objectives. The study also shows the wide range of considerations which the planner must take into account if he is to be successful; political, social and economic factors all influenced the final G.L.D.P. proposals. The section is not a straightforward description of the plan itself, although many of its main features are brought out, but rather it looks at its implications and the criticisms levelled against it.

The Greater London Development Plan had its origins in the pre-1968 town and country planning legislation and for this reason it evolved as something between a town and a structure plan (Foster and Whitehead [1973]). The G.L.D.P. is of particular interest to the economist, not only because it was concerned with the largest urban concentration in the country and the nation's capital, but for a number of important features associated with it. It was an attempt, admittedly a very limited one, to develop planning objectives for the city and to evolve an over-all plan. Second, a considerable amount of economic discussion and analysis emanated from the subsequent appraisal of the Plan and this, in turn, produced further technical and theoretical controversy. Finally, the inquiry into the Plan – the Layfield Inquiry as it is now known – was the most thorough assessment ever undertaken of urban planning proposals in this country; the Inquiry itself took 237 separate days spread over two years, cost £1 million and produced two large volumes of conclusions and technical appendices.

The background to the Plan partly explains some of its inconsistencies and many of the weaknesses in its foundations which were highlighted by the Committee of Inquiry. The Plan began when the Greater London Council was formed in 1963 under the London Government Act. Two points of importance stem from this; first, the 1963 Act gave the G.L.C. only partial planning powers, thirty-two large borough councils and the City of London having extensive powers within their own areas. Second, the initial planning was undertaken within the framework of the 1947 Town and Country Planning Act which required the production of what was essentially a 'town plan' (a cartographical picture of the lay-out of the city at some future date). Part way through the planning process, however, a new act in 1968 called for a 'structure plan' which, in written form, presents the authority's objectives, alternative strategies and evaluations of these strategies with respect to the stated objectives. The result of these difficulties was a seventy-seven page *Statement* (Greater London Council [1969a]) accompanied by nine large-scale maps, which verbally and visually depicted how London would change by 1981. (A more popular presentation of the proposals is to be found in Greater London Council [1969b].) The plan presented in February 1969, therefore, was neither a town plan in the sense of the 1947 Act nor a structure plan but rather fell between the two stools.

The underlying aims of London's planners, as set out in the *Statement*, can be summarised under seven headings (Greater London Council [1969a] p. 12).

(1) To liberate and develop, so far as planning can, the enterprise and activities of London, promoting efficiency in economic life and vitality in its society and culture.

(2) To treasure and develop London's character – capital of the

nation, home and work place of millions, focus of the British tradition.

(3) To conserve and develop London's fabric of buildings, spaces and communications, protecting the best while modernising what is out of date or inferior.

(4) To promote a balance between homes, work and movement as principal elements upon whose relationship London's over-all prospects depend.

(5) To participate in necessary measures of decentralisation and help forward the part that London plays in national and regional development.

(6) To encourage continual improvement in metropolitan environments and make them congenial and efficient in the service of London's people.

(7) To unite the efforts of all who can help to realise these aims and to give new inspiration to the onward development of London's genius.

The Layfield Committee acknowledged the problems which had confronted the G.L.C. in drawing up the Plan but nevertheless it concluded: 'we consider the Metropolitan Structure Plan in its present form dangerous and largely useless, and we recommend that you (i.e. the Minister) should not approve it.' In general the Panel criticised the Plan on a number of important points (Department of the Environment [1973] para. 2.17).

(a) *The plan was over-ambitious*, 'for example, it assumes that [the G.L.C.'s] policies can alter settled population trends, and in employment it tries to forecast supply and demand for substantial periods ahead and to translate these into terms of floor space allocations for various sectors of London. No policies by a local authority can effectively change settled population trends in the short term, and the G.L.C. had neither the information to make employment forecasts nor the ability to relate them to floor space.'

(b) *The general treatment was not consistent*: 'The information obtained upon which the Plan was founded differed widely in degrees of specificity and depth. . . . The plan making authority tended to concentrate in the Plan upon those proposals which it had power to carry through itself.'

(c) *There was a failure to relate information to policy*: in particular, 'one of the most notable features of the G.L.D.P. is the independence of the policies in the Plan from the facts gathered in the Report Studies and other documents'.

(*d*) *There were general problems of defining objectives and aims and in relating them to policy*: for example, 'We found it extremely difficult to discover what the precise aims were that many of the policies in the G.L.D.P. were supposed to fulfil', and 'The G.L.D.P. Written Statement is full of statements of aims which do not mean anything because they can mean anything to anyone.'

Rather than go into detail on all of these points, some of which involve issues well outside of the realms of economics, we now turn to look at four important subjects which attracted the particular attention of the Inquiry and which are of greatest interest to urban economists.

(*a*) *The Objectives and Instruments of Urban Economic Policy*

The broad strategy of the Plan (set out in Section 2 of the *Statement*) was vague: 'It is the council's intention to do everything within its powers to maintain London's position as the capital of the nation and one of the world's great cities' was the primary objective and unexceptional in itself; it was the method proposed to achieve this goal that created the problem (Wilcox [1971]). The G.L.C. reversed previous thinking and, instead of advocating further movements of jobs out of the capital and the strengthening of green-belt powers, proposed to reduce outward migration and to check the decline in employment by relaxing floor-space controls and regulating the granting of Office Development Permits. The G.L.C.'s case centred around the argument that the continued decline in London's population was depriving the city of young, skilled, well-educated people, families with young children and workers with the best prospects and was leaving behind the old, the less skilled and the disadvantaged. Continued out-migration, it was argued, would place an increasing burden on those remaining whilst reducing their ability to bear it.

The Inquiry's Report lays one detailed and one fundamental objection to this proposal. Layfield argues that regulating the number of floor-space permits granted is an inefficient and ineffective policy instrument and suggests a range of alternatives (para. 5.86), for example the rehabilitation of 'worn-out' areas, improved access to jobs, planned emigration, better transport facilities for goods, the development of new sources of employment, and so on. Similarly, it was critical of the proposed use of Office Development Permits – considered too negative. The Report, though, goes into no detail of how effective the alternatives are or how costly they would prove if introduced.

Accepting this detailed criticism, the Inquiry then proceeded to question the legitimacy of the G.L.C.'s attempt to develop an employment policy as part of a structure plan and objected to the notion that the raising of *per capita* incomes constituted a relevant objective. The objection centred on the idea that the Plan should have concentrated on land use. As Foster and Whitehead [1973] have argued, however, this is a rather strange and, in terms of evolving planning techniques, retrograde step. First, the G.L.C. was attempting to devise a total plan for the city, embracing social, economic and land-use perspectives, and because of the clear inter-relationships between economic and social objectives and physical planning, this was not unreasonable. The Layfield objection implies the need for a number of separate plans each concentrating on a different aspect of urban activity. Intuitively, in the light of the numerous interdependencies involved, this proposal of separate plans seems inefficient.

Second, the Layfield Committee seemed worried that any conscious attempt by the G.L.C. to increase the over-all level of incomes in London would have serious repercussions elsewhere in the economy – there was, however, no objection to increasing the relative *per capita* incomes of some sections of the population within the city itself. Foster and Whitehead point to the need for an over-all assessment of G.L.C. policies, both in relation to the needs of London and the country as a whole, to ensure there is a net benefit to the nation. Not all attempts to raise *per capita* incomes in London would be at the expense of other regions and would consequently be desirable – only the measures which reduce incomes elsewhere and induce 'beggar-my-neighbour' policies are harmful. In summary, Layfield should have looked at the question of compensation from London to the adversely affected regions rather than condemn the G.L.C.'s objective *per se*.

(b) The Appropriate Population Size of London
The population of London declined from 8·6 million in 1939 to 8 million in 1961 and to 7·4 million in 1971, although there has been

a rise in the number of households since the early 1960s as incomes have risen and people have got married earlier. The Layfield Inquiry assumed this downward trend would continue, giving a population of between 6·37 and 6·55 million in 1981 and about 6 million a decade later. Besides conscious attempts to reduce the population ever since the Barlow Commission of 1939 (Royal Commission on the Distribution of Industrial Population [1940]), the decline in the number of people living in the capital is also a result of outward migration to suburbs where it is possible to live without having to endure the social costs associated with the inner Metropolitan Area but at the same time enjoy many of the benefits and facilities of the city (Richardson [1973] pp. 200–13).

The G.L.D.P. did not contain proposals to further hasten the depopulation process, stating that this would lead to unemployment and the lowering of real incomes both absolutely and relatively to other regions. In addition, even if the population was decreased further, the G.L.C. argued, this would not reduce the city's role as an international and regional centre and these commitments would become increasingly difficult to fulfil. The existing migration was already having an impact and, by reducing the rateable value of property in the city, was forcing up rate levels to meet the needs of local public expenditure. The Inquiry Panel rejected this scepticism on the part of the G.L.C. towards further population reductions, maintaining that, 'taking costs and benefits together, they clearly lend to a general view that continuation of decreases in employment and population at recent rates will produce a greater increase in net benefit than would a retardation in the rate of decline' (para. 5.45). Layfield's justification for this view (which is contained in Appendix H of the *Report*) rests primarily on the belief that one can relate city size to overcrowding which in turn is directly correlated with social cost.

Without clear empirical evidence it is impossible to evaluate the validity of these two views. The G.L.D.P. did not discuss the size question in terms of external economies and diseconomies associated with particular population levels (see Chapter 6) and, although the Layfield Inquiry made some attempt at this sort of approach, it eventually submitted to the conventional idea that London is too big *per se*. The Plan and Inquiry also ignored the fundamental issue of whether it would be beneficial for the South-east as a whole if London declined and it has been suggested that Layfield was remiss in not recommending a central government examination of this question (Foster and Whitehead [1973] p. 449).

(c)   *The G.L.D.P. Transport Proposals*

The G.L.C.'s proposals for extensive investment in transport infrastructure resulted in considerable controversy – 90 per cent of the objections to the G.L.D.P. involved its transport proposals. In particular there was penetrating debate over the urban motorway plans; these involved ring motorways approximately three, seven and twelve miles from the city centre (a fourth outside the G.L.C.'s boundaries being planned by the Department of the Environment) linked together by a number of radial motorways and high-quality roads. The Plan contained little of importance with respect to other forms of transport although the approval of the Fleetline and extensions of the underground system to Heathrow following the publication of the *Statement* does add weight to the G.L.C.'s claim that their long-term transport planning is flexible (Thomson [1971]). (One should perhaps also add that the G.L.C. only took full responsibility for London Transport in 1970 and hence one would expect plans for public transport to be somewhat vague.)

The literature on the transport content of the G.L.D.P. is formidable, and whatever the shortcomings of the proposals themselves, the work undertaken (both by the G.L.C. and the Inquiry Panel) into this aspect of the Plan represents one of the most comprehensive attempts to tackle the urban transport problem in an economic manner. The problem was basically one of cost–benefit analysis, the objective being to find the best way of coping with the rapidly growing number of cars in the city. As some critics have pointed out, however – and this seems to be supported by Table 8.1 presented earlier – road-traffic congestion is not the only transport problem in London. The majority of passenger-miles travelled in the capital are either undertaken in public transport or on foot, but the Plan says little about difficulties of overcrowding and inconvenience in these spheres. The G.L.C. would presumably counter this by saying that the relief afforded by the new roads would improve the situation elsewhere in the transport system.

The motorway proposals evoked considerable hostility amongst both those directly affected and pressure groups generally opposed to the over-all social and environmental costs of the scheme. Arguments were on two levels, the first centring around the objections to the private-transport bias of the proposals on the one hand and the second questioning the detailed alignment of the roads on the other.

The Layfield Inquiry rejected many of the motorway proposals although it retained the most controversial, the Motorway Box (Ringway 1). The Panel pointed to the low return on all of the proposed urban motorways – Ringway 1 offering only 5·4 per cent compared with the 10 per cent return needed on government investments – and questioned the logic of many of the G.L.C.'s arguments presented to support them. The Report maintains that 'such a lavish provision of orbital roads will in our view either result in a situation in which they are not utilised to their full capacity, and hence be a waste of valuable resources, or alternatively, and more probably they will encourage inessential movements by road which otherwise would either not take place or would take place by some alternative mode'.

Despite its low return, the Inquiry accepted the Motorway Box project because of the 'important environmental advantages gained by the canalisation of traffic that would otherwise use secondary and local roads remains unaccounted for in money terms'. This argument is open to several criticisms (see Foster [1973]). The construction of this urban motorway around Central London could well divert traffic from other roads but in doing so it would create bottlenecks on its approach roads with a decline in environmental standards for areas adjacent to them. As Foster says, 'It is not building Ringway 1 that will enhance the environmental quality of central London, but traffic restraint and environmental traffic planning.' There are far more cost-efficient and effective methods of discouraging heavy lorries and excessive numbers of cars from the city centre than the construction of an expensive inner ring road. Indeed the attraction of the Motorway Box to through traffic will depend upon the degree of restraint in the central area and there appeared no guarantee this would be forthcoming. (More recently, in 1974, proposals for restraining traffic by means of daily tickets has been examined suggesting a change of heart by the G.L.C.)

The Panel of Inquiry felt that co-ordination of public transport was impossible under the existing administrative framework and suggested the creation of a new co-ordinating body to remove the built-in differences between the approaches of the G.L.C., British Rail and London Transport. The Panel felt that 'The plain truth is that London depends heavily on its public transport system and, if it is to go on working as a civilised urban community it needs to maintain the system at least in its present form, and, if at all possible, in a much better form.'

(d)   The Housing Policies of the G.L.C.

London has a considerable housing problem with both an acute shortage of accommodation (half the homeless families in England and Wales are in London) and a high proportion of sub-standard dwellings, some 69 per cent of the housing stock being built before 1920. Some indication of the size of the problem is given by Table 11.1 where the housing situation in London during 1966 is compared to that in the other major U.K. conurbations.

TABLE 11.1   *The housing situation in the major U.K. conurbations*

	Ratio of households/dwellings	Sharing Households nos	total (per cent)
London	1·12	635,000	24
West Midlands	1·00	39,000	5
Merseyside	1·01	29,000	7
South-east Lancashire	0·98	25,000	3
West Yorkshire	0·96	11,000	2

SOURCE: Henney [1974] p. 88

Although the situation had improved since the early 1950s, much still needed to be done and consequently housing played an important part in G.L.C. policies. It should be noted that the G.L.C. does not directly control housing developments or densities within the various London boroughs but still has broad powers to transfer population from the more congested boroughs both to less congested outer ones and to town-development schemes elsewhere in the country. A major limitation with this administrative structure is that there is no single waiting list for housing in London nor a common criteria for allocation of public accommodation between boroughs.

To solve the housing problems the G.L.C. made the following proposals:

(1) To give 'first priority' to the eradication of slums, overcrowding and 'lamentable domestic environments';

(2) To provide as many new dwellings as a good standard of environment will allow;

(3) To give 'first priority' to the improvement of the Housing Problem Areas;

(4) To call for a gradual redistribution of population, particularly to Outer London;

(5) To encourage private-enterprise and housing-association building; and

(6) To provide for a continued flow of about 20,000 residents a year to expanding towns.

The Layfield Panel strongly criticised the G.L.D.P. housing proposals as 'thin and unconvincing', pointing especially to the lack of integration with other policies, the incorrect objective of stemming the out-migration from the city and the numerous and serious omissions in the *Statement*. Much of the debate concerning housing centred around the differing views of Layfield and the G.L.C. over the future population size of London (see Clark [1973]). In particular, the Panel stated thus: 'we entirely accept that as many homes should be built as possible to deal with those housing problems which cannot be met by dispersing population from London, but we do not accept that building houses in order to keep up the population, or slow the rate of decline in population within London, is justified.' There were, however, also fundamental differences in the over-all economic approaches adopted by the G.L.C. and the Inquiry Panel.

The G.L.D.P. did not attempt to develop a model explaining the demand for housing (the quantitative base) but rather estimated the probable future number of households and did so on very shaky assumptions (Foster and Whitehead [1973]). Layfield suggested a more reasonable approach would be to initially determine this quantitative base and then assess the effectiveness of alternative housing strategies against it. As in practice this is difficult to actually do, the Panel proposed an alternative where the need for housing is estimated independently and compared with some loose notion of a reasonable standard of housing. In fact this hardly solves the problem since the concepts of 'need' and 'standard' are as vague and nebulous as the demand pattern itself.

The second suggestion of the Panel is that a central body should be established to co-ordinate building in London since 'the interests of the boroughs and the G.L.C. are, quite naturally, in conflict' (para. 6.107). This housing authority would also be responsible for co-ordinating the public housing stock in London and, in particular, for managing a single 'waiting list' for the metropolis. Such a body may reduce the conflicts between the G.L.C. and other authorities and also provide some economies of scale in planning and management but it reduces the flexibility of control in relation to local requirements. In addition, the proposal does not quantitatively consider the diseconomies of centralised control, especially the costs of achieving the flow of information necessary for decision-making at the centre and the loss of impetus for local experimentation in the provision of public housing. A thorough cost–benefit analysis of the advantages of such a body is required.

11.4 Conclusions

Town planning has advanced a long way in a comparatively short time. In the last two decades of the nineteenth century the first great planners (or 'seers' as Peter Hall prefers to call them) appeared. These planners, influenced considerably by American experience, were concerned with individual planning ventures and were in many ways experimenters rather than planners. Examples of their efforts. which spanned the years 1880–1928, were Saltaire near Bradford (Titus Salt), Bournville outside Birmingham (George Cadbury), Port Sunlight near Birkenhead (William Lever) and perhaps best known of all, Welwyn Garden City in Hertfordshire (Ebenezer Howard).

Legislation assisting planners was only passed at the beginning of the century, the Town Planning Act of 1909 being the first of any practical significance. Since that time, a large number of Acts have been passed affecting the role of the planner and the degree of intervention permitted in urban markets. Despite the general acceptance of planning today and the resources put into it, the contemporary problems of traffic congestion and urban sprawl remain with us. The inability to cope with these problems is partly the result of ideological disputes amongst planners themselves. There has been a continual conflict between those desiring greater physical planning controls, as envisaged under the 1947 Town and Country Planning Act, and those favouring a market-orientated approach, as contained in the Planning Acts of 1953, 1954 and 1959. Today the dispute seems to have been settled in favour of the former school and, with the passing of the 1968 Act, the government seems firmly committed to extensive programmes of urban planning.

The general approach to planning has also changed with time and it is no longer simply seen as an exercise in allocating land to particular uses determined by some ultimate ideal city design. Planning is now an on-going operation involving economic and social considerations with the objective of not only improving the welfare of those living in the city but fitting into a more grandiose scheme to benefit the nation as a whole. The current problem is to incorporate these economic and social ideals into a framework which has traditionally been concerned with engineering and physical problems and to produce a satisfactory synthesis of ideas that can provide a firm basis for future planning.

References

P. J. BARKER and K. J. BUTTON [1974], *Cost–Benefit Analysis and its Recent Applications*, Loughborough Papers on Recent Developments in Economic Policy and Thought, no. 5 (Loughborough University).

G. CLARK [1973], 'The Layfield Report and the G.L.D.P.', *Journal of the Royal Town Planning Institute* (April) pp. 160–2.

Department of the Environment [1973], *Greater London Development Plan: Report of the Panel of Inquiry* (London: H.M.S.O.).

D. DONNISON [1972], 'Ideas for Town Planners', *Three Banks Review* (December) pp. 3–27.

C. D. FOSTER [1972], *Politics, Finance and the Role of Economics* (London: Allen & Unwin).

C. D. FOSTER [1973], 'An Inquiry into the Layfield Inquiry', *The Times* (21 February).

C. D. FOSTER and M. E. BEESLEY [1963], 'Estimating the Social Benefits of Constructing an Underground Railway in London', *Journal of the Royal Statistical Society* pp. 46–56.

C. D. FOSTER and C. M. E. WHITEHEAD [1973], 'The Layfield Report on the Greater London Development Plan', *Economica* (November) pp. 442–54.

M. I. GOODMAN and E. C. FREUND [1968], *Principles and Practice of Urban Planning* (London: International City Managers Association).

Greater London Council [1969a], *Greater London Development Plan Statement* (London: G.L.C.).

Greater London Council [1969b], *Tomorrow's London* (London: G.L.C.).

P. HALL [1974], *Urban and Regional Planning* (Harmondsworth: Penguin).

A. HENNEY [1974], 'The Housing Situation in the U.K.', *Moorgate and Wall Street Review* (Autumn) pp. 61–90.

J. T. HUGHES and J. KOZLOWSKI [1968], 'Threshold Analysis – an Economic Tool for Town and Regional Planning', *Urban Studies* (June) pp. 132–43.

J. KOZLOWSKI and J. T. HUGHES [1967], 'Urban Threshold Theory and Analysis', *Journal of the Town Planning Institute* (February) pp. 55–60.

W. LEAN [1967], 'Economic Studies and Assessment of Town Development', *Journal of the Town Planning Institute* (April) pp. 148–52.

N. LICHFIELD [1966a], *Cost–Benefit Analysis in Town Planning: a Case Study of Cambridge* (Cambridgeshire and Isle of Ely County Council).

N. LICHFIELD [1966b], 'Cost–Benefit Analysis in Town Planning: a Case Study of Swanley', *Urban Studies* (November) pp. 215–250.

N. LICHFIELD [1969], 'Cost–Benefit Analysis in Urban Expansion – a Case Study: Peterborough', *Regional Studies*, pp. 123–55.

N. LICHFIELD and H. CHAPMAN [1968], 'Cost-Benefit Analysis and Road Proposals for a Shopping Centre – a Case Study: Edgeware', *Journal of Transport Economics and Policy* (September) pp. 280–320.

N. LICHFIELD and H. CHAPMAN [1970], 'Cost–Benefit Analysis in Urban Expansion – a Case Study: Ipswich', *Urban Studies* (June) pp. 153–89.

A. R. PREST and R. TURVEY [1965], 'Cost–Benefit Analysis: a Survey', *Economic Journal* (December) pp. 683–735.

D. J. REYNOLDS [1966], *Economics, Town Planning and Traffic* (London: Institute of Economic Affairs).

H. W. RICHARDSON [1973], *The Economics of Urban Size* (Farnborough: Saxon House).

Royal Commission on the Distribution of Industrial Population [1940], *Report* (London: H.M.S.O.).

J. M. THOMSON [1971], 'Transport: the Motorway Proposals', in *Planning for London*, ed. J. Hillman (Harmondsworth: Penguin).

D. WILCOX [1971], 'The Greater London Development Plan', in *Planning for London*, ed. J. Hillman (Harmondsworth: Penguin).

A. WILLIAMS [1972], 'Cost–Benefit Analysis: Bastard Science? and/or Insidious Poison in the Body Politick?', *Journal of Public Economics* (August) pp. 199–225.

INDEX